AN ENCYCLOPEDIA OF AMERICAN POLITICS

AN ENCYCLOPEDIA OF

EDWIN VALENTINE MITCHELL

AMERICAN POLITICS

GREENWOOD PRESS, PUBLISHERS
WESTPORT, CONNECTICUT

Copyright 1946 by Edwin Valentine Mitchell

Reprinted with the permission
of Doubleday & Company, Inc.

First Greenwood Reprinting 1968
Second Greenwood Reprinting 1971

Library of Congress Catalogue Card Number 69-10135

SBN 8371-0171-9

Printed in the United States of America

Acknowledgments. GRATEFUL ACKNOWLEDGMENT is made to former Ambassador Hugh Gibson and Miss Margaret Hensey of the editorial staff of Doubleday and Company for their suggestions and criticisms.

I am also greatly obliged to DeWitt Mackenzie of the Associated Press for his interest and help, and to Lewis Copeland and Barrows Mussey for their aid. Special thanks are due Miss Terry West for assisting with the research.

To William H. Blake, General Solicitor of the Public Service of New Jersey, I am deeply indebted for the loan of many useful books, especially Brown and Strauss's *A Dictionary of American Politics*, published in 1888, from which I have drawn much material concerning the earlier years of American political history.

I also wish to thank the New York Public Library and its staff, who have been extremely resourceful and helpful.

E. V. M.

AN ENCYCLOPEDIA OF AMERICAN POLITICS

Abjuration is the renunciation under oath of the allegiance which one owes to a sovereign or state. Aliens applying for citizenship in the United States are required to declare on oath or affirmation before the court where they apply that, among other things, they entirely renounce and abjure all allegiance and fidelity to any foreign sovereign or state, and particularly the sovereign or state whereof before they were subjects or citizens.

Abolitionists—Persons who sought to abolish the institution of slavery were called Abolitionists. The first society dedicated to freeing the slaves was formed in Pennsylvania in 1744. A similar society was organized in New York in 1785, among the presidents of which were John Jay and Alexander Hamilton. Rhode Island followed in 1786 and Maryland in 1789. Before the end of Washington's first term there were societies in Connecticut, Virginia, and New Jersey. All they did was to petition Congress.

Public opinion was stirred by the publication in 1831 of *The Liberator,* an uncompromising anti-slavery paper edited by William Lloyd Garrison of Massachusetts. Feeling ran high on both sides. Elijah P. Lovejoy, an abolition editor, was murdered by a mob at Alton, Illinois, in 1837. The following year Pennsylvania Hall in Philadelphia was burned. In 1839 the Abolitionists who desired to put political candidates in the field organized the Liberty party and nominated James G. Birney for President. In 1844 the party polled enough votes to cause the defeat of Henry Clay. In 1848 and 1852 they voted with the Free Soil party, and after that with the Republicans.

Acceptance Speech—Although preparations for the presidential race get under way as soon as the party nominating conventions

1

have been held, the campaign does not actually open until a month or two later, when the candidates are officially notified of their nominations and make their acceptance speeches. However, on July 2, 1932, Governor Franklin D. Roosevelt of New York flew to Chicago while the Democratic national convention was still in session, to be notified of his nomination for the presidency and to make his acceptance speech.

Acceptance speeches attract more attention than do the party platforms, as they reflect the personal views of the nominees, which, in the event of victory, are more likely to be put into effect than are the platforms. While candidates usually accept the platforms adopted by their parties, they do not necessarily stand squarely upon them but frequently go on frolics of their own concerning particular planks.

Accidental President—Sobriquet of John Adams and Millard Fillmore, the former because he was elected President by only three electoral votes, the latter because as Vice-President he succeeded to the presidency on the death of President Taylor.

Adams, John, the second President and the only Federalist to hold that office, was born in that part of Braintree, Massachusetts, which is now the city of Quincy, October 19, 1735, and died there July 4, 1826, the same day on which Thomas Jefferson died. He was graduated from Harvard College and soon afterward admitted to the bar. He was elected to the Massachusetts Legislature in 1770, and from 1774 to 1777 served in the Continental Congress. In the latter year he went to France as Minister of the United States. At the close of the Revolution he was one of the commissioners who negotiated the peace treaty. In 1785 he was sent to England to represent this country. Returning to America in 1788, he was elected Vice-President under Washington, and on the retirement of Washington in 1797 he was chosen President over Jefferson by three electoral votes. (See *President by Three Votes.*)

The principal events during his administration were the difficulties with France, which brought us to the brink of war with that country (see *X Y Z Mission*), and the passage of the Alien and

Sedition Laws (*q.v.*), which were the subject of much popular clamor. While Adams's policy toward France averted war, it made him unpopular with a portion of his party, as did other acts of his administration, and the end of his term saw the Federalist party divided and beaten at the polls.

During his administration Washington died and the seat of the national government was transferred to Washington. He was the first President to live in the White House. He left Washington the day of Jefferson's inauguration without participating in the ceremonies. (See *Midnight Judges*.) His dying words were, "Thomas Jefferson still survives." But unknown to Adams, Jefferson had died a few hours before on the same day—the fiftieth anniversary of the Declaration of Independence, which both had signed.

Adams, John Quincy, the sixth President of the United States, was a son of John Adams, the second President. He was born in what is now the city of Quincy, Massachusetts, July 11, 1767, and died in Washington, February 23, 1848. He was educated in Europe and also at Harvard. He was admitted to the bar in 1791, and in 1794, during Washington's administration, he became Minister to the Hague and later to Portugal. Under his father he was Minister to Prussia. He was elected state senator in Massachusetts, and in 1803 became a Federalist senator at Washington, where he backed the embargo, for which he was censured by the state legislature. He immediately resigned and joined the Republican (Democratic-Republican) party, and by his new friends was sent as Minister, first to Russia and then to Great Britain. In 1817 he became Secretary of State under Monroe, whom he helped to formulate the Monroe Doctrine. He also negotiated the Florida Purchase.

In 1825 he was elected by the House of Representatives to succeed Monroe. His enemies charged that his election was the result of a corrupt political bargain with Henry Clay, but this has never been proved. (See *Contested Elections*.) Adams, who served as President from 1825 to 1829, was defeated for a second term by Andrew Jackson. In 1831 he was elected to the House of Representatives, in which he served until his death, seventeen years later. He was stricken while in the chamber of the House.

When it was suggested to him that to be a congressman after having been President was rather degrading, Adams said, "No person can be degraded by either serving the people as a representative in Congress, or as a selectman of his town."

Adams and Clay Republicans—In 1825 the Federalist party was of no influence—the Democratic-Republican was the only real party. In it there were two factions, the supporters of President John Quincy Adams and his lieutenant, Henry Clay, known as above; and the followers of Andrew Jackson, known as Jackson Republicans, or Jackson Men. The Adams and Clay Republicans ultimately became Whigs.

Admission of States—"New states," says the Constitution (Article IV, Section 3), "may be admitted to the Union; but no new state shall be formed or erected within the jurisdiction of any other state; nor any state be formed by the junction of two or more states or parts of states, without the consent of the legislatures of the states concerned as well as of Congress."

Although in a few cases the people residing in a territory of the United States have drawn up a constitution and asked to be admitted as a state, the usual procedure is for the people to petition Congress, which, if favorably inclined, passes an enabling act authorizing the drafting of a constitution and prescribing conditions which must be complied with before statehood will be granted. Upon the fulfillment of these conditions Congress passes a resolution admitting the new state, which enters the Union on an equal footing with all the other states. The United States Supreme Court has held that Congress cannot impose political restrictions on a new state, because if it were permitted to do so, "the Union, through the power of Congress to admit new states, might come to be a union of states of unequal power."

The table which follows shows the dates on which the first thirteen states ratified the Constitution, the dates on which the rest were admitted to the Union, and the dates on which the Southern states were readmitted after the Civil War.

No.	States	Date of Ratification or Admission	Date of Readmission
1	Delaware	December 7, 1787	
2	Pennsylvania	December 12, 1787	
3	New Jersey	December 18, 1787	
4	Georgia	January 2, 1788	July 15, 1870
5	Connecticut	January 9, 1788	
6	Massachusetts	February 6, 1788	
7	Maryland	April 28, 1788	
8	South Carolina	May 23, 1788	June 25, 1868
9	New Hampshire	June 21, 1788	
10	Virginia	June 25, 1788	January 26, 1870
11	New York	July 26, 1788	
12	North Carolina	November 21, 1789	June 25, 1868
13	Rhode Island	May 29, 1790	
14	Vermont	March 4, 1791	
15	Kentucky	June 1, 1792	
16	Tennessee	June 1, 1796	July 24, 1866
17	Ohio	March 1, 1803	
18	Louisiana	April 8, 1812	June 25, 1868
19	Indiana	December 11, 1816	
20	Mississippi	December 10, 1817	February 23, 1870
21	Illinois	December 3, 1818	
22	Alabama	December 14, 1819	June 25, 1868
23	Maine	March 15, 1820	
24	Missouri	August 10, 1821	
25	Arkansas	June 15, 1836	June 22, 1868
26	Michigan	January 26, 1837	
27	Florida	March 3, 1845	June 25, 1868
28	Texas	December 29, 1845	March 30, 1870
29	Iowa	December 28, 1846	
30	Wisconsin	May 29, 1848	
31	California	September 9, 1850	
32	Minnesota	May 11, 1858	
33	Oregon	February 14, 1859	
34	Kansas	January 29, 1861	
35	West Virginia	June 20, 1863	
36	Nevada	October 31, 1864	
37	Nebraska	March 1, 1867	
38	Colorado	August 1, 1876	
39	North Dakota	November 2, 1889	
40	South Dakota	November 2, 1889	
41	Montana	November 8, 1889	
42	Washington	November 11, 1889	
43	Idaho	July 3, 1890	
44	Wyoming	July 10, 1890	
45	Utah	January 4, 1896	
46	Oklahoma	November 16, 1907	
47	New Mexico	January 6, 1912	
48	Arizona	February 14, 1912	

Agriculture, Department of—This executive department of the Federal Government was created by act of Congress on May 15, 1862, and was originally in charge of the Commissioner of Agriculture. His title was changed to the Secretary of Agriculture on February 8, 1889, and he became a member of the Cabinet. All matters relating to the agricultural industry are directed by the Secretary, whose functions entail agricultural research, extension education, marketing, conservation, credit, etc. Weather reports and crop reports and estimates are made available through this department. Laws covering marketing are administered by the Secretary, as is also the subsidization and insuring of crops. Packing plant inspection is the concern of the department, which also enforces the Pure Food and Drug Act. Information services are maintained and much literature is disseminated.

Among the principal bureaus and offices of the department are Agricultural Research Administration, which co-ordinates and directs the scientific work of the department and is composed of the Bureau of Animal Industry, Bureau of Dairy Industry, Bureau of Human Nutrition and Home Economics, Bureau of Plant Industry, Soils, and Agricultural Engineering, Bureau of Agricultural and Industrial Chemistry, Bureau of Entomology and Plant Quarantine, and the Office of Experiment Stations. The Forest Service, which has charge of the national forests, conducts researches and surveys. The Rural Electrification Administration is concerned with the use of electric current to promote efficiency on farms and other rural enterprises. The Farm Credit Administration makes available to farmers a public source of credit at reasonable rates.

Alabama—Known as the "Cotton State." State flower, goldenrod. Population, 2,832,961. Area, 51,609 square miles. Capital, Montgomery. Was admitted to the Union as a state in 1819. In January 1861 Alabama seceded but was readmitted in June 1868. For a considerable period after the Civil War party strife was rampant, but in the late seventies the state began to prosper. It is a Democratic state and has nine representatives in Congress.

Alaska—Population, 72,524. Area, 586,400 square miles. Capital, Juneau. Purchased from Russia in 1867 for approximately $7,000,-

ooo. Became an organized territory of the United States Government by an act of Congress in 1912. One delegate represents the territory in Washington.

Alexander the Coppersmith—Nickname bestowed on Alexander Hamilton by persons dissatisfied with the copper cents coined in 1793 at his suggestion as Secretary of the Treasury.

Alien and Sedition Laws—At the time of troubles which this country had with France in 1798 there was a considerable section of the populace in sympathy with France, and attacks of the most scurrilous nature were continually made against the President and Congress. This state of things was the occasion for the passage of the above-named bills. The first Alien Bill lengthened the period of residence for the purpose of naturalization to fourteen years. All aliens thereafter to come into the country were to be registered, and the certificate of registration was to be the only proof of residence. Alien enemies could never become citizens.

Another bill gave the President power, in case of war with a foreign nation or danger of invasion by it, to seize or expel all resident alien citizens of that nation. Still another bill, signed by the President in June, gave him power to send away any alien whom he thought dangerous to the country; if after being ordered away he were found here he might be imprisoned for three years and could never become a citizen; aliens so imprisoned could be removed from the country by the President's order, and on voluntarily returning be imprisoned at the President's discretion; the act provided for various details concerning the carrying out of its intention and gave the United States courts cognizance of cases arising thereunder. The action of the law was limited to two years.

The Sedition Bill was passed in July and declared anyone that in any way hindered any officer of the United States in the discharge of his duty, or opposed any of its laws, to be guilty of a high crime and misdemeanor, punishable by a maximum fine of five thousand dollars and maximum imprisonment of five years; further, writing, printing, or publishing any false, scandalous, and malicious writing against Congress or the President, or aiding therein, was made pun-

7

ishable by a maximum fine of two thousand dollars and maximum imprisonment of two years; but the truth of the matter, if proved, was to be a good defense. This act was to expire in March 1801.

The opposition aroused by these bills was enormous, and though the prosecutions under them were very few, they made Adams's administration and the Federal party very unpopular. Hamilton had in vain tried to prevent the party from committing this blunder.

Alien Registration Act—The Alien Registration Act passed June 28, 1940, requires aliens over fourteen years of age who reside in the United States to be registered and fingerprinted and the Department of Justice notified of each change of address. All aliens entering the country on and after August 27, 1940, must likewise be registered and fingerprinted if they intend to stay in the United States more than twenty-nine days.

"All We Ask Is to Be Let Alone"—Jefferson Davis used these words in his message to the Confederate Congress in March 1861, when he referred to Northern preparations to oppose secession.

Allegiance in its political sense is the duty of obedience which a man owes his country. Paramount allegiance is owed by every citizen of the United States to the national government. The idea that he owed allegiance to his state first and to the Union only secondarily, which was part of the doctrine of state sovereignty, was settled by the Civil War. A foreigner cannot become a naturalized citizen of the United States without first renouncing allegiance to his former government. (See *Abjuration*.)

Alphabet Soup—Contemptuous term for the multiplicity of New Deal agencies which were known by their initials, such as NRA, AAA, WPA, RFC, SEC, etc.

Amendments to the Constitution—Provision for amending the Constitution is made in Article V. This may be done whenever two thirds of both houses deem it necessary, or on the application of the legislatures of two thirds of the states, in which case a convention for proposing amendments is called. Amendments become valid parts of the Constitution when ratified by the legislatures of three fourths of the states, or by conventions in three fourths of them, as the one or other mode of ratification is proposed by Congress. By the same article the Constitution was made unamendable prior to 1808 on these points: so as to prohibit immigration as existing in 1787, or so as to permit the levying of capitation or other direct taxes by Congress except in proportion to the census. The only point remaining unamendable at present is that "no state, without its consent, shall be deprived of its equal suffrage in the Senate." For the twenty-one amendments which have been adopted since the Constitution came into force, see that instrument itself.

America—All the early presidents of the United States pronounced America as if it were spelled Americay, and so general was this pronunciation that in the songs and poetry of the period the word was generally rhymed with words having the *ay* ending.

America First Committee—An organization of persons opposed to our entry into World War II. Their chief spokesman was Colonel Charles A. Lindbergh. In a speech delivered at a rally held at Manhattan Center, New York City, on April 23, 1941, he said: "I ask you to look at the map of Europe today and see if you can suggest any way in which we could win this war if we entered it. Suppose we had a large army in America, trained and equipped. Where would we send it to fight? The campaigns of this war show only too clearly how difficult it is to force a landing, or to maintain an army, on a hostile coast. . . . Suppose we had an air fleet we could send to Europe. Where could it operate? Some of our squadrons might be based in the British Isles, but it is physically impossible to base enough aircraft in the British Isles alone to equal in strength the aircraft that can be based on the continent of Europe. . . .

"Over 100,000,000 people in this nation are opposed to entering this war. If the principles of democracy mean anything at all, that is reason enough for us to stay out. If we are forced into a war against the wishes of an overwhelming majority of our people, we will have proved democracy such a failure at home that there will be little use fighting for it abroad."

American Legion—This is a patriotic organization which was formed in Paris in March 1919, at the suggestion of Colonel Theodore Roosevelt, Jr. Its membership is made up of men and women who served in the armed forces of the United States in World Wars I and II. One of its main purposes is to get as many benefits as possible for its members, particularly the disabled. It is strongly in favor of conscription both in wartime and peacetime, and is a strong proponent of the government plan to train youths of the country for national security. In 1945 the membership totaled approximately 1,700,000, of which 600,000 were World War II veterans.

American's Creed—On April 3, 1918, the House of Representatives, in behalf of the American people, accepted a creed which was written by William Tyler Page, who was then Clerk of the House. It reads as follows:

"I believe in the United States of America as a Government of the people, by the people, for the people; whose just powers are derived from the consent of the governed; a democracy in a republic; a sovereign Nation of many sovereign States; a perfect union, one and inseparable; established upon those principles of freedom, equality, justice and humanity for which American patriots sacrificed their lives and fortunes.

"I therefore believe it is my duty to my country to love it; to support its Constitution; to obey its laws; to respect its flag, and to defend it against all enemies."

American Whigs—In England, before the American Revolution and after it, too, the Whigs were the party that struggled against the extension of the royal prerogative; the Tories upheld it. So it naturally followed that Americans opposing the oppression of Great Britain likewise took the name of Whigs. They were known as American Whigs. The name was first used in New York in 1768. The name Tory was by contrast employed to designate partisans of Great Britain. After the Revolution there was thus but one party, the Whig. The estates of some of the Tories had been confiscated, others had left the country, and those who remained were left without a cause. The Whigs soon broke up into factions, the Strong-Government Whigs and the Particularists, and these respectively gave rise to the Federalists and Republicans.

Ananias Club—In 1906, when Theodore Roosevelt was President, the newspapers frequently mentioned the Ananias Club, proposing for membership those persons who had criticized the President and whom he had dubbed liars.

Annapolis Convention—In September 1786 commissioners from five states met at Annapolis, Maryland, for the purpose of securing uniformity of commercial regulations among the states. The call had been sent to all states by a commission authorized by the Virginia legislature at the instigation of Madison. But with representatives from only five states attending, the convention was powerless to accomplish its object. The meeting, however, proved more than a barren requital to the participants, for the unanimous adoption by the delegates of a report drawn up by Hamilton, who represented New York, proposing a convention of delegates from the thirteen states to meet in Philadelphia the following May, led Congress to issue the call for the Convention of 1787 that framed the Constitution.

Annexations—At the commencement of our existence as a nation the territory of the United States comprised all our present territory between the Atlantic on the east, the Mississippi on the west, British America on the north, and the thirty-first degree of north latitude on the south, with a few slight differences owing to subsequent rearrangements of boundary lines. There have since been a number of additions made to our territory which have brought it to its present extent.

I LOUISIANA—Before the year 1763, France owned what was known as the Province of Louisiana, a vast region which comprised, east of the Mississippi, the territory south of the thirty-first degree of north latitude and as far east as the Perdido River, and, west of the Mississippi, the whole of the present Louisiana, Arkansas, Missouri, Iowa, Nebraska, South Dakota, Montana, and Oklahoma, part of North Dakota, that part of Minnesota west of the Mississippi,

Wyoming and Colorado east of the Rocky Mountains and north of the Arkansas River, and all but a small southwestern section of Kansas.

By the Treaty of Paris of 1763, which closed our French and Indian War, the French territory east of the Mississippi passed to England, and that west of the Mississippi to Spain. By the Treaty of Paris of 1783, which ended the Revolution, England gave Florida back to Spain. During the first years of our national history, therefore, Spain owned the western shore of the Mississippi and both shores at its mouth. It was soon seen that our citizens who were settling along the Mississippi would have their commerce threatened and hampered by Spain, especially as that country at first refused us the free navigation of the river. It was not until 1795 that a treaty was negotiated by Thomas Pinckney whereby Spain granted us free navigation of the river and the right to use New Orleans, or some other place which would be provided, as a place of deposit for merchandise.

In 1800 a secret treaty was negotiated between France and Spain by which the latter "retroceded" to France the Province of Louisiana. Napoleon, then First Consul of France, threatened to send an army and fleet to New Orleans. It was feared that French ambition in Louisiana and Spanish designs in Florida would ultimately prove hurtful to us.

In 1802 the right of deposit in New Orleans was taken away, and no other place was designated. The western portion of the United States clamored for governmental action. Congress appropriated $2,000,000 for the purchase of New Orleans, and President Jefferson, in January 1803, sent James Monroe as minister extraordinary with discretionary powers to act with our Minister to France, Robert R. Livingston, in the purchase. Napoleon at this time found himself burdened with debt and threatened with an English war, and proposed to sell the whole Province of Louisiana. A convention to that effect was speedily arranged and signed on April 30, 1803, by Livingston and Monroe for the United States and Barbé-Marbois for France. The price agreed upon to be paid was $15,000,000, of which $3,750,000 were claims of our citizens against France, which the United States agreed to assume.

The people of the United States as a whole rejoiced, though the Federalists claimed that the measure was unwarranted by the Constitution, and even Jefferson thought a constitutional amendment would be necessary. The purchase, however, was finally accepted without an amendment and was generally acquiesced in. An early session of Congress was called for October 17, 1803. Two days later the treaty was ratified by the Senate, and on October 25 the House passed a resolution to carry it into effect by a vote of ninety to twenty-five, the Federalists voting in the minority. Napoleon accepted 6 per cent bonds, payable in fifteen years, for this territory, which more than doubled the area of the United States.

Concerning this purchase, Livingston is said to have exclaimed: "We have lived long, but this is the noblest work of our whole lives." And Napoleon is said to have remarked: "I have just given to England a maritime rival that will, sooner or later, humble her pride." Portions of the boundary line of this purchased territory were in dispute for a long time, but so far as Spain was concerned, the differences of opinion were settled by the treaty of 1819 (see next section), and the treaty of 1846 with Great Britain settled the remainder. The region acquired by this purchase was divided into the Territory of Orleans and the Territory of Louisiana.

II FLORIDA—When Great Britain in 1763 acquired that part of Louisiana east of the Mississippi from France, and Florida from Spain (see preceding section), she joined her portion of Louisiana to Florida and divided West Florida from East Florida by the Apalachicola River. Both of these passed to Spain in 1783.

Spain claimed that when, in 1800, she "retroceded" Louisiana to France, she gave back only what she had obtained from that country, and that West Florida, which she obtained from England, still remained hers. The United States maintained that Spain had given to France the whole original extent of Louisiana, and that Florida west of the Perdido was a part of our purchase from France in 1803.

Our government did not press this claim till 1810, but then, under direction of the President, Governor Claiborne of the Territory of Orleans, took possession of all West Florida except Mobile, and in 1813 General Wilkinson obtained possession of Mobile also. There was a growing desire in the United States to seize East Florida.

Congress as early as 1811 passed secret acts authorizing the President to take "temporary possession" of it, though nothing came of this. In 1814 and 1818 Jackson made raids into the coveted territory, which seemed to show to Spain the danger her territory was in. She did not think it worth defending, and on February 22, 1819, the Spanish Minister in Washington signed a treaty by which Florida was ceded to the United States. Our government in return assumed claims of its citizens against Spain to the amount of $5,000,000 and accepted the Sabine River as the eastern boundary of Mexico. By the same treaty Spain accepted the forty-second degree of north latitude as the northern limit to her claims of territory west of the Rocky Mountains. The United States Senate at once ratified this treaty, but Spain delayed till early in 1821, and in July of that year possession was surrendered.

III TEXAS—Previous to 1819 the United States had claimed as part of the Louisiana Purchase the region known as Texas as far as the Rio Grande River, but by the Spanish treaty of that year yielded its claim. Soon afterward, inhabitants of the United States began to remove to Texas, where they obtained grants of land and settled. It thus grew into a state which was closely allied to the United States.

This migration to Texas and the subsequent annexation were part of the political scheme of the South to maintain its power in Congress by the addition of slave territory to offset the creation of free states in the North. In 1827 and 1829, Clay and Calhoun tried to obtain Texas by purchase, offering $1,000,000 and $5,000,000, but without success.

In March 1836, Texas, dissatisfied with the government of Mexico, declared its independence. A short war followed. The Mexicans committed massacres at Goliad and the Alamo, but on April 10, at San Jacinto, Santa Anna, the Mexican President, with five thousand men, was badly defeated by seven hundred men under General Sam Houston, the commander of the Texan forces.

Santa Anna agreed to a treaty which recognized the independence of Texas. This was not ratified by Mexico, but in March 1837 the United States recognized the independence of the Republic of Texas, and soon England, France, and Belgium did likewise. In 1837

Texas made application to Congress for annexation, but with no immediate result. The presidential campaign of 1844 turned largely on this question. The Democratic convention nominated Polk, who favored annexation, instead of Van Buren, who opposed it. Clay, the Whig candidate, was also supposed to be against the project.

In the meantime, Secretary of State Calhoun had negotiated a treaty of annexation with Texas in April 1844, including the territory between the Nueces and Rio Grande rivers, disputes as to which finally led to the Mexican War. This treaty failed of ratification at the hands of the Senate. Polk was elected, partly by reason of the votes thrown away on Birney, but his election was taken as a sign of popular approval of annexation, and Congress and Tyler's administration now became attached to the project.

Early in 1845 Congress authorized the President to negotiate a treaty of annexation. Tyler hastened to accomplish the object, though without a treaty, and on the last day of his term sent a special messenger to Texas. This emissary on June 18 secured the consent of the Congress of Texas, which was ratified by a popular vote on July 4. A resolution for the admission of Texas as a state was passed in the House of Representatives by a vote of 141 to 56 on December 16, 1845, and in the Senate by a vote of 31 to 13 on December 22, and Texas was declared a state of the Union on December 29, 1845.

IV NEW MEXICO AND UPPER CALIFORNIA—The name New Mexico was originally applied to the territory now known as Utah, Nevada, and large portions of Arizona, Colorado, and New Mexico. Upper California comprised what is now the state of California. These regions, which belonged to Mexico, were conquered during the Mexican War, and by the treaty of 1848, which ended that contest, passed to the United States. Our government paid to Mexico for this cession $15,000,000 and assumed debts due from Mexico to our citizens amounting to $3,250,000. A portion of this acquisition (that part of New Mexico east of the Rio Grande) was claimed by Texas, and one of the provisions of Henry Clay's Omnibus Bill, passed in 1850, provided for the payment of $10,000,000 to Texas in satisfaction of her claim.

V GADSDEN PURCHASE—Disputes still remained with reference

15

to those portions of Arizona and New Mexico south of the Gila River, and Mexican troops were sent thither. Trouble was averted, however, by the Gadsden Treaty, December 30, 1853, so called because it was negotiated by our Minister to Mexico, General James Gadsden. By this treaty the United States obtained the disputed territory, for which we paid $10,000,000.

VI ALASKA—By a treaty of March 30, 1867, ratified by the Senate on June 20 of the same year, Russia ceded to the United States what is now the Territory of Alaska. The price paid was $7,200,000.

VII The Hawaiian Islands voluntarily became a territory of the United States in 1898, this country assuming the Hawaiian national debt of $4,000,000.

VIII The United States purchased the Danish West Indies, known as the Virgin Islands, from Denmark in 1917 for $25,000,000.

"Another County Heard From"—A phrase which came into general use during the presidential campaign of 1876, when the election returns from Florida and other doubtful states were reported at a vexingly slow rate.

Anthem, National—Congress designated the words and music of "The Star-Spangled Banner" as the national anthem on March 3, 1931. The tune of "The Star-Spangled Banner," which was originally a German drinking song, was very popular in the first decades of the nineteenth century, first under its name of "To Anacreon in Heaven," then as a political song called sometimes "Adams and Liberty" and sometimes "Jefferson and Liberty." Setting Key's words to this tune was much like using the tune of the "Beer Barrel Polka" for a patriotic hymn.

Anti-Federal Junto—When the Constitution was before the country for adoption and it was proposed in the Pennsylvania Legislature to call a convention to ratify it, nineteen of the members walked out, leaving the House without a quorum. But enough were dragged back to enable the House to do business. Sixteen of those who withdrew signed, in September 1787, an address against the Constitution which was so full of absurd misstatements that it was treated as a ridiculous piece of work, and the signers and their followers became known as the Anti-Federal Junto.

Anti-Masonic Party—This party was composed of persons who refused to vote for Masons because they believed the members of the society placed the laws of their fraternity above those of their country and were therefore unfit to hold public office.

Enormous excitement was caused in 1826 when William Morgan of Batavia, New York, who had declared his intention of publishing a book disclosing the secrets of Freemasonry, was arrested for a trifling debt. On his release he was seized and taken in a closed carriage to Fort Niagara. Here he disappeared and was never heard from again. A body found in the river below Niagara Falls sometime afterward was said to be his, and the public generally believed that the Masons were responsible for the abduction and slaying of Morgan. So strong did the prejudice against them become that, even though the National Republican party in New York named a state ticket without any Masons on it, an Anti-Masonic convention was held and a ticket to oppose Freemasonry nominated. Relatively few votes were polled by the party at first, but it grew rapidly, spreading to other states, and in 1831 held a national convention at which William Wirt of Maryland was nominated for President and Amos Ellmaker of Pennsylvania for Vice-President. Vermont gave its electoral vote to this ticket. The party was absorbed soon after by the Whig party but remained a powerful clique. It continued as a separate party only in Pennsylvania, where its nominee won the governorship in 1835. (See *Good Enough Morgan Till After Election.*)

Anti-Monopoly Party—At a convention held at Chicago on May 14, 1884, the Anti-Monopoly Organization of the United States nominated Benjamin F. Butler of Massachusetts for President. The platform adopted at the meeting demanded economical government and the enactment and enforcement of equitable laws, including an interstate commerce law, the establishment of labor bureaus providing industrial arbitration, the direct election of United States

17

senators, a gradual income tax, payment of the national debt as it matured, and fostering care for agriculture. It denounced the tariff and the grant of lands to corporations. The Greenback Labor party endorsed the candidacy of Butler, and the joint ticket was called the People's party. In the election it polled 130,000 votes.

Anti-Nebraska Men were the Northern Whigs who in 1854 opposed the Kansas-Nebraska Bill. Joined by Democrats of similar views, this faction controlled the House in the Thirty-fourth Congress, and it was from them that the Republican party sprang. (See *Kansas-Nebraska Bill.*)

Anti-War Democrats—A term applied to the minority members of the early Democratic party who sided with the Federalists in their opposition to the War of 1812. The extremists who favored peace at any price were called Submission Men.

During the Civil War the Democratic party was the peace party. At its national convention, August 29, 1864, a resolution was passed declaring it to be "the sense of the American people that after four years of failure to restore the Union by the experiment of war . . . immediate efforts be made for the cessation of hostilities, with a view to an ultimate convention of the States . . . to the end that . . . peace may be restored on the basis of the Federal Union of the States." The members of the party who approved of this view were called Anti-War Democrats. Those who disapproved and sided with the Republicans were called War Democrats.

Arizona—"Valentine State." State flower, saguaro cactus. Population, 499,261. Area, 113,909 square miles. Capital, Phoenix. Admitted to the Union as the forty-eighth state in 1912, since which time it has been Democratic in national elections, except in 1920, 1924, and 1928. It has two representatives in Congress.

Arkansas—Often called the "Bear State." State flower, apple-blossom. Population, 1,949,387. Area, 53,102 square miles. Capital, Little Rock. Admitted to the Union as a state in 1836. Seceded in May 1861, but was readmitted in June 1868. For a period after the

Civil War there was much unrest and political conflict until 1874, when a new constitution went into effect. It is a Democratic state. Besides its two senators, it has seven representatives in Congress.

Armageddon—Theodore Roosevelt, in seeking the presidential nomination in June 1912, made one of the most impressive speeches of his career at a pre-convention rally in Chicago. The following paragraph is from his speech:

"We fought in honorable fashion for the good of mankind; fearless of the future, unheeding of our individual fates, with unflinching heart and undimmed eyes; we stand at Armageddon, and we battle for the Lord."

Arm-in-Arm Convention—When the Republican supporters of President Johnson's reconstruction policy met at Philadelphia in August 1866, the members from Massachusetts and from South Carolina entered the convention together at the head of the delegates, arm in arm, and this gave rise to the name.

Arsenal of Democracy—When the Axis powers ran roughshod over country after country in the early part of World War II, President Franklin D. Roosevelt acted in a realistic fashion and laid down the principle that the preservation of Britain and the British Navy were necessary to American safety. He traded fifty over-age destroyers to Britain in exchange for naval and air-base sites in the western Atlantic. Selective service soon became a law, naval and air programs were accelerated, industry was put on a wartime basis, and America then became, in Roosevelt's own words, the great Arsenal of Democracy. The speech in which he used the phrase was broadcast from the White House on December 29, 1940.

Arthur, Chester A.—Upon the death of Garfield, Chester Arthur became our twenty-first President and held that office from 1881 to 1885. He was a tall, handsome man of distinguished appearance, and his impeccable manners served him well in social gatherings.

Because of his past associations with the Republican party, Arthur had been accused of being a "machine politician," but the presidency

19

brought out the best in him. Conservative but not lacking in good judgment, he gave the country a satisfactory administration. It is interesting to note that in 1883, during his term of office, the Pendleton Civil Service Act was passed. It was a bill which stood contrary to most of his previous political principles, but he gave it his full support.

He was born in Fairfield, Vermont, on October 5, 1830. In 1848 he was graduated from Union College and for a time taught school in Pownall, Vermont. Then he studied law in New York City, where he was admitted to the bar in 1854. After practicing law for a few years in New York he served in the Civil War as quartermaster general of New York in charge of getting troops raised and equipped. In 1871 he was appointed collector of the Port of New York and filled that office until 1878, when President Hayes removed him for political reasons. In 1880, as the running mate of Garfield on the Republican ticket, he was elected Vice-President.

He died in New York City on November 18, 1886, less than two years after he had retired from the presidency.

Articles of Confederation—On June 11, 1776, the Colonial Congress, assembled in Philadelphia, resolved to appoint a committee, consisting of one member from each colony, to prepare a form of confederation to be entered into between the colonies. The committee reported, a few changes were made in the wording of the document that they submitted, and on November 15, 1777, it was agreed to by Congress. It was submitted to the states for ratification, and it was provided that it should be conclusive when signed by the delegates of all the states, as these should authorize the ratification.

On July 9, 1778, it was signed in behalf of New Hampshire, Massachusetts Bay, Rhode Island and Providence plantations, Connecticut, New York, Pennsylvania, Virginia, and South Carolina. It was signed for North Carolina on July 21, for Georgia on July 24, and for New Jersey on November 26. One delegate of Delaware signed on February 12, 1779, and the other two on May 5. On March 1, 1781, the delegates of Maryland signed, and on the next day Congress assembled under its new powers.

By this instrument, known as the Articles of Confederation, the

United States was governed before the adoption of the Constitution. While these articles gave to Congress power to perform many of the acts of a sovereign government, they gave to it no power to enforce its own commands, and as a consequence it was impossible in spite of strenuous efforts to raise revenue. The debt, principal and interest, fell into arrears, the soldiers of the Revolution remained unpaid, and Congress could not even induce the states to give it power to retaliate on nations bent on ruining our trade. The attendance of members in Congress grew smaller and smaller, and it required an especial appeal to have the quorum necessary for the ratification of the treaty of peace with Great Britain. On July 14, 1788, the ratification by nine states of the present Constitution (prepared by the Convention of 1787) was announced by Congress. After January 1789 the attendance of a few members, who met and adjourned from day to day, gave a nominal existence to Congress, and on March 2, two days before the time fixed for the beginning of the new government, even this pretense of existence was dropped and the old Congress was dead. The following is the text of these articles:

ARTICLES OF CONFEDERATION AND PERPETUAL UNION

Between the States of New Hampshire, Massachusetts Bay, Rhode Island and Providence Plantations, Connecticut, New York, New Jersey, Pennsylvania, Delaware, Maryland, Virginia, North Carolina, South Carolina and Georgia.

ARTICLE I The style of this confederacy shall be, "THE UNITED STATES OF AMERICA."

ARTICLE II Each State retains its sovereignty, freedom and independence, and every power, jurisdiction and right, which is not, by this confederation, expressly delegated to the United States in Congress assembled.

ARTICLE III The said States hereby severally enter into a firm league of friendship with each other, for their common defense, the security of their liberties, and their mutual and general welfare; binding themselves to assist each other against all force offered to, or attacks made upon them, or any of them, on account of religion, sovereignty, trade, or any other pretense whatever.

ARTICLE IV The better to secure and perpetuate mutual friendship and intercourse among the people of the different States in this Union, the free inhabitants of each of these States, paupers, vagabonds and fugitives from justice excepted, shall be entitled to all privileges and immunities of free citizens in the several States; and the people of each State shall have free ingress and egress to and from any other State, and shall enjoy therein all the privileges of trade and commerce, subject to the same duties, impositions and restrictions as the inhabitants thereof respectively; provided, that such restrictions shall not extend so far as to prevent the removal of property imported into any State to any other State of which the owner is an inhabitant; provided, also, that no imposition, duties or restriction shall be laid by any State on the property of the United States, or either of them.

If any person guilty of, or charged with treason, felony or other high misdemeanor in any State, shall flee from justice, and be found in any of the United States, he shall, upon demand of the governor or executive power of the State from which he fled, be delivered up and removed to the State having jurisdiction of his offense.

Full faith and credit shall be given in each of these States to the records, acts and judicial proceedings, of the courts and magistrates of every other State.

ARTICLE V For the more convenient management of the general interests of the United States, delegates shall be annually appointed in such manner as the Legislature of each State shall direct, to meet in Congress on the first Monday in November, in every year, with a power reserved to each State to recall its delegates, or any of them, at any time within the year, and send others in their stead for the remainder of the year.

No State shall be represented in Congress by less than two, nor by more than seven members, and no person shall be capable of being a delegate for more than three years in any term of six years, nor shall any person, being a delegate, be capable of holding any office under the United States for which he, or another for his benefit, receives any salary, fees or emolument of any kind.

Each State shall maintain its own delegates in a meeting of the States, and while they act as members of the committee of the States.

In determining questions in the United States in Congress assembled, each State shall have one vote.

Freedom of speech and debate in Congress shall not be impeached or questioned in any court or place out of Congress; and the members of Congress shall be protected in their persons from arrest and imprisonment during the time of their going to and from, and attendance on Congress, except for treason, felony, or breach of the peace.

ARTICLE VI No State, without the consent of the United States in Congress assembled, shall send any embassy to, or receive any embassy from, or enter into any conference, agreement, alliance or treaty with any king, prince or State; nor shall any person holding any office of profit or trust under the United States, or any of them, accept of any present, emolument, office or title of any kind whatever, from any king, prince or foreign State; nor shall the United States in Congress assembled, or any of them, grant any title of nobility.

No two or more States shall enter into any treaty, confederation or alliance whatever, between them, without the consent of the United States in Congress assembled, specifying accurately the purposes for which the same is to be entered into, and how long it shall continue.

No State shall lay any imposts or duties which may interfere with any stipulations in treaties entered into by the United States in Congress assembled, with any king, prince or State, in pursuance of any treaties already proposed by Congress to the courts of France and Spain.

No vessels of war shall be kept up in time of peace by any State, except such number only as shall be deemed necessary by the United States in Congress assembled, for the defense of such State or its trade; nor shall any body of forces be kept up by any State, in time of peace, except such number only as in the judgment of the United States in Congress assembled, shall be deemed requisite to garrison the forts necessary for the defense of such State; but every State shall always keep up a well-regulated and disciplined militia, sufficiently armed and accoutered, and shall provide and constantly have ready for use, in public stores, a due number of field-pieces and tents, and a proper quantity of arms, ammunition and camp equipage.

No State shall engage in any war, without the consent of the United States in Congress assembled, unless such State be actually invaded by enemies, or shall have received certain advice of a resolution being formed by some nation of Indians to invade such State, and the danger is so imminent as not to admit of a delay till the United States in Congress assembled can be consulted; nor shall any State grant commissions to any ship or vessels of war, nor letters of marque or reprisal, except it be after a declaration of war by the United States in Congress assembled, and then only against the Kingdom or State, and the subjects thereof, against which war has been so declared, and under such regulations as shall be established by the United States in Congress assembled, unless such State be infested by pirates, in which vessels of war may be fitted out for that occasion, and kept so long as the danger shall continue, or until the United States in Congress assembled shall determine otherwise.

ARTICLE VII When land forces are raised by any State for the common defense, all officers of, or under the rank of colonel, shall be appointed by the Legislature of each State, respectively, by whom such forces shall be raised, or in such manner as such State shall direct, and all vacancies shall be filled up by the State which first made the appointment.

ARTICLE VIII All charges of war, and all other expenses that shall be incurred for the common defense, or general welfare, and allowed by the United States in Congress assembled, shall be defrayed out of a common treasury, which shall be supplied by the several States in proportion to the value of all land within each State, granted to or surveyed for, any person, as such land and the buildings and improvements thereon shall be estimated, according to such mode as the United States in Congress assembled shall from time to time direct and appoint. The taxes for paying that proportion shall be laid and levied by the authority and direction of the Legislatures of the several States within the time agreed upon by the United States in Congress assembled.

ARTICLE IX The United States in Congress assembled shall have the sole and exclusive right and power of determining on peace and war, except in the cases mentioned in the sixth article: Of sending and receiving ambassadors: Entering into treaties and alliances; provided that no treaty of commerce shall be made whereby the legislative power of the respective States shall be restrained from imposing such imposts and duties on foreigners as their own people are subjected to, or from prohibiting the exportation or importation of any species of goods or commodities whatever: Of establishing rules for deciding, in all cases, what captures on land or water shall be legal; and in what manner prizes taken by land or naval forces in the service of the United States shall be divided or appropriated: Of granting letters of marque or reprisal in times of peace: Appointing courts for the trial of piracies and felonies committed on the high seas; and establishing courts, for receiving and determining, finally, appeals in all cases of captures; provided, that no member of Congress shall be appointed a judge of any of the said courts.

The United States in Congress assembled shall also be the last resort, on appeal, in all disputes and differences now subsisting, or that hereafter may arise, between two or more States, concerning boundary, jurisdiction, or any other cause whatever; which authority shall always be exercised in the manner following: Whenever the legislative or executive authority, or lawful agent, of any State, in controversy with another, shall present a petition to Congress, stating the matter in question, and praying for a hearing, notice thereof shall be given, by order of Congress, to the legislative or executive authority of the other State in controversy; and a day assigned for the appearance of the parties by their lawful agents, who shall then be directed to appoint, by joint consent, commissioners or judges, to constitute a court for hearing and determining the matter in question; but if they cannot agree, Congress shall name three persons, out of each of the United States, and from the list of such persons each party shall alternately strike out one, the petitioners beginning, until the number shall be reduced to thirteen; and from that number, not less than seven, nor more than nine, names, as Congress shall direct, shall, in the presence of Congress, be drawn out, by lot; and the persons whose names shall be so drawn, or any five of them, shall be commissioners or judges, to hear and finally determine the controversy, so always as a major part of the judges, who shall hear the cause, shall agree in the determination. And if either party shall neglect to attend at the day appointed, without showing reasons which Congress shall judge sufficient, or being present shall refuse to strike, the Congress shall proceed to nominate three persons out of each State; and the secretary of Congress shall strike in behalf of such party absent or refusing; and the judgment and sentence of the court, to be appointed in the manner before prescribed, shall be final and conclusive. And if any of the parties shall refuse to submit to the authority of such court, or to appear, or defend their claim or cause, the court shall, nevertheless, proceed to pronounce sentence or judgment, which shall in like manner be final and decisive; the judgment, or sentence, and other proceedings, being in either case, transmitted to Congress, and, lodged among the acts of Congress, for the security of the parties concerned: Provided that every commissioner, before he sits in judgment, shall take an oath, to be administered by one of the judges of the Supreme or Superior Courts of the State where the cause shall be tried, "Well and truly to hear and determine the matter in question, according to the best of his judgment, without favor, affection, or hope of reward:" Provided, also, that no State shall be deprived of territory for the benefit of the United States.

All controversies concerning the private right of soil claimed under different grants of two or more States, whose jurisdiction, as they may respect such lands, and the States which passed such grants are adjusted, the said grants or either of them being at the same time claimed to have originated antecedent to such settlement of jurisdiction, shall, on the petition of either party to the Congress of the United States, be finally determined, as near as may be, in the same manner as is before prescribed for deciding disputes respecting territorial jurisdiction between different States.

The United States, in Congress assembled, shall have the sole and exclusive right and power of regulating the alloy and value of coin struck by their own authority, or by that of the respective States: Fixing the standard of weights and measures throughout the United States: Regulating the trade and managing all affairs with the Indians, not members of any of the States; provided that the legislative right of any State, within its own limits, be not infringed or violated: Establishing and regulating post-offices from one State to another, throughout all the United States, and exacting such postage on the papers passing through the same as may be requisite to defray the expenses of the said office: Appointing all officers of the land forces in the service of the United States, excepting regimental officers: Appointing all the officers of the naval forces, and commissioning all officers whatever in the service of the United States: Making rules for the government and regulation of the land and naval forces, and directing their operations.

The United States in Congress assembled shall have authority to appoint a committee, to sit in the recess of Congress, to be denominated A COMMITTEE OF THE STATES, and to consist of one delegate from each State; and to appoint such other committees and civil officers as may be necessary for managing the general affairs of the United States under their direction: To appoint one of their number to preside; provided, that no person be allowed to serve in the office of president more than one year in any term of three years: To ascertain the necessary sums of money to be raised for the service of the United States, and to appropriate and apply the same for defraying the public expenses: To borrow money, or emit bills on the credit of the United States, transmitting every half year to the respective States an account of the sums of money so borrowed or emitted: To build and equip a navy: To agree upon the number of land forces, and to make requisitions from each State for its quota, in proportion to the number of white inhabitants in such State, which requisition shall be binding; and thereupon the Legislature of each State shall appoint the regimental officers, raise the men, and clothe, arm and equip them, in a soldier-like manner, at the expense of the United States; and the officers and men so clothed, armed and equipped, shall march to the place appointed, and within the time agreed on, by the United States in Congress assembled; but if the United States in Congress assembled shall, on consideration of circumstances, judge proper that any State should not raise men, or should raise a smaller number than its quota, and that any other State should raise a greater number of men than its quota thereof, such extra number shall be raised, officered, clothed, armed and equipped, in the same manner as the quota of such State; unless the Legislature of such State shall judge that such extra number cannot be safely spared out of the same; in which case they shall raise, officer, clothe, arm and equip, as many of such extra number as they judge can be safely spared; and the officers and men so clothed, armed and equipped shall march to the place appointed, and within the time agreed on, by the United States in Congress assembled.

The United States in Congress assembled shall never engage in a war, nor grant letters of marque and reprisal in time of peace, nor enter into any treaties or alliances, nor coin money, nor regulate the value thereof, nor ascertain the sum and expenses necessary for the defense and welfare of the United States, or any of them, nor emit bills, nor borrow money on the credit of the United States, nor appropriate money, nor agree upon the numbers of vessels of war to be built or purchased, or the number of land or sea forces to be raised, nor appoint a commander-in-chief of the army or navy, unless nine States assent to the same; nor shall a question on any other point, except for adjourning from day to day, be determined, unless by the votes of a majority of the United States in Congress assembled.

The Congress of the United States shall have power to adjourn at any time within the year, and to any place within the United States, so that no period of adjournment be for a longer duration than the space of six months, and shall publish the journal of their proceedings monthly, except such parts thereof relating to treaties, alliances, or military operations as in their judgment require secrecy; and the yeas and nays of the delegates of each State, on any question, shall be entered on the journal, when it is desired by any delegate; and the delegates of a State, or any of them, at his or their request, shall be furnished with a transcript of the said journal, except such parts as are above excepted, to lay before the legislatures of the several States.

ARTICLE X The committee of the States, or any nine of them, shall be authorized to execute, in the recess of Congress, such of the powers of Congress as the United States in Congress assembled, by the consent of nine States, shall, from time to time, think expedient to vest them with; provided that no power be delegated to the said committee, for the exercise of which, by the Articles of Confederation, the voice of nine States, in the Congress of the United States assembled, is requisite.

ARTICLE XI Canada, acceding to this Confederation, and joining in the measures of the United States, shall be admitted into and entitled to all the advantages of this Union; but no other colony shall be admitted into the same unless such admission be agreed to by nine States.

ARTICLE XII All bills of credit emitted, moneys borrowed, and debts contracted by or under the authority of Congress, before the assembling of the United States, in pursuance of the present Confederation, shall be deemed and considered as a charge against the United States, for payment and satisfaction whereof the said United States and the public faith are hereby solemnly pledged.

ARTICLE XIII Every State shall abide by the determinations of the United States in Congress assembled, on all questions which, by this Confederation, are submitted to them. And the Articles of this Confederation shall be inviolably observed by every State; and the

Union shall be perpetual. Nor shall any alteration at any time hereafter be made in any of them, unless such alteration be agreed to, in a Congress of the United States, and be afterward confirmed by the legislatures of every State.

And whereas, it hath pleased the great Governor of the world to incline the hearts of the Legislatures we respectively represent in Congress to approve of, and to authorize us to ratify, the said Articles of Confederation and Perpetual Union:

KNOW YE, That we, the undersigned delegates, by virtue of the power and authority to us given for this purpose, do, by these presents, in the name, and in behalf, of our respective constituents, fully and entirely ratify and confirm each and every of the said Articles of Confederation and Perpetual Union, and all and singular the matters and things therein contained. And we do further solemnly plight and engage the faith of our respective constituents, that they shall abide by the determinations of the United States in Congress assembled, on all questions, which, by the said Confederation, are submitted to them; and that the articles thereof shall be inviolably observed by the States we respectively represent; and that the Union shall be perpetual.

In witness whereof, we have hereunto set our hands in Congress.

Done at Philadelphia, in the State of Pennsylvania, the ninth day of July, in the year of our Lord one thousand seven hundred and seventy-eight, and in the third year of the Independence of America.

[Here follow the signatures of the delegates from New Hampshire, Massachusetts Bay, Rhode Island and Providence Plantations, Connecticut, New York, New Jersey, Pennsylvania, Delaware, Maryland, Virginia, North Carolina, South Carolina, and Georgia. Forty-eight in all.]

"As Maine Goes, So Goes the Nation"—See *Hell-Bent for Election.*

Ashburton Treaty, The, was drawn up by Lord Ashburton, Commissioner from Great Britain, and Daniel Webster, Secretary of State under Tyler. It was signed in Washington, August 9, 1842, ratified by the Senate on the twentieth of the same month, and proclaimed by the President on the tenth of the following November. Besides settling the northeast boundary, it provided that the United States should make common cause with Great Britain in suppressing the slave trade, and also provided for the extradition of persons charged with certain crimes. (See *Northeast Boundary*.)

"Ask Nothing but What Is Right"—President Jackson in his instructions to Louis McLane, his first Minister to England in 1831, stated what his conception of our foreign policy should be when he said, "Ask nothing but what is right; submit to nothing that is wrong."

Assassinations, Political—Three presidents of the United States have been assassinated—Lincoln, Garfield, and McKinley.

Lincoln was shot while attending a performance of *Our American Cousin* in Ford's Theater, Washington, on Good Friday, April 14, 1865. His assailant, John Wilkes Booth, an actor of Southern sympathies, was shot to death in a barn near Fredericksburg, Virginia, April 26, by Sergeant Boston Corbett of the United States Army. Four persons, one woman and three men, were tried and hanged for their part in the crime.

On July 2, 1881, four months after his inauguration, James A. Garfield was shot and fatally wounded in the waiting room of the Baltimore and Potomac Railroad Station in Washington by Charles J. Guiteau, a Chicago lawyer and disappointed office seeker. The President survived until September 19, when he died from the effects of the wound. Guiteau was tried, convicted, and hanged in the district jail in Washington, June 30, 1882.

McKinley was shot at the Pan-American Exposition in Buffalo, New York, September 6, 1901, dying in Buffalo on September 14. His assassin was Leon Czolgosz, an anarchist, who fired twice at the President at point-blank range as the President was about to shake hands with him. Czolgosz had concealed his pistol under a handkerchief. Found guilty of murder, he was electrocuted in the state prison in Auburn, New York, October 29, 1901.

Theodore Roosevelt was wounded by a crank who shot at him just as he was entering a hall in Milwaukee to deliver a speech, October 14, 1912. Roosevelt was then running independently for President, and in spite of the bullet in his breast spoke to the crowd gathered to hear him.

30

An Italian-born anarchist, Joseph Zangara, fired at Franklin D. Roosevelt in Miami, Florida, February 15, 1933, but because of the quick action of a woman who seized Zangara's arm the President-elect was unharmed. The bullet, however, struck Mayor Anton J. Cermak of Chicago, and several others in the crowd were also wounded by Zangara. Cermak died of his wound March 6. Zangara was electrocuted March 20, 1933, after he had pleaded guilty and been found sane.

Other sensational American political assassinations were those of Mayor Carter Harrison, Sr., of Chicago in 1893, and Governor William Goebel of Kentucky in 1900. On September 8, 1935, United States Senator Huey P. Long was shot by Dr. Carl Austin Weiss in the Louisiana State Capitol at Baton Rouge and died two days later. Long's personal guards killed Weiss.

Assembly, Right of—The right of the people peaceably to assemble and to petition the government for a redress of their grievances is expressly preserved by the First Amendment to the Constitution (Article I of the Bill of Rights), and by most, if not all, state constitutions. But there is a distinction between the right of the people to meet for the peaceful discussion of their affairs and the assembly which has for its object the commission of acts of violence against persons or property, resisting the execution of the laws, disturbing the public order, or perpetrating acts creating public terror or alarm. Assemblies of this kind are unlawful and are not protected.

Atlantic Charter—A joint declaration of peace aims of the United States and Britain was signed "somewhere on the Atlantic" by President Franklin D. Roosevelt and Prime Minister Winston Churchill early in August 1941. An official statement, covering the meeting, was issued in Washington on August 14 and contained eight points. The text of the statement follows:

The President of the United States and the Prime Minister, Mr. Churchill, representing His Majesty's Government in the United Kingdom, have met at sea.

The President and the Prime Minister have had several confer-

31

ences. They have considered the dangers to world civilization arising from the policies of military domination by conquest upon which
the Hitlerite government of Germany and other governments associated therewith have embarked, and have made clear the steps
which their countries are respectively taking for their safety in the
face of these dangers.

They have agreed on the following Declaration:

The President of the United States of America and the Prime
Minister, Mr. Churchill, representing His Majesty's Government in
the United Kingdom, being met together, deem it right to make
known certain common principles in the national policies of their
respective countries on which they base their hopes for a better future
for the world.

FIRST—Their countries seek no aggrandizement, territorial or other;

SECOND—They desire to see no territorial changes that do not accord with the freely expressed wishes of the peoples concerned;

THIRD—They respect the right of all peoples to choose the form of
government under which they will live; and they wish to see sovereign rights and self-government restored to those who have been
forcibly deprived of them;

FOURTH—They will endeavor, with due respect for their existing
obligations, to further the enjoyment by all States, great or small,
victor or vanquished, of access, on equal terms, to the trade and to
the raw materials of the world which are needed for their economic
prosperity;

FIFTH—They desire to bring about the fullest collaboration between all nations in the economic field with the object of securing,
for all, improved labor standards, economic adjustment and social
security;

SIXTH—After the final destruction of the Nazi tyranny, they hope
to see established a peace which will afford to all nations the means
of dwelling in safety within their own boundaries, and which will
afford assurance that all the men in all the lands may live out their
lives in freedom from fear and want;

SEVENTH—Such a peace should enable all men to traverse the
high seas and oceans without hindrance;

EIGHTH—They believe that all of the nations of the world, for
realistic as well as spiritual reasons, must come to the abandonment

of the use of force. Since no future peace can be maintained if land, sea or air armaments continue to be employed by nations which threaten, or may threaten, aggression outside of their frontiers, they believe, pending the establishment of a wider and permanent system of general security, that the disarmament of such nations is essential. They will likewise aid and encourage all other practicable measures which will lighten for peace-loving peoples the crushing burden of armaments.

FRANKLIN D. ROOSEVELT

Dated August 14, 1941.   WINSTON S. CHURCHILL

Attorney General of the United States—This office was created by act of Congress on September 24, 1789, but the Attorney General was not made a member of the Cabinet until 1814. On the organization of the Department of Justice in 1870, the Attorney General was placed at its head, and all United States district attorneys and marshals were brought under his control. In the absence of the Attorney General his place is taken by the Solicitor General. The Attorney General seldom appears in cases before the courts, but leaves this work to other attorneys in his department. Like the other members of the Cabinet, the Attorney General is appointed by the President and confirmed by the Senate. In the presidential succession he stands fourth among the Cabinet members, the Secretary of State, the Secretary of the Treasury, and the Secretary of War preceding him in the order named. (See *Justice, Department of.*)

Australian Ballot—The Australian ballot was introduced into the United States from Australia in 1888, and in one form or another it is used today in practically every state of the Union. Printed at government expense, it lists the names of all candidates and is not placed in the voter's hands until he reaches the polls. The voter, after secretly marking his ballot, deposits it in the ballot box. Originally the Australian ballot made no party distinctions but printed the names of the candidates under the head of each office, and the voter went through the list, marking his choice in each instance. Following the lead of Massachusetts, a number of states adopted the system of labeling candidates with the names of their party. But now in most states candidates are grouped according to parties, and the person wishing to vote the straight party ticket does so by simply placing a mark in the circle at the top of the column of the party he prefers. If he wishes to split his ticket he does so by scratching some names and marking others instead.

Bachelor President—Name applied to our only unmarried President—James Buchanan. At the time of his first inauguration Grover Cleveland was a bachelor, but shortly afterward—June 2, 1886—was married in the White House.

Backbone of a Chocolate Éclair—Just before the Spanish-American War, when President McKinley was endeavoring to effect a peaceful solution of the Cuban problem, Theodore Roosevelt said that McKinley did not have the backbone of a chocolate éclair.

Band Wagon—The band wagon always headed the old-time circus parade, and the phrase "climbing on the band wagon" means that one joins in the popular procession. In politics people like to be on the winning side, and when there is a stampede toward a candidate whose chances of success look bright those who join him are said to climb on the band wagon.

Bank Holiday—One of Franklin D. Roosevelt's first acts upon becoming President in 1933 was to proclaim a bank holiday. Every financial repository in the country was closed for ten days during a readjustment period.

Bank of the United States—There have, in the history of this country, been two banks named Bank of the United States, the first from 1791 to 1811, the second from 1816 to 1836. The incorporation of the first of these was a part of Hamilton's financial scheme, and it aroused great opposition. Jefferson, Madison, and others who subsequently formed and became the leaders of the Republican party were foremost in the opposition, which was based on the lack of power on the part of Congress to charter any such institution.

The attitude of public men on this measure was among the first indications of the direction in which party lines would tend. Jefferson and the future Republicans demanded a strict construction of

34

the Constitution and denied the grant of any such power to Congress in that instrument. Hamilton maintained that the right to charter a corporation was one of the inherent privileges of a sovereign power, that the Federal Government was a sovereign power and need not therefore have such authority specifically granted, and that the step was "within the sphere of the specified powers" of the government enumerated by the Constitution. The bill incorporating the bank became law in 1791. The bank was to continue for twenty years; its capital was to be $10,000,000, of which $2,000,000 was to be subscribed by the government. In return the government was to receive a loan of $2,000,000, repayable in yearly installments of $200,000. Congress agreed to charter no other bank within twenty years. The public subscriptions were to be payable one quarter in coin and three quarters in 3 or 6 per cent national-debt certificates. The bank was authorized to establish branches, and its notes were to be received in payments to the United States.

Although Jefferson had originally opposed the bank on the ground of the unconstitutionality of its charter, he nevertheless, while President, recognized its constitutionality by signing various acts affecting it, and in the courts the legitimacy of its existence was never questioned. Its efforts to obtain a renewal of its charter from the United States at the expiration of its existence in 1811 were unsuccessful, as were the efforts to prolong its life by a Pennsylvania state charter, and so it went out of existence.

The head office of the bank was at Philadelphia. The government stock in the bank was sold to English bankers in 1802 at a premium of 57 per cent. The bank had paid dividends averaging over 8 per cent per annum; while in liquidation it was bought out by Stephen Girard of Philadelphia, one of the stockholders, and continued by him as a private institution.

In 1816 the second Bank of the United States was incorporated. Public sentiment had been inclined in favor of such a renewal by the financial difficulties attending the War of 1812, but although the subject was broached as early as 1814, it was two years later before the act passed. This time it was the Federalists who were opposed to it, and by in turn supporting and opposing each of two rival plans, they had compassed the defeat of both.

The powers of the bank were much the same as those of the first. Its capital stock was $35,000,000, payable one fifth in cash and four fifths in government stock. It was to have the custody of public funds, and five of the twenty-five directors were to be appointed by the government. Mismanagement brought the bank into a precarious position, and the new bank president was obliged, as a matter of necessity, largely to curtail its loans. The stringency thus created awakened considerable feeling against the bank.

The first intimation of any connection of the bank with politics was the demand of certain of President Jackson's political friends for the removal of the president of a New England branch who was politically obnoxious to them. The president of the bank, Nicholas Biddle, refused, denying any connection of his institution with politics. President Jackson was opposed to the bank, and his messages to Congress in 1829, 1830, and 1831 expressed strong dislike of the institution. In 1832 a bill to recharter passed both houses but was vetoed by the President and failed to pass over the veto. The elections of that year produced a House whose majority supported the President. On the plea that the bank was not safe, the President now removed the government deposits and placed them with state banks, which were called Banks of Deposit, and nicknamed "Pet Banks." In this he was supported by the House, which decided against a renewal of the charter and ordered an investigation of the bank. Of this nothing came. The bank was chartered by the state of Pennsylvania, and was thereafter known as Nicholas Biddle's United States Bank. Another attempt to establish such a bank was made in 1844, while Tyler was President. Two bills having that end in view passed Congress, but they were both vetoed.

Bicameral System—A legislature consisting of two distinct houses, such as the Senate and the House of Representatives at Washington. Both chambers concur in enacting legislation.

Bill of Rights—The first ten amendments to the Constitution are called the American Bill of Rights. These amendments were proposed at the first session of the First Congress of the United States which was begun and held in New York City, March 4, 1789, and were declared in force December 15, 1791. The resolution submitting the amendments to the states for ratification was as follows:

> The conventions of a number of the States having, at the time of their adopting the Constitution, expressed a desire, in order to prevent misconstruction or abuse of its powers, that further declaratory and restrictive clauses should be added, and as extending the ground of public confidence in the government will best insure the beneficent ends of its institution:
>
> *Resolved,* by the Senate and House of Representatives of the United States of America in Congress assembled, two-thirds of both Houses concurring, that the following articles be proposed to the legislatures of the several States, as amendments to the Constitution of the United States; all or any of which articles when ratified by three-fourths of the said legislatures, to be valid to all intents and purposes, as part of said Constitution.

Here follow the amendments (see *Constitution of the United States*) designed to protect, among other things, the freedom of religion, speech, and the press, the rights of assembly, petition, bearing arms, and trial by jury, and the right to compensation for private property taken for public uses. (See *Assembly, Right of; Eminent Domain; Petition, Right of.*)

These protective provisions are also a part of most of the state constitutions.

Black Cockade—During the troubles with France in 1797, when war seemed inevitable, the Federalists wore black cockades in their hats in contrast to the tricolor French cockades affected by the Republicans. The black cockade had been a part of the Continental uniform during the Revolution. In the days of the party's decline the Federalists were referred to reproachfully as Black Cockade Federalists.

Black Horse Cavalry—An old-time political term for corrupt legislators who band together for the purpose of exacting money from persons interested in the passage of a measure by threatening to defeat it if their demands are not met.

37

Black Laws—Prior to the abolition of slavery, many Northern states passed laws which exacted certain requirements of the Negroes or placed restrictions upon them as requisite for their residence in a state. For example, Negroes had to have certificates of their freedom placed on file; they could not testify in court when white men were involved in the case; they were not eligible to join the militia, could not attend public schools, and must present bonds for their good behavior.

Black Republicans—A term originating in the controversy over slavery. Southerners applied it particularly to the anti-slavery members of the Republican party.

Black Umbrella Boys—In the presidential campaign of 1940, Secretary of the Interior Harold L. Ickes branded those Republicans who favored appeasing the European dictators as Black Umbrella Boys. The allusion was to the umbrella-carrying habit of Prime Minister Neville Chamberlain of Great Britain, who signed the pact of Munich with Hitler and Mussolini, which he said meant "peace in our time."

Bloody Shirt—"Waving the bloody shirt" was a phrase often heard after the Civil War to describe the attempts of Republican political orators to get votes by appealing to the prejudices and passions engendered by the war.

Blue Laws—Social life was sternly regulated in colonial times, particularly in New England, where the moral code was extremely rigid. Laws were passed enforcing church worship, forbidding smoking in the public streets, prohibiting theatrical exhibitions, and the like. When the first collection of laws for the government of the colony of Connecticut was published in 1650, they were issued in blue paper covers and were given the name of blue laws.

A renegade tory, Reverend Samuel Peters, who was driven from the colony, published what purported to be a selection from these laws in 1781, and many persons came to believe that the blue laws of Connecticut actually contained such ridiculous regulations as that no husband should kiss his wife, and no mother her children, on the

Sabbath or on Fast Day; that a beer barrel should be whipped if it worked on Sunday; that on that day no one should cook food, make beds, sweep house, cut hair, or shave himself, and that every male of the colony should have his hair cut round by a cap, or, if a cap was wanting, then by the scooped-out shell of a half pumpkin.

Nowadays the term is applied to laws of a puritanical nature.

Blue Light Federalists—During the War of 1812 two frigates under the command of Commodore Stephen Decatur were bottled up in New London Harbor by the British. Attempts to run the blockade at night failed because, according to Decatur, the British fleet was warned each time by blue signal lights burned at the mouth of the harbor. These signals, it was charged, were given by Federalists opposed to the war, and from this incident the name arose.

Boodle—An old-time slang expression for money used for purposes of political bribery.

Border States—The northern tier of Southern slave states lying next to the free states of the North. They were Delaware, Maryland, Virginia, Kentucky, and Missouri, but sometimes North Carolina, Tennessee, and Arkansas were included under the name. It was from the Border States that the bitterest complaints came of the non-execution of the fugitive slave laws. These states did not want a political issue made of the slavery question and favored such parties as the American party and the Constitutional Union party, which stood for neutrality on the question. Of the Border States proper, Virginia was the only one that seceded at the time of the Civil War.

Boss System—The control exercised by professional politicians or "bosses" over nominations and elections, and their secret direction of the policies and processes of government, is known in the United States as the "boss system."

This system, sometimes called "invisible government," is most commonly practiced in state and local governments. There, more easily than in national affairs, the boss can establish a smooth-running, close-knit "machine," drawing his supporters from the ranks

39

of partisan workers who will give their services at primaries and elections in return for petty public offices and other political favors. Often times not only these workers, but the actual candidates for nomination or election, are tools of the "boss."

The widespread development of the "boss system" in this country is primarily due to the fact that the average citizen is not sufficiently interested in all the many elections held and the many elective officials to be chosen. Bosses have been quick to take advantage of this condition, though direct primaries, the initiative, the referendum, and the recall have challenged the professional politician's unfair and often destructive influence and power.

The most notorious boss in American politics was William M. Tweed, the head of Tammany Hall. He and his so-called "ring" were exposed, and in 1872 Tweed was convicted of stealing millions of dollars from the city of New York. (See *Ward Eight.*)

Bourbons—A term used in American politics during the nineteenth century to characterize statesmen and politicians who obstinately refused to keep step with the times and clung to dead issues and opposed changes of every kind. The name came from the house of Bourbon, which ruled France for two centuries, from 1589 to the period of the French Revolution in 1789. Its kings were rankly reactionary and learned nothing from experience. The term was revived during President Franklin D. Roosevelt's administration, when it was applied, synonymously, to those persons whom he called "economic royalists" (*q.v.*).

Brain Trust—During his first term and the early days of the New Deal, President Franklin D. Roosevelt had a number of unofficial personal advisers outside his Cabinet who, because many of them were college professors, were known as the Brain Trust. (See *Kitchen Cabinet; Tennis Cabinet.*)

Bretton Woods Conference—Delegates from forty-four nations, at the invitation of President Franklin D. Roosevelt, met at Bretton Woods, New Hampshire, on July 1, 1944, for the purpose of working out details for an international fund designed to hold financial transactions throughout the world on an even keel in the postwar period. The fund (International Monetary Fund) was to amount to $8,800,000,000. Another subject before the delegates was a proposal for an approximate $10,000,000,000 bank (International Bank for Reconstruction and Development) fund to be used for stimulating the flow of long-term credit which it was felt would be required to bring some semblance of order out of the war's chaos and damage, and to speed the industrial development of the peacetime world.

The International Monetary Fund works this way: All forty-four participating nations agreed to contribute on a predetermined basis to the fund. Other non-members may join later. Based on the existing control of gold stocks and other factors, the United States agreed to contribute the largest share—$2,750,000,000. Britain's portion was $1,300,000,000; Russia's was $1,200,000,000; China's, $550,-000,000; and France's, $450,000,000.

One of the main purposes of the fund is to maintain a stable world currency whereby trading can be conducted without interference from currency restrictions or wide fluctuations in exchange rates. Nations needing loans to get back to some semblance of normalcy are to be served by the International Bank.

One of the main objects of the bank is to aid governments and private corporations to make loans by guaranteeing, either in whole or in part, loans negotiated with private bankers. The bank was to have a capital of $9,100,000,000, and each nation was to be asked to advance 20 per cent of its allotment. The United States' share of the bank's capitalization is $3,175,000,000, 20 per cent of which is $635,000,000. This amount was to be deposited with the Federal Reserve Bank of New York to the credit of the International Bank. The plan provided that the other nations deposit their share in their own central banks. Each nation is to bear its share of any losses incurred by the International Bank.

The United States was the first nation to adopt the Bretton Woods Agreement, the Senate voting 61 to 16 on July 19, 1945.

Broad Seal War—In the election of 1838 there was a close contest in New Jersey between the six Democratic candidates for Congress and the six Whig candidates. Representatives to Congress

41

were then elected from New Jersey on a general ticket. The Democrats had a majority of about one hundred votes out of a total of 57,000; but because of certain irregularities the State Board of Canvassers gave the election certificates under the broad seal of the state to the Whig candidates. Since the House without New Jersey's representatives stood 118 Whigs to 119 Democrats, the control of the House hinged on the outcome of the controversy, which became known as the Broad Seal War. Great confusion followed, but a compromise Speaker was finally chosen, and eventually the Democratic members were seated.

Brother Jonathan—A general name formerly applied to the people of the United States. Its origin is said to be as follows: General Washington found soon after taking command of the Continental Army that it was sadly in need of many articles. Jonathan Trumbull, the elder, at that time governor of Connecticut, was a friend of Washington and one in whose judgment Washington had great confidence. During a consultation on the state of the Army, Washington suggested that "Brother Jonathan," meaning Trumbull, should be consulted. This advice was followed, and Trumbull devised the means of procuring what was desired. The story was told in the Army, and the reply to a demand for any article was invariably advice to ask "Brother Jonathan." The phrase became proverbial.

Buchanan, James, the fifteenth President of the United States, was born in Franklin County, Pennsylvania, April 23, 1791, and died in Lancaster, Pennsylvania, June 1, 1868. Following his graduation from Dickinson College, he studied law and was admitted to the bar. During his early political career he was a Federalist, but about 1826 he became a member of the Democratic party. He was a member of the Pennsylvania Legislature in 1814, and from 1820 to 1830 served in Congress. In the latter year he became Minister to Russia. On his return in 1834 he entered the Senate, where he remained until 1845. He was Secretary of State under Polk from 1845 to 1849. In 1852 he went abroad again, this time as Minister to Great Britain, but two years later he returned to the United States. In 1856 he was the Democratic candidate for President, winning the election in a three-cornered fight against John C. Frémont, the Republican candidate, and Millard Fillmore, the nominee of the American or Know-Nothing party. The popular vote was Buchanan 1,927,955, Frémont 1,391,555, Fillmore 934,816.

His administration was marked by the Dred Scott Decision, John Brown's raid on Harpers Ferry, and other events leading up to the Civil War. President Buchanan was anxious to preserve peace, but his leading Cabinet members were Southerners who seemed to overawe him. Largely because of his lack of energy and his opinion that the Federal Government could not interfere to keep any state in the Union by force, the nation was not prepared to meet the crisis. The presidential election of 1860 was unusually bitter, the South threatening to secede if Lincoln was elected. After the announcement of his success they went to work to destroy the Union, and before President Buchanan left the White House the Confederacy had been formed.

Buck and Breck—Popular nickname for the Democratic presidential candidates in 1856—James Buchanan and John C. Breckenridge.

Buckshot War—In 1838 the defeated Democratic candidate of a congressional district in Pennsylvania claimed Whig frauds in the North Liberties district as the cause of his defeat. Thereupon the ten Democratic return judges threw out the vote of that district, thus electing their member. The seven Whig judges met apart from the Democrats and gave certificates to the Whig candidates for Congress and also to the Whig candidates for the Legislature, although these latter had considered themselves fairly defeated.

This proceeding was part of a scheme to elect a Whig senator. The Whig certificates reached the Secretary of State first, and he, also a Whig, declared his intention of recognizing them until discredited by investigation. The House met December 4 at Harrisburg; armed partisans of both sides were in town; two separate organizations of the House took place, side by side, amid great confusion. Governor Ritner, a Whig, declared the city in the hands of a mob and sought the aid of United States troops from their com-

43

mander and then from President Van Buren. In both cases he met with refusal.

After a time several Whigs seceded to the Democratic House, which had succeeded in keeping possession of the chamber and records, and the House was recognized by the State Senate, when the other Whigs joined them; all but Thaddeus Stevens, who did not attempt to join until May 1839. The House then declared his seat vacant, and he was obliged to be again elected before he was finally admitted. The remark of a Whig member that the mob "should feel ball and buckshot before the day is over" is said to have given rise to the name.

Bull Moose—Followers of Theodore Roosevelt, when he chose to run in the presidential election of 1912, were known as Bull Moose adherents. The party symbol was a bull moose. In a letter written to Mark Hanna in 1900, Roosevelt said, "I am as strong as a bull moose," and this remark apparently led to the nickname. The political group which supported Roosevelt became known as the Bull Moose party.

Buncombe, to Speak for—Talking for political effect has come to be described as "speaking for Buncombe." The phrase originated during the debates on the Missouri Compromise, when Felix Walker, congressional representative from North Carolina, insisted on speaking, despite protests from the other members, upholding his right to be heard because he had to "make a speech for Buncombe," one of the counties in the state he represented.

Bureaucrat—The popular conception of a bureaucrat is that of a government officeholder who forgets that he is a public servant and assumes an undue importance to the annoyance and obstruction of the public. One of the arguments used in favor of the spoils system and periodic changes in government personnel is that other systems tend to create a bureaucracy composed of indifferent officials.

Burr Conspiracy—Aaron Burr was born in Newark, New Jersey, February 6, 1756, and died in New York on September 14, 1836. He was graduated from the College of New Jersey and served in the Continental Army in the Revolution, reaching the rank of colonel. He was subsequently admitted to the bar and moved to New York City. In 1791 he was elected to the United States Senate. He had a genius for political organization and soon brought his party, the anti-Federalists, into a state of efficient discipline. The Federalists called him, with a small number of young men of his party who gathered about him, the Little Band. It was to his efforts that the success of his party in the presidential contest of 1800 was due.

Burr was elected Vice-President, serving from 1801 to 1805. In 1804 a coalition was arranged between the New England Federalists, who were hopeless of victory in the South, and Burr's followers. As a part of this scheme, Burr was first nominated for governor against the candidate of the Clintons, the Livingstons, and the Schuylers, the great New York families that had been supreme in that state. Alexander Hamilton's personal efforts did much to defeat Burr; the celebrated duel between the two followed, ending, as is well known, in Hamilton's death. This is the last of Burr in politics.

In consequence of Burr's duel with Hamilton, Burr was indicted in New York and New Jersey for murder. He went West and made an extensive tour, in the course of which he made preparations for a gigantic but mysterious scheme. The real object of this is unknown. It was either to separate the Mississippi Valley from the rest of the Union and erect it into a new nation, or to conquer Mexico.

In 1806 he gathered a number of reckless persons about him and started for the region of Texas, ostensibly on a colonizing expedition. President Jefferson issued a proclamation warning citizens against joining the expedition. Burr was arrested by Jefferson's orders, brought back to Virginia, and indicted there by a United States grand jury for treason and for a misdemeanor, based on his course in levying war within this country on a friendly nation, but it was hoped that Burr could also be shown to have had treasonable designs against the unity of this country. He was acquitted of treason for want of jurisdiction, on the failure of the evidence required by Article III, Section 3, Clause 1, of the Constitution; he was also acquitted of misdemeanor. He was bound over to present himself for trial in Ohio, but the matter was pressed no further.

45

Cabinet—The term "Cabinet" is applied collectively to the heads of the executive departments of the Federal Government. No mention is made of the Cabinet in the Constitution, but that instrument (Article II, Section 2) authorizes the President to "require the opinion, in writing, of the principal officer in each of the executive departments, upon any subject relating to the duties of their respective offices." As originally constituted, the Cabinet consisted of only three members, the Secretary of State, the Secretary of War, and the Secretary of the Treasury. Washington called on them not only for their opinions on matters relating to their departments, but also consulted them on national affairs in general. Gradually the Cabinet became an advisory board to the President, meeting with him regularly in conferences over which he presided, as is still the case today. The importance of the members as a part of the executive branch of the Federal Government was recognized, and they were placed in the line of presidential succession (*q.v.*). Only six Cabinet appointments have been turned down by the Senate, and there have been only a few withdrawals.

Although it has frequently been suggested that the members of the Cabinet be given seats in one of the houses of Congress, either with or without a vote but with the right of debate, the suggestion has not been carried out. Appointed by the President, members of the Cabinet hold office through an administration or at their own or the President's pleasure. In addition to the ten heads of the various departments, the Vice-President may sit at Cabinet meetings, which are held in secret. (See *Brain Trust; Kitchen Cabinet; Tennis Cabinet.*)

California—Familiarly known as the "Golden State." State flower, golden poppy. Population, 6,907,387. Area, 158,693 square miles. Capital, Sacramento. Admitted as a state of the Union in 1850. Normally Republican in national politics, but went Democratic in 1880 and 1892 and in 1912 swerved to the new Progressive party. In 1916 the state again went Democratic, and also in 1932, 1936, 1940, and 1944. Herbert Hoover, who became the thirty-first President of the United States, was a native of California. The state has twenty-three Representatives in Congress.

Campaign Cigars given by candidates to voters during political campaigns, presumably to curry favor with them, are popularly supposed to be of a peculiarly cheap and vile brand. "What this country needs," remarked Vice-President Thomas R. Marshall to the Chief Clerk of the United States Senate, "is a good five-cent cigar."

Campaign Expenditures—During the past century the cost of electing a President has risen prodigiously. The Democrats spent less than $25,000 to elect James Buchanan in 1856. In 1860 it cost the Republicans $100,000 to elect Abraham Lincoln. By the end of the century millions were being spent, with the Republican party possessing the largest war chest. In the Wilson-Hughes campaign of 1916, the Republicans spent more than six millions to about two millions spent by the Democrats. This was the first presidential campaign in which the winner spent less than the loser. In March 1945, the Senate was informed by the chairman of the Senate Campaign Investigating Committee that the 1944 campaigns for President cost $23,000,000.

Presidential and congressional candidates are now required by Federal law to file sworn statements in Washington accounting for all campaign contributions and expenditures, and so are the organizations supporting them, including, since the passage of the 1944 tax bill, labor unions. Under the Hatch Act (see *Political Activity Act*) any person who directly or indirectly makes contributions in aggregate amount in excess of $5,000 during any calendar year or in connection with any campaign for nomination or election, to or on behalf of any candidate to an elective Federal office, or to or on behalf of any committee or other organization engaged in furthering, advancing, or advocating the nomination or election of any candidate for any such office or the success of any national political party is guilty of pernicious political activity and shall be fined not less than $5,000 and also sentenced to the penitentiary for not exceeding five years.

Various states now have corrupt practices acts which require detailed accounts of campaign contributions and expenses. Amounts candidates may spend are limited, and their financial statements are open to public inspection.

Campaign Manager—A presidential candidate always chooses his own campaign manager, who is then made chairman of the national committee. The manager is usually an experienced and astute politician, a master organizer with a talent for handling people, and a gift for turning every situation and incident arising during a campaign to the candidate's advantage. Some presidential candidates direct their own campaigns, but as a rule the fight is conducted by the manager.

Candidate—A political candidate is one who seeks public office. The word is of Latin derivation meaning white-robed, from the fact that those who sought public offices in Rome wore loose white robes or togas. A candidate puts his character in issue and must expect to have the full light of publicity play upon it.

Capital of the United States—The first national capital was New York City. The agricultural members of Congress desired a change because they feared the influence of surrounding commercial interests on legislation. Philadelphia was objected to by the Southern members because the Quakers were urging the abolition of slavery. A compromise was finally made by which the capital was to be Philadelphia for ten years, and after that a district ceded by Maryland and Virginia to the national government. Accordingly the seat of government was removed to Philadelphia in 1790.

In the meantime, Maryland, in 1788, and Virginia, in 1789, had ceded a district ten miles square lying on both sides of the Potomac, which was first known as the Federal City and afterward, in 1791, obtained the name of the Territory of Columbia, the city being known as the city of Washington. On November 17, 1800, the government was removed to Washington, where it has since remained. The city at that time was a curious combination of huts and half-finished buildings of greater pretension, with a small population. (See *Seat of Government; District of Columbia.*)

Carpetbaggers—Southern whites gave this name to the Northern whites who flocked to the South after the Civil War to take an active part in politics. Among them were many Federal officeholders and others whose intent was to qualify for elective offices after a short residence in the South. They organized and controlled most of the Negro vote. Since the majority of them were only temporary sojourners in the South, they took with them only such effects as they could carry in a carpetbag, and that is how the name arose.

Caucus—This word is said to have been first applied to political meetings held in Boston just before the Revolution, when bad feeling existed between the citizens and the British soldiers quartered on the town. Many shipyard workers, including calkers or men who drive oakum into the seams of vessels, attended these gatherings, which were derisively labeled calkers' meetings, a term that through corruption became simply caucus. Other derivations have been suggested, but whatever its true origin, the term is now applied to any meeting of a political party or faction held to determine upon a future united course of action with respect to policies or candidates in a pending election.

Local party caucuses are held in some places to name delegates to larger political assemblies, and uninstructed state delegations to national nominating conventions hold caucuses to determine which candidate or candidates they will support. Legislative caucuses are privately held meetings of party members to decide what course the party will take in the legislative chamber. In national politics these caucuses began to be held about 1805. Presidential nominations were formerly made by congressional party caucuses, but this system was displaced in the 1820s.

Censure of the President by Congress—The first resolution censuring a President of the United States was passed by the Senate on March 28, 1834. President Jackson had given great offense to Congress by the highhanded way in which he disposed of the United States Bank (*q.v.*). Since the President had too many friends in Congress to make it possible to impeach him, the Senate determined to inflict an extrajudicial condemnation on him. Accordingly, after debating the question hotly for three months, it resolved by a vote of 26 to 20 "that the President, in the late executive proceedings in relation to the public revenue, has assumed upon himself authority and power not conferred by the Constitution and laws, but in derogation of both."

President Jackson became very indignant over this resolution and protested in a special message sent to the Senate on April 15. He contended that it accused him of perjury in violating his oath of office and was thus an indirect and illegal method of impeachment against which he had no opportunity to defend himself. But the Senate refused to receive the protest or record it in the journal. Senator Benton of Missouri immediately gave notice that he would bring forward every year a resolution to expunge the vote of censure. After a struggle lasting three years the supporters of President Jackson succeeded in passing Benton's expunging resolution, and the resolution of censure was marked around on the journal with broad black lines and a memorandum reading, "Expunged by order of the Senate, this 16th day of January, 1837."

The House censured President Tyler for vetoing the Tariff Bill of 1842. This was done in the report of the committee to which his veto message had been referred. It censured the President for improper use of the veto power. Tyler protested against this as Jackson had done before him, but since he had as a senator voted against the reception of Jackson's protest, the reply of the House was to send him a copy of the Senate resolution in the Jackson case.

Charter Oak, The—More or less familiar to every schoolboy is the story of this famous tree in which Captain Wadsworth hid King Charles's charter of the old colony of Connecticut, when Sir Edmund Andros in 1687 demanded its surrender in the name of his master, King James II. From the time of its first settlement Connecticut had chosen its own rulers and magistrates. It had never had a royal governor or judge, and the rights and privileges it had always enjoyed were confirmed by the charter which Charles II granted to the colony in 1662. Cotton Mather called it "the freest Charter under the cope of Heaven." But when King Charles died in 1685, there was a change in the colonial policy of the home government. James II appointed Sir Edmund Andros colonial governor of New England and ordered him to demand the surrender of the Connecticut charter and, if it was not surrendered, to seize it. After long consideration the charter or a copy of it was placed on the council table in Hartford, but when Sir Edmund reached for the precious document the lights were suddenly extinguished and in the ensuing black-out the charter was smuggled away and hidden in the hollow oak. When news of the Revolution in England reached Connecticut, the people of Connecticut resumed their government under the provisions of the old charter. It had never been vacated by any judgment or decree in the royal courts, nor had it been abrogated by voluntary surrender. On the contrary, the spiriting away and hiding of the charter in the ancient oak showed the determination of the people not to surrender it.

Many souvenirs were made from the wood of the historic tree when it was blown down during a storm, August 21, 1856. Among these were a nine-pound ham, said to have been a mouth-watering imitation, several pianos, numerous walking sticks and napkin rings, chessmen, a chair in which the lieutenant governor of Connecticut now sits while presiding over the State Senate, and bushels of nutmegs.

Checks and Balances—This phrase refers to those features of our system of national government whereby each branch of the government acts as a check or balance on the others in securing laws desired by the people and in accordance with the Constitution, and in securing their proper enforcement. Thus the Senate, which by reason of the longer terms of its members is not so likely to be influenced by the popular whims and prejudices of the moment as the House of Representatives, acts as a check on attempts at hasty or demagogic action by the latter. The House, reflecting more immediately the popular will, is a check on legislation which might be proposed by the Senate in defiance of the principles of a government according to the wishes of a majority of the people. The veto power of the President is a check on hasty or improper action by Congress but cannot prevent the passage of laws for which there is an overwhelming demand, as shown by a two thirds majority of both houses; and should the President fail to execute the laws or otherwise misconduct the duties of his office, he is liable to impeachment. Lastly, the Supreme Court of the United States is the final arbiter of the constitutionality of enacted laws, which cannot be enforced should it decide that these violate the Constitution.

Cherokee Case—The Indian tribes known as the Creeks and the Cherokees possessed large tracts of land in what are now the states of Georgia and North Carolina, and the territory to the west of them. From time to time treaties had been made with these Indians by which much of this land had been ceded to the United States. Among these were the Hopewell Treaty of 1785 and the Holston Treaty of 1791; the first of these instruments had, among other things, recognized the Cherokees as a nation possessing its own laws and all the other attributes of nationality; the second had guaranteed to them all lands not thereby ceded.

When Georgia in 1802 ceded her western territory to the United States, the latter agreed to extinguish Indian titles to lands in the state proper as soon as it could peaceably and reasonably be done, but the Cherokees could not be induced to surrender their lands. The state therefore claimed the right to extend its own laws over all its territory and passed acts depriving the Cherokees of their courts and other machinery of government; these were followed by acts dividing the Cherokee land into counties and, after allotting 160 acres to each head of a Cherokee family, providing for the distribution of the remainder by lot among the people of the state. Notwithstanding the treaties, President Jackson took the ground that as the state was sovereign the United States could not interfere.

The question now came up before the United States Supreme Court in the following way: A Cherokee named Tassels was sentenced to be hanged under the laws of Georgia for killing another Indian on the Cherokee lands. The United States Supreme Court granted a writ of error requiring the state to show cause why the case should not go to the Cherokee courts. This writ was disregarded, and the Indian was hanged. There the matter was dropped.

Again, two missionaries were convicted of entering the Cherokee territory without having complied with certain requirements demanded by Georgia enactments regarding these lands. Their case was carried to the United States Supreme Court on a writ of error, and the judgment of the court held the provisions of our Indian treaties as paramount to the state laws. But the decision was never enforced. Jackson is reported to have said: "Well, John Marshall [the Chief Justice] has made his decision; now let him enforce it."

The Cherokee case is important as the first instance of successful nullification of United States laws by a state. The Indians were finally persuaded to move to the Indian Territory, and by 1838 the last had left the state.

Cipher Dispatches—The presidential election of 1876 was long doubtful; the change of a single electoral vote would have turned the result. After the election a number of cipher dispatches were discovered which, on translation, proved to have been sent by persons closely identified with Samuel J. Tilden, relating to corrupt agreements for the purchase of electoral votes in Florida and Oregon for the Democratic party. The allegations were investigated by a congressional committee, which concluded that, while at least one of the Florida Canvassing Board was purchasable, still Tilden was not implicated in any attempts to purchase him, even if these were made. The minority report, being that of the Republican members of the investigating committee, concluded that the charges of corruptibility on the part of members of canvassing boards were "but the slanders of foiled suborners of corruption." They regarded the proofs of attempted corruption as conclusive and did not hesitate to indicate their belief that Tilden had knowledge of the matter. In a card dated October 16, 1878, Tilden denied in most emphatic terms all connection with the matter.

Citizens—According to the act of Congress which went into effect January 13, 1941, the following persons are at birth deemed to be nationals and citizens of the United States.

Section 201. The following shall be nationals and citizens of the United States at birth:

(a) A person born in the United States and subject to the jurisdiction thereof;

(b) A person born in the United States to a member of an Indian, Eskimo, Aleutian, or other aboriginal tribe: Provided, That the granting of citizenship under this subsection shall not in any manner impair or otherwise affect the right of such person to tribal or other property;

(c) A person born outside of the United States and its outlying

53

possessions of parents both of whom are citizens of the United States and one of whom has resided in the United States or one of its outlying possessions, prior to the birth of such person;

(d) A person born outside of the United States and its outlying possessions of parents one of whom is a citizen of the United States who resided in the United States or one of its outlying possessions prior to the birth of such person, and the other of whom is a national, but not a citizen of the United States;

(e) A person born in an outlying possession of the United States of parents one of whom is a citizen of the United States who resided in the United States or one of its outlying possessions prior to the birth of such person;

(f) A child of unknown parentage found in the United States, until shown not to have been born in the United States;

(g) A person born outside the United States and its outlying possessions of parents one of whom is a citizen of the United States who, prior to the birth of such person, has had ten years' residence in the United States or one of its outlying possessions, at least five of which were after attaining the age of sixteen years, the other being an alien: Provided, That, in order to retain such citizenship, the child must reside in the United States or its outlying possessions for a period or periods totaling five years between the ages of thirteen and twenty-one years: Provided further, That, if the child has not taken up a residence in the United States or its outlying possessions by the time he reaches the age of sixteen years, or if he resides abroad for such a time that it becomes impossible for him to complete the five years' residence in the United States or its outlying possessions before reaching the age of twenty-one years, his American citizenship shall thereupon cease.

The preceding provisos shall not apply to a child born abroad whose American parent is at the time of the child's birth residing abroad solely or principally in the employment of the Government of the United States or a bona fide American, educational, scientific, philanthropic, religious, commercial, or financial organization, having its principal office or place of business in the United States, or an international agency of an official character in which the United States participates, for which he receives a substantial compensation;

(h) The foregoing provisions of subsection (g) concerning retention of citizenship shall apply to a child born abroad subsequent to May 24, 1934.

Section 202. All persons born in Puerto Rico on or after April 11, 1899, subject to the jurisdiction of the United States, residing on the effective date of this Act in Puerto Rico or other territory over which the United States exercises rights of sovereignty and not citizens of the United States under any other Act, are hereby declared to be citizens of the United States.

Section 203. (a) Any person born in the Canal Zone on or after February 26, 1904, and whether before or after the effective date of this Act, whose father or mother or both at the time of the birth of such person was or is a citizen of the United States, is declared to be a citizen of the United States.

(b) Any person born in the Republic of Panama on or after February 26, 1904, and whether before or after the effective date of this Act, whose father or mother or both at the time of the birth of such person was or is a citizen of the United States employed by the Government of the United States or by the Panama Railroad Company, is declared to be a citizen of the United States.

Section 204. Unless otherwise provided in Section 201, the following shall be nationals, but not citizens of the United States at birth:

(a) A person born in an outlying possession of the United States of parents one of whom is a national, but not a citizen, of the United States;

(b) A person born outside the United States and its outlying possessions of parents both of whom are nationals, but not citizens, of the United States, and have resided in the United States or one of its outlying possessions prior to the birth of such person;

(c) A child of unknown parentage found in an outlying possession of the United States, until shown not to have been born in such outlying possession.

Section 205. The provisions of Section 201, subsections (c), (d), (e), and (g), and Section 204, subsections (a) and (b), hereof apply, as of the date of birth, to a child born out of wedlock, provided the paternity is established during minority, by legitimation, or adjudication of a competent court.

In the absence of such legitimation or adjudication, the child, whether born before or after the effective date of this Act, if the mother had the nationality of the United States at the time of the child's birth, and had previously resided in the United States or one of its outlying possessions, shall be held to have acquired at birth her nationality status.

City Manager—See *Municipal Government.*

Civil Service—The civil service system in the United States embraces those persons employed in the civil administration of the government. The military and persons elected to office are not in this category, nor are those who are employed in either the judicial or legislative branches of the central government. The staffs of all the agencies in the executive branch of the government are chosen through civil service examinations, with the exception of those employed in the Foreign Service of the State Department, the Federal Bureau of Investigation, the Commissioned Corps of the Public Health Service, and the Tennessee Valley Authority. These agencies, however, have merit systems of their own.

Prior to 1883 anyone desiring to enter the government service had to have some political backing or "pull." On January 16, 1883, President Arthur approved the Civil Service Act, and a commission consisting of three persons was set up with powers to inaugurate a system of merit under which selections for appointments were made according to fitness for the positions. Political and religious considerations had no bearing on the tests.

The central office of the Civil Service Commission is in Washington, D.C., and there are a dozen or more regional offices throughout the country. Upward of a half million persons annually take the examinations given by the Commission. Positions under the civil service are divided into five groups, within each of which are a number of grades carrying different salaries. The five main groups are: clerical, administrative, and fiscal; professional; sub-professional; crafts, protective, and custodial; and clerical-mechanical. In June 1945 the persons in the Civil Service numbered close to 3,000,000.

Cleveland, Grover—Grover Cleveland was our twenty-second and twenty-fourth President. He was the only President re-elected after a defeat and the first Democrat elected after the Civil War. In 1884 he defeated James G. Blaine by a close margin with the help of the mugwump vote, a group of disgruntled Republicans who had protested the nomination of Blaine. In 1888 he was defeated by Benjamin Harrison but was returned to the Chief Executive office by popular demand in 1892.

Son of a minister and one of nine children, Mr. Cleveland was born on March 18, 1837, in Caldwell, New Jersey. He left school at sixteen, when his father died, and clerked for a short time in a store in Clinton, New York. Later he taught with an older brother in New York City at the Institute for the Blind. From there he went to Buffalo, where he studied law and was admitted to the bar in 1859. In 1863 Cleveland was made assistant district attorney of Erie County. He was defeated for district attorney in 1865 but was elected sheriff in 1870. In 1881 he became mayor of Buffalo. A fine record in public office advanced him to governor of New York in 1882, and from that position he rose to the presidency.

Although not a man of brilliant qualities, he was of sterling character. Truth and honesty were almost a mania with him. He had sound judgment, splendid courage, and great independence. On the eve of the election in 1888 he sacrificed his chances for victory when he boldly opposed, publicly, the high customs duties at that time in force in the United States. He had been warned that it would be folly to take sides on such a controversial issue then, but he defied his advisers, saying, "I care more for principle than the presidency."

His fearless, uncompromising ways made Cleveland too tactless, outspoken, and intolerant to be a truly great statesman, although he was tremendously admired for these very qualities. The Tammany organization hated this man who fought corrupt political rings and ignored party machines. At a Democratic national convention in Chicago his nomination was strongly opposed by the Tammany faction. General Bragg of Wisconsin arose from his chair and said, "We love him for the enemies he has made."

Cleveland improved civil service. He approved the establishment of the Interstate Commerce Commission while he was President. He was opposed to imperialism on principle and was therefore against the annexing of Hawaii by the United States and our taking sides in Cuba's struggle for independence from Spain. Cleveland was far-sighted in his concern for the welfare of the country and forced the repeal of the Sherman Silver Bill passed by the Harrison administration.

Efficient and industrious in office, a man of great vigor and back-bone, Cleveland was inclined to be gruff in manner and aggressive in action. His close friends tell us that in private life he was warm-hearted, gentle, and very religious. He was devoted to his wife, whom he married in his second year of presidency. It was the first marriage ever performed in the White House.

His parting words shortly before he died in Princeton, New Jersey, on June 24, 1908, were, "I have tried so hard to do right."

Clintonians—In New York State the Clinton family was originally opposed to the adoption of the Constitution; the Livingstons and Schuylers favored it. Alexander Hamilton was a connection of the Schuylers, and Morgan Lewis of the Livingstons. Aaron Burr had at first been a lukewarm Federalist. The Clintons were naturally at once of the Republican (Democratic-Republican) party; about 1800 they were joined by the Livingstons, or Lewisites, and Burr and his followers, the Burrites.

The union of the Burrites with the others was not firm, and, dissension following, their influence rapidly waned, the national administration recognizing and aiding the other faction. About 1807 a split in the Republican party in the state led to the ascendancy of the Clintons over the Lewisites, the state patronage being freely used by the Clintons to accomplish their object. The Lewisites and Burrites now joined hands and declared against George Clinton and in favor of Madison for the presidency to succeed Jefferson. The combination of the Lewisites and Burrites is usually known as the "Martling Men," from their meeting place in New York City—Martling's Long Room.

The Clinton faction was known as the Clintonians. These latter were thus naturally opposed to the administration, and their dislike of the respective measures on commerce at this period threw them toward the Federalists, with whom the Clintonians now frequently acted, jointly supporting De Witt Clinton for the presidency in 1812. His friends issued an address, known as the Clintonian platform, in which they attacked the congressional caucus and the Virginia influence.

Madison had the support of Jefferson, and his supporters were known in consequence as Jefferson Democrats. A split among the Clintonians now threw De Witt Clinton and the Federalists still

58

more closely together, but in 1815 this coalition was defeated and the Federalists finally destroyed, Clinton and the others of his party now became reconciled, and in 1817 he was elected governor.

The Martling Men had about 1812 revivified the Tammany organization and had become known as the "Bucktails," a name derived from the Tammany insignia of a buck's tail worn in the hat instead of a feather.

On his election in 1817 Clinton inaugurated the canal policy which ended in giving to the state the Erie Canal. The Bucktails naturally opposed this policy, and the name Bucktail came to be applied to any opponent of the canals. Among the prominent Clintonians had been Daniel D. Tompkins and Martin Van Buren, who had joined the Bucktails.

About 1822 the Bucktails came to be recognized as the regular Republican (Democratic-Republican) party of the state. In the election of that year the Clintonians were defeated. In 1824, however, the removal of Clinton from the post of canal commissioner created a reaction in his favor, and he was elected governor in that year and again in 1826. The lead of the Bucktails had passed to the Albany Regency.

In 1828 Clinton died, leaving his faction leaderless. It had always been a personal party. Clinton tolerated no equals. The position of his family had enabled him to carry out his desires, but the increase in the voting population had rendered it more and more difficult, and the entirely popular and democratic faction had supplanted him.

Cloture—The so-called Cloture Rule of the United States Senate was adopted March 8, 1917. Under this rule an end may be put to debate on a bill provided two thirds of the members present concur. The rule is invoked when sixteen senators sign a petition asking that debate be ended. The petition to apply cloture must be voted on by the Senate at 1 P.M. the second calendar day after it is filed. If two thirds of the members present vote for cloture, then no senator can talk more than one hour on the bill, but since there are ninety-six senators the debate can still go on for ninety-six hours.

Cloture has been applied only four times since 1917, although nearly two dozen attempts have been made to invoke it. It was first applied November 15, 1919, to limit debate on the Versailles Treaty. The second application was January 22, 1926, on the World Court. The next was February 15, 1927, on the McFadden Banking Bill, and the fourth, February 28, 1927, on a measure to create a Bureau of Customs and Prohibition. The Cloture Rule of the Senate was adopted to prevent filibusters. (See *Filibuster*.)

Coalition—When two or more political factions or parties agree to act together for some common purpose the alliance is called a coalition and the individuals composing it coalitionists. In Congress coalitions are often formed between members of the two major parties who are particularly interested in the passage or defeat of certain legislation because of the effect which it will have on their constituents.

Coffin Handbills—In the presidential campaign of 1824 between John Quincy Adams and Andrew Jackson, General Jackson was charged with most of the crimes in the calendar, including half a dozen murders. The Adams supporters issued handbills decorated with coffins, called "coffin handbills," on which were printed the stories of the hanging of two Englishmen in Florida while Jackson was territorial governor, and several others. The Jackson or Democratic party multiplied the handbills to show how their candidate was maligned. Hanging a couple of Englishmen did not affect the popularity of Jackson, who had also killed a number at New Orleans, and he was triumphantly elected despite the coffin handbills.

Colonization—It was the object of the colonization societies to aid and encourage free Negroes to systematic colonization of the western coast of Africa. It was hoped thus to counteract and ultimately to suppress the slave trade. The idea seems to have originated as early as 1770 with the Reverend Samuel Hopkins, D.D., of Newport, but it was not until January 1, 1817, that the American Colonization Society was formally organized. Among its presidents were James Madison and Henry Clay.

Some few Negroes had previously immigrated to the British

Negro colony of Sierra Leone, but in 1820 the first organized attempt was made to found a colony. This was at Sherbro Island. The location proving unfortunate, land was purchased on the main land at Cape Mesurado, and early in 1822 colonists landed there. Between nine and ten thousand persons were sent there up to 1856. In 1847 the colony declared itself an independent republic under the name of Liberia. The colonization movement was at first encouraged by the slaveholders, as it tended to relieve the South of its free Negroes; but as slaves became more valuable, fewer were freed by their masters, and these latter, from regarding slavery as an institution to be merely tolerated, came to assert the doctrine of its essential righteousness. Under these circumstances colonization fell into disfavor in the South, while in the North the Abolitionists regarded all such schemes as immoral temporizing.

Colorado—At times referred to as the "Centennial State" because it was admitted to the Union in 1876. State flower, columbine. Population, 1,123,269. Area, 104,247 square miles. Capital, Denver. More often than not this state is Republican. It has four representatives in Congress.

Commander in Chief—The Constitution (Article II, Section 2) makes the President the Commander in Chief of the Army and Navy, and of the militia of the several states when called into the service of the United States. State constitutions also bestow this title on the governors of the states, though their authority is restricted to their respective states.

Commerce, Department of—Congress created the Department of Commerce and Labor on February 14, 1903. In 1913 the department was divided into the Department of Commerce and the Department of Labor, and the secretaries of the two departments were given portfolios in the Cabinet. Fostering, promoting, and developing the foreign and domestic commerce of the United States is the principal function of the Secretary of Commerce. Within his province also is the development of mining, manufacturing, and shipping, as well as fishing industries and facilities for transportation throughout the country. The department may investigate organizations and corporations which are engaged in interstate commerce, with the exception of railroads. Enforcing the laws for the protection of life and property on the water is within the department's jurisdiction. The department has charge of patents, applies standards of weights and measures, and collects and publishes much statistical information. Coast and geodetic surveys are under the Department of Commerce, which also has charge of the development of civil aeronautics.

Its main bureaus, offices, and divisions include the Bureau of the Census, Bureau of Foreign and Domestic Commerce, Civil Aeronautics Administration, the Coast and Geodetic Survey, Inland Waterways Corporation, National Bureau of Standards, National Inventors Council, the Patent Office, and the Weather Bureau. Standards, rules, and regulations for air traffic are prescribed by the Civil Aeronautics Board, which can suspend and revoke safety certificates.

Commission Government—See *Municipal Government.*

Commissioners, Resident—See *Resident Commissioners.*

Committees—To facilitate the work of Congress, the Senate and the House each have a number of standing committees which deal with various matters coming before Congress. When a bill is introduced it is referred to the committee which deals with the particular subject covered by the measure. These committees are extremely powerful as they can practically doom a measure by sidetracking it, or they can report it adversely, in which case its chances of passing are slim. By the same token, if a committee desires the passage of a bill it can exert great influence in its favor. The real work of Congress is done mostly in committee.

Formerly the Speaker of the House appointed the committees (see *Speaker*), but now they are elected, as they are in the Senate. The actual make-up of the committees, however, is a prearranged party matter. In the Senate the chairmanships of the committees go by seniority. Both the Senate and the House have the power to summon witnesses to testify before committees.

Joint committees are standing committees of both houses which work together. Select committees are appointed for the purpose of investigating particular matters. Committees of conference are appointed by both houses to confer on points in dispute between the two chambers.

The principal standing committees of the Senate are: Agriculture and Forestry, Appropriations, Banking and Currency, Commerce, Education and Labor, Finance, Foreign Relations, Interstate Commerce, Judiciary, Military Affairs, Naval Affairs, and Rules. In the House they are: Appropriations, Banking and Currency, Foreign Affairs, Immigration and Naturalization, Judiciary, Labor, Military Affairs, Naval Affairs, Rules, and Ways and Means.

The Legislative Reorganization Act of 1946, which Senator Robert M. La Follette, Jr., described as a "legislative miracle," reduced the number of Senate committees from 48 to 19 and House committees from 35 to 15. Under the old system House members averaged membership on more than two committees each, but now they can serve on only one. Senators formerly averaged membership on six committees each, but under the new setup no senator can serve on more than two committees.

Committees, National—See *National Committees.*

Communist Party in the United States—The American Communist party was established in 1919 and was made up of a radical element of dissenters of the American Socialist party. Not long afterward, James Reed, a Harvard University graduate imbued with radical theories, formed the Communist Labor party. The two groups merged about a year later to form the United Communist party.

The Federal Government went after the Communists and their movement, which was beginning to make marked progress, and they were forced to take cover. In 1921 the Workers' party came into being, but owing to the continued activity of Federal and state agencies, it was constrained to carry on its work surreptitiously.

However, when the national election came around in 1924 the party polled over 36,000 votes, and in the presidential year of 1928 they had a ticket headed by William Z. Foster. Their platform urged the formation of a government of farmers and workers and of a Communist society whereby "the means of production will not be the property of the few." The economic depression with its accompanying unemployment on a large scale brought about a Communist revival, and gains were made in the membership. A special congressional committee which investigated the activities of the Communists and Bolshevists in 1930 estimated the communistic membership, with sympathizers, at 500,000.

Earl Russell Browder, who was general secretary of the Communist party, was made the party's presidential candidate in 1936 and 1940. In the latter year he received a four-year sentence for passport fraud and was sent to the Atlanta penitentiary. President F. D. Roosevelt commuted his sentence in 1942.

The attitude of the Communists toward the war in Europe underwent a decided change after the German armies had invaded Russia in 1941; and when Roosevelt ran for re-election in 1944, Browder, who prior to that had been anti-Roosevelt, urged his followers to keep Roosevelt in office.

On May 20, 1944, the American Communist party, after a twenty-five-year existence, dissolved and gave way to what was termed a non-party association for political education, but announced its support of Roosevelt for a fourth term. The temporary name of the new organization was to be Communist Political Association. Browder at the time said the Communists had an enrollment of 80,000 members. In May 1945, Browder announced that the American Communists were making an inventory of their position with a view to resuming direct political activity. He was at that time president of the year-old Communist Political Association. In 1946 he lost the leadership of the organization.

Compromise of 1850—For more than a year after the termination of the Mexican War the new territory acquired had remained under military rule. But in 1850 California adopted a constitution prohibiting slavery and then applied for admission. The slave states would not agree to admit her unless a new slave state was also formed.

At the same time the organization of the newly acquired territory came up for discussion. Henry Clay then proposed a compromise which, having been referred to a select committee of thirteen, of which he was chairman, was reported by them in substantially the same shape as proposed. It provided for:

1. The postponement of the admission of new states to be formed out of Texas until demanded by such state.

2. The admission of California as a free state.

3. The organization, without the Wilmot Proviso, of all territory acquired from Mexico and not included in California, as the territories of New Mexico and Utah.

4. The combination of the last two measures in one bill.

5. The establishment of the boundaries of Texas and the payment to her of $10,000,000 for the abandonment of her claim to New Mexico.

6. More effectual laws for the return of fugitive slaves.

7. Abolishing the slave trade in the District of Columbia, but leaving slavery there undisturbed.

These measures all became laws and together were commonly known as the Omnibus Bill. It is charged that the indemnity of $10,000,000, the payment of which raised the market value of Texas securities from twenty or thirty to nearly par, was not without influence in the passage of the bill. The Kansas-Nebraska Bill (*q.v.*), passed in 1854, virtually repealed this compromise.

Compromises of the Constitution—On three points the convention of 1787, framing the Constitution, came to a stage at which further progress seemed impossible. From this sprang three compromises. The result of the first was the present system of a Senate containing two members from each state, regardless of size, and a House whose members are apportioned to the population. Rhode Island was never represented in the convention, and New Hampshire not until after the disposition of this subject. There were, therefore, eleven states, and these were divided as follows: Virginia, Massachusetts, Pennsylvania, North Carolina, South Carolina, and

Georgia, known as the "large states," against New York, Maryland, Connecticut, New Jersey, and Delaware, known as the "small states." The former desired representation according to population, the *national system;* the latter by states, or the *federative system.* A compromise was effected, the present system being the result.

One of the most serious evils of the Confederation was the powerlessness of Congress to regulate commerce. The commercial states were all in favor of giving to Congress complete control of this subject, nor were the other states generally opposed to this, except that the Southern states, whose industries consisted almost exclusively of the cultivation of rice, tobacco, and a few other articles, objected strenuously to any possibility by which an export tax could at any time be imposed on these articles, as any such proceeding would tend to cripple the entire state. The second compromise was accordingly made, complete control over commerce being given to Congress, except that a tax on exports was prohibited. (Article I, Section 4, Clause 5.)

The third compromise was on the question of slavery. Georgia and South Carolina refused to enter the Union if the slave trade was to be prohibited or discriminated against. It was then that Article I, Section 9, Clause 1, was agreed on, forbidding Congress to prohibit the slave trade prior to the year 1808 but permitting the imposition of a tax thereon not to exceed ten dollars a head. The other concessions to the slave states were Article IV, Section 2, Clause 2, concerning the return of fugitive slaves, and Article I, Section 2, Clause 3, giving representation in Congress to the number of inhabitants *plus three fifths of the slaves.* The consideration for these concessions was the elimination of the following section: "No Navigation Act shall be passed without the assent of two thirds of the members present in either house."

Confederate States, The—The name adopted by the states that seceded in 1861. Delegates from six of these states met at Montgomery, Alabama, February 4, 1861, and formed a provisional government under the above name. The delegates to the convention had been appointed by the different state conventions, and not elected by the people. The government thus established adopted provisionally the Constitution of the United States, making in it such changes as suited their purpose, and declared all the laws of the United States in force until repealed. The legislation of the provisional Congress (consisting of one house only) dealt with the carrying on of the war, the raising of money, and the adoption of a permanent constitution.

In February 1862, this constitution having been adopted by all the states, an election was held under it, and Jefferson Davis and Alexander H. Stephens (the provisional President and Vice-President) were chosen. They were inaugurated February 22, 1862. The capital had been removed to Richmond, Virginia, and there it remained during the war. The influence of Congress on the course of events was small, all the real power being in the hands of the President, who made his influence felt in every department. The surrender of Lee in 1865 put an end to the Civil War, and at the same time to the Confederacy. Most of the changes that the Confederacy made in the Constitution were made for the purpose of securing explicit recognition of slavery and of the sovereignty of the states.

Congress is the legislative branch of the Federal Government. All legislative powers granted by the Constitution are vested in Congress, which consists of the Senate and the House of Representatives. The powers of Congress are set forth in Article I, Section 8, of the Constitution. Since the Constitution is a document of enumerated powers, all powers not expressly granted therein to Congress, or prohibited to the states, are reserved to the states or to the people.

The Senate is composed of two senators from each state, irrespective of size or population, but the members of the House are apportioned on the basis of population. The qualifications for members of the Senate and the House differ, and senators are elected for terms of six years, while representatives are chosen for only two. Each house is, according to the Constitution, "the judge of the elections, returns, and qualifications of its own members." Colloquially, the word "Congress" is used to indicate the House of Representatives as distinguished from the Senate. Traditionally, the

Senate is the more conservative chamber, acting as a brake on the more volatile House of Representatives. The Senate also provides the means of defending the smaller states from possible encroachments of the larger. To safeguard the smaller states, the Constitution provides that "no state without its consent shall be deprived of its equal suffrage in the Senate."

Although the two houses sit separately, both must consent to legislation. Bills that have passed both houses are sent to the President, who may either sign or veto them, or do neither, in which case the bill becomes a law after ten days, unless Congress has previously adjourned and the President, therefore, cannot return it. If Congress adjourns before the ten days have elapsed and the President' fails to sign the bill, it automatically dies. This is the so-called pocket veto. The veto of the President is the only check upon the power of Congress to legislate within the scope of its authority, but Congress can override the veto by a two-thirds majority vote of each house. Legislation exceeding the constitutional power of Congress will be declared unconstitutional by the Supreme Court if that body is appealed to by either party to any controversy arising from an attempt to enforce such laws.

Congress is said to be in session when both Senate and House meet for the transaction of business, but the Senate may be called in extra session without the House to consider matters which are exclusively the business of the Senate, such as the ratification of treaties, the trial of impeachments, and the confirmation of appointments. (See *Senate; House of Representatives.*)

Congressional Record—The Constitution (Article I, Section 5) says, "Each house shall keep a journal of its proceedings, and from time to time publish the same, excepting such parts as may, in their judgment, require secrecy." When Congress is in session the proceedings of the House and Senate are published daily in the *Congressional Record,* which each member of Congress is allowed to send free to fifty persons.

Congressman—Members of the Senate and the House of Representatives are congressmen, but a member of the Senate is usually called a senator and a member of the House a congressman. The official title of a member of the House of Representatives is representative. (See *Delegates.*)

Connecticut—Nicknamed "Nutmeg State." State flower, mountain laurel. Population, 1,709,242. Area, 5,009 square miles. Capital, Hartford. One of the original states of the Union. The first popular constitution made in America was framed in Connecticut. In politics Connecticut has been considered a doubtful state. It has six representatives in Congress.

Connecticut Compromise—One of the greatest problems the Founding Fathers had to deal with at the Constitutional Convention of 1787 was the question of representation in Congress. The large states wanted representation wholly on a basis of population, but the small states were opposed to being thus overridden. At length, after a protracted and inconclusive debate, the Connecticut delegation—Johnson, Sherman, and Ellsworth—advanced very strong arguments in favor of a scheme for representation in the lower house in proportion to population and equal representation in the upper house. This plan was finally accepted by the larger states. Because the Connecticut delegates were largely instrumental in securing its adoption, this compromise came to be known as the "Connecticut Compromise."

Conservatives—A name assumed by certain political parties in many nations. These parties are sometimes actually, and always avowedly, opposed to changes from old and established forms and practices. In United States history these names have never been in general use, but in Van Buren's administration the name was applied to those Democrats who at the special session of Congress in September 1837 opposed the establishment of the subtreasury system. In the Congress that met in December 1839 they had practically disappeared. The name was also assumed by Southern whites during the reconstruction period following the Civil War, to show their adherence to the old state governments, the abolition

69

of which by Congress they opposed. In Virginia the name was in use until 1872. The name was also used in the North during this period. The Democrats applied it to themselves to draw moderate Republican votes.

Constitution of the United States—The government of this country under the Articles of Confederation had been a failure, and the remedy suggested by many was by means of a convention of the states. This was proposed in 1781 in a pamphlet by Pelatiah Webster, and within the next few years the legislatures of New York and Massachusetts adopted resolutions of similar tenor. In 1786 a resolution of the Virginia Legislature, growing out of a desire to regulate commerce on Chesapeake Bay and the connected waters, was passed, appointing commissioners to meet representatives of the other states for the purpose of considering the commercial condition of the United States.

This commission, to which only five states sent delegates, reported the fault to be with the Articles of Confederation and recommended a convention of all the states to amend them, without which step they despaired of any improvement in the condition of trade. Their report was approved by Congress, and on May 25, 1787, the representatives of seven states met and elected as their chairman George Washington, the delegate of Virginia. All the states except Rhode Island were ultimately represented in the convention.

The first plan proposed was that of Edmund Randolph of Virginia, known as the Virginia Plan. It consisted of fifteen resolutions and provided for two houses, one elected by the people, the other elected by the first house from nominations made by the state legislatures. Congress was to have a veto power on state laws and power to coerce delinquent states; it was also to choose the executive. These are the salient features in which the plan differed from the Constitution as ultimately adopted.

Charles Pinckney of South Carolina introduced a plan, the original of which has been lost and the only record of which, a copy furnished by Pinckney more than thirty years later, is not believed to be entirely accurate. In its general features it resembled the Virginia Plan, but it differed from the latter in being more nearly like the present Constitution. It was known as the South Carolina Plan.

On June 13 the committee of the whole reported a modification of the Virginia Plan in nineteen resolutions, the most striking change being that the power to coerce a state was not granted to Congress. On June 14 the convention adjourned in order to enable William Paterson of New Jersey to introduce what was known as the Jersey Plan, the main features of which were as follows: Congress was to continue as a single house, but with additional powers; it was to elect the executive; acts of Congress and treaties were to be paramount to state laws, and the executive was to have power to coerce refractory individuals and states.

Hamilton suggested a plan whereby, among other provisions, the Senate and President were to hold office for life, but his plan had no supporters. On July 24 the various resolutions and plans were referred to a committee of detail, from which, on August 6, a draft of a constitution in twenty-three articles was reported.

After debate of more than a month, during which the clause permitting the slave trade for twenty years, the fugitive slave clause, and the electoral system clause were inserted, the draft was referred to a committee consisting of Gouverneur Morris, Johnson, Hamilton, Madison, and King. This committee, most of whose work was done by Morris, on September 13 reported the Constitution in substantially its present form. Some trifling changes were made by the convention, which then adopted the instrument, and after deciding against a new convention to consider amendments suggested by the states, the convention adjourned on September 17. The Constitution, accompanied by a request that it be submitted to the states for ratification, was sent to Congress, by whom copies were sent to the state legislatures. The Constitution, as finally adopted, was signed by but thirty-nine out of the fifty-five delegates. The proceedings of the convention were secret. Its papers were placed in Washington's custody, subject to the disposal of the new Congress, and in 1796 they were deposited with the State Department.

71

CONSTITUTION OF THE UNITED STATES

PREAMBLE

We the People of the United States, in Order to form a more perfect Union, establish Justice, insure domestic tranquillity, provide for the common defense, promote the general Welfare, and secure the Blessings of Liberty to ourselves and our Posterity, do ordain and establish this Constitution for the United States of America.

ARTICLE I

Section 1. All legislative Powers herein granted shall be vested in a Congress of the United States, which shall consist of a Senate and House of Representatives.

Section 2. The House of Representatives shall be composed of Members chosen every second Year by the People of the several States, and the Electors in each State shall have the Qualifications requisite for Electors of the most numerous Branch of the State Legislature.

No Person shall be a Representative who shall not have attained the Age of twenty-five Years, and been seven Years a Citizen of the United States, and who shall not, when elected, be an Inhabitant of that State in which he shall be chosen.

[1][Representatives and direct Taxes shall be apportioned among the several States which may be included within this Union, according to their respective Numbers, which shall be determined by adding to the whole Number of free Persons, including those bound to Service for a Term of Years, and excluding Indians not taxed, three-fifths of all other Persons.] The actual Enumeration shall be made within three Years after the first Meeting of the Congress of the United States, and within every subsequent Term of ten Years, in such Manner as they shall by Law direct. The Number of Representatives shall not exceed one for every Thirty Thousand, but each State shall have at Least one Representative; and until such enumeration shall be made, the State of New Hampshire shall be entitled to choose three, Massachusetts eight, Rhode Island and Providence Plantations one, Connecticut five, New York six, New Jersey four, Pennsylvania eight, Delaware one, Maryland six, Virginia ten, North Carolina five, South Carolina five, and Georgia three.

---

[1]The clause included in brackets is amended by the Fourteenth Amendment, Section 2.

When vacancies happen in the Representation from any State, the Executive Authority thereof shall issue Writs of Election to fill such Vacancies.

The House of Representatives shall choose their Speaker and other Officers; and shall have the sole Power of Impeachment.

Section 3. The Senate of the United States shall be composed of two Senators from each State, chosen by the Legislature thereof,[2] for six Years; and each Senator shall have one Vote.

Immediately after they shall be assembled in Consequence of the first Election, they shall be divided as equally as may be into three Classes. The Seats of the Senators of the first Class shall be vacated at the Expiration of the second Year, of the second Class at the Expiration of the fourth Year, and the third Class at the Expiration of the sixth Year, so that one-third may be chosen every second Year; and if Vacancies happen by Resignation, or otherwise, during the Recess of the Legislature of any State, the Executive thereof may make temporary Appointments until the next Meeting of the Legislature, which shall then fill such Vacancies.

No Person shall be a Senator who shall not have attained to the Age of thirty Years, and been nine Years a Citizen of the United States, and who shall not, when elected, be an Inhabitant of that State for which he shall be chosen.

The Vice President of the United States shall be President of the Senate, but shall have no Vote, unless they be equally divided.

The Senate shall choose their other Officers, and also a President pro tempore, in the Absence of the Vice President, or when he shall exercise the office of President of the United States.

The Senate shall have the sole Power to try all Impeachments. When sitting for that Purpose, they shall be on Oath or Affirmation. When the President of the United States is tried, the Chief Justice shall preside: And no Person shall be convicted without the Concurrence of two-thirds of the Members present.

Judgment in Cases of Impeachment shall not extend further than to removal from Office, and disqualification to hold and enjoy any office of Honor, Trust or Profit under the United States: but the Party convicted shall nevertheless be liable and subject to Indictment, Trial Judgment and Punishment, according to Law.

Section 4. The Times, Places and Manner of holding Elections for Senators and Representatives, shall be prescribed in each State

[2]Replaced by the Seventeenth Amendment.

by the Legislature thereof; but the Congress may at any time by Law make or alter such Regulations, except as to the Places of choosing Senators.

[3]The Congress shall assemble at least once in every Year and such Meeting shall be on the first Monday in December, unless they shall by Law appoint a different Day.

Section 5. Each House shall be the Judge of the Elections, Returns and Qualifications of its own Members, and a Majority of each shall constitute a Quorum to do Business; but a smaller Number may adjourn from day to day, and may be authorized to compel the attendance of absent Members, in such Manner, and under such Penalties as each House may provide.

Each House may determine the Rules of its Proceedings, punish its Members for disorderly Behavior, and, with the Concurrence of two-thirds, expel a Member.

Each House shall keep a Journal of its Proceedings, and from time to time publish the same, excepting such Parts as may in their judgment require Secrecy; and the Yeas and Nays of the Members of either House on any question shall, at the Desire of one-fifth of those present, be entered on the Journal.

Neither House, during the Session of Congress, shall, without the consent of the other, adjourn for more than three days, nor to any other Place than that in which the two Houses shall be sitting.

Section 6. The Senators and Representatives shall receive a Compensation for their Services, to be ascertained by Law, and paid out of the Treasury of the United States. They shall in all Cases, except Treason, Felony and Breach of the Peace, be privileged from Arrest during their Attendance at the Session of their respective Houses, and in going to and returning from the same; and for any Speech or Debate in either House, they shall not be questioned in any other Place.

No Senator or Representative shall, during the Time for which he was elected, be appointed to any civil Office under the Authority of the United States, which shall have been created, or the Emoluments whereof shall have been increased during such time; and no Person holding any Office under the United States, shall be a Member of either House during his Continuance in Office.

Section 7. All Bills for raising Revenue shall originate in the

---

[3]The clause has been replaced by the Twenty-second Amendment, Section 2.

House of Representatives; but the Senate may propose or concur with Amendments as on other Bills.

Every Bill which shall have passed the House of Representatives and the Senate, shall, before it becomes a Law, be presented to the President of the United States; if he approves he shall sign it, but if not he shall return it, with his Objection to that House in which it shall have originated, who shall enter the Objections at large on their Journal and proceed to reconsider it. If after such Reconsideration two-thirds of that House shall agree to pass the Bill, it shall be sent, together with the Objections, to the other House, by which it shall likewise be reconsidered, and if approved by two-thirds of that House it shall become a Law. But in all such Cases the Votes of both Houses shall be determined by Yeas and Nays, and the Names of the Persons voting for and against the Bill shall be entered on the Journal of each House respectively. If any Bill shall not be returned by the President within ten Days (Sundays excepted) after it shall have been presented to him, the Same shall be a Law in like Manner as if he had signed it, unless the Congress by their Adjournment prevent its Return, in which Case it shall not be a Law.

Every Order, Resolution, or Vote to which the Concurrence of the Senate and House of Representatives may be necessary (except on a question of Adjournment) shall be presented to the President of the United States; and before the Same shall take Effect, shall be approved by him, or being disapproved by him, shall be repassed by two-thirds of the Senate and House of Representatives, according to the Rules and Limitations prescribed in the Case of a Bill.

Section 8. The Congress shall have Power to lay and collect Taxes, Duties, Imposts and Excises, to pay the Debts and provide for the common Defense and general Welfare of the United States; but all Duties, Imposts and Excises shall be uniform throughout the United States.

To borrow Money on the credit of the United States;

To regulate Commerce with foreign Nations, and among the several States, and with the Indian Tribes;

To establish an uniform Rule of Naturalization, and uniform Laws on the subject of Bankruptcies throughout the United States;

To coin Money, regulate the Value thereof, and of foreign Coin, and fix the Standard of Weights and Measures;

To provide for the Punishment of counterfeiting the Securities and current Coin of the United States;

To establish Post Offices and post Roads;

To promote the Progress of Science and useful Arts, by securing for limited Times to Authors and Inventors the exclusive Right to their respective Writings and Discoveries;

To constitute Tribunals inferior to the Supreme Court;

To define and punish Piracies and Felonies committed on the high Seas, and Offences against the Law of Nations;

To declare War, grant Letters of Marque and Reprisal, and make Rules concerning Captures on Land and Water;

To raise and support Armies, but no Appropriation of Money to that Use shall be for a longer Term than two Years;

To provide and maintain a Navy;

To make Rules for the Government and Regulation of the land and naval Forces;

To provide for calling forth the Militia to execute the Laws of the Union, suppress Insurrections and repel Invasions;

To provide for organizing, arming, and disciplining, the Militia, and for governing such Part of them as may be employed in the Service of the United States, reserving to the States respectively the Appointment of the Officers, and the Authority of training the Militia according to the discipline prescribed by Congress;

To exercise exclusive Legislation in all Cases whatsoever, over such District (not exceeding ten Miles square) as may, by Cession of particular States, and the Acceptance of Congress, become the Seat of the Government of the United States, and to exercise like Authority over all Places purchased by the Consent of the Legislature of the State in which the Same shall be, for the Erection of Forts, Magazines, Arsenals, dock-Yards, and other needful Buildings;—And

To make all Laws which shall be necessary and proper for carrying into Execution the foregoing Powers, and all other Powers vested by this Constitution in the Government of the United States, or in any Department or Officer thereof.

Section 9. The Migration or Importation of such Persons as any of the States now existing shall think proper to admit, shall not be prohibited by the Congress prior to the Year one thousand eight hundred and eight, but a Tax or duty may be imposed on such importation, not exceeding ten dollars for each Person.

The Privilege of the Writ of Habeas Corpus shall not be suspended, unless when in Cases of Rebellion or Invasion the Public Safety may require it.

No Bill of Attainder or ex post facto Law shall be passed.

No Capitation, or other direct, tax[4] shall be paid, unless in Proportion to the Census or Enumeration herein before directed to be taken.

No Tax or Duty shall be laid on Articles exported from any State.

No Preference shall be given by any Regulation of Commerce or Revenue to the Ports of one State over those of another; nor shall Vessels bound to, or from, one State be obliged to enter, clear, or pay Duties in another.

No Money shall be drawn from the Treasury, but in Consequence of Appropriations made by Law; and a regular Statement and Account of the Receipts and Expenditures of all public Money shall be published from time to time.

No Title of Nobility shall be granted by the United States: And no Person holding any Office of Profit or Trust under them, shall, without the Consent of the Congress, accept of any present, Emolument, Office, or Title, of any kind whatever, from any King, Prince, or foreign State.

Section 10. No State shall enter into any Treaty, Alliance, or Confederation; grant Letters of Marque and Reprisal; coin Money, emit Bills of Credit; make any Thing but gold and silver Coin a Tender in Payment of Debts; pass any Bill of Attainder, ex post facto Law, or Law impairing the Obligation of Contracts, or grant any Title of Nobility.

No State shall, without the Consent of the Congress, lay any Imposts or Duties on Imports or Exports, except what may be absolutely necessary for executing its inspection Laws; and the net Produce of all Duties and Imposts, laid by any State on Imports or Exports, shall be for the Use of the Treasury of the United States; and all such Laws shall be subject to the Revision and Control of the Congress.

No State shall, without the Consent of Congress, lay any Duty of Tonnage, keep Troops, or ships of War in time of Peace, enter into any Agreement or Compact with another State, or with a foreign Power, or engage in War, unless actually invaded, or in such imminent Danger as will not admit of delay.

ARTICLE II

Section 1. The executive Power shall be vested in a President of the United States of America. He shall hold his Office during the

---

[4]See Sixteenth Amendment.

Term of four Years, and, together with the Vice President, chosen for the same term, be elected, as follows:

Each State shall appoint, in such Manner as the Legislature thereof may direct, a Number of Electors, equal to the whole Number of Senators and Representatives to which the State may be entitled in the Congress; but no Senator or Representative, or Person holding an Office of Trust or Profit under the United States, shall be appointed an Elector.

[5][The electors shall meet in their respective States, and vote by ballot for two Persons, of whom one at least shall not be an Inhabitant of the same State with themselves. And they shall make a List of all the Persons voted for, and of the Number of votes for each; which List they shall sign and certify, and transmit sealed to the Seat of the Government of the United States, directed to the President of the Senate. The President of the Senate shall, in the Presence of the Senate and House of Representatives, open all the Certificates, and the Votes shall then be counted. The Person having the greatest Number of Votes shall be the President, if such a Number be a Majority of the whole Number of Electors appointed; and if there be more than one who have such Majority, and have an equal Number of Votes, then the House of Representatives shall immediately choose by Ballot one of them for President; and if no Person have a Majority, then from the five highest on the List the said House shall in like Manner choose the President. But in choosing the President the Votes shall be taken by States, the Representation from each State having one Vote; A quorum for this Purpose shall consist of a Member or Members from two-thirds of the States, and a Majority of all the States shall be necessary to a Choice. In every Case, after the Choice of the President, the Person having the greatest Number of Votes of the Electors shall be the Vice President. But if there should remain two or more who have equal Votes, the Senate shall choose from them by Ballot the Vice President.]

The Congress may determine the Time of choosing the Electors, and the Day on which they shall give their Votes; which Day shall be the same throughout the United States.

No Person except a natural born Citizen, or a Citizen of the United States, at the time of the Adoption of this Constitution, shall be eligible to the Office of President; neither shall any Person be eligible to that Office who shall not have attained the Age of thirty-five

---

[5]This clause has been replaced by the Twelfth Amendment.

Years, and been fourteen Years a Resident within the United States.

In Case of the Removal of the President from Office, or of his Death, Resignation, or Inability to discharge the Powers and Duties of the said Office, the same shall devolve on the Vice President, and the Congress may by Law provide for the Case of Removal, Death, Resignation, or Inability, both of the President and Vice President, declaring what Officer shall then act as President, and such Officer shall act accordingly, until the Disability be removed, or a President shall be elected.

The President shall, at stated Times, receive for his Services, a Compensation, which shall neither be increased nor diminished during the Period for which he shall have been elected, and he shall not receive within that Period any other Emolument from the United States, or any of them.

Before he enter on the Execution of his Office, he shall take the following Oath or Affirmation:—"I do solemnly swear (or affirm) that I will faithfully execute the Office of President of the United States, and will to the best of my Ability, preserve, protect and defend the Constitution of the United States."

Section 2. The President shall be Commander in Chief of the Army and Navy of the United States, and of the Militia of the several States, when called into the actual Service of the United States; he may require the Opinion, in writing, of the principal Officer in each of the Executive Departments, upon any Subject relating to the Duties of their respective Offices, and he shall have Power to grant Reprieves and Pardons for Offenses against the United States, except in Cases of Impeachment.

He shall have Power, by and with the Advice and Consent of the Senate, to make Treaties, provided two-thirds of the Senators present concur; and he shall nominate, and by and with the Advice and Consent of the Senate, shall appoint Ambassadors, other public Ministers and Consuls, Judges of the Supreme Court, and all other Officers of the United States, whose Appointments are not herein otherwise provided for, and which shall be established by Law; but the Congress may by Law vest the Appointment of such inferior Officers, as they think proper, in the President alone, in the Courts of Law, or in the Heads of Departments.

The President shall have Power to fill up all Vacancies that may happen during the Recess of the Senate, by granting Commissions which shall expire at the end of their next Session.

Section 3. He shall from time to time give to the Congress Information of the State of the Union, and recommend to their Consideration such Measures as he shall judge necessary and expedient; he may, on extraordinary Occasions, convene both Houses, or either of them, and in Case of Disagreement between them, with Respect to the Time of Adjournment, he may adjourn them to such Time as he shall think proper; he shall receive Ambassadors and other public Ministers; he shall take Care that the Laws be faithfully executed, and shall Commission all the Officers of the United States.

Section 4. The President, Vice President and all civil Officers of the United States, shall be removed from Office on Impeachment for, and Conviction of Treason, Bribery, or other high Crimes and Misdemeanors.

ARTICLE III

Section 1. The judicial Power of the United States, shall be vested in one supreme Court, and in such inferior Courts as the Congress may from time to time ordain and establish. The Judges, both of the supreme and inferior Courts, shall hold their Offices during good Behavior and shall, at stated Times, receive for their Services, a Compensation, which shall not be diminished during their continuance in Office.

Section 2. The Judicial Power shall extend to all Cases, in Law and Equity, arising under this Constitution; the Laws of the United States, and Treaties made, or which shall be made, under their Authority;—to all Cases affecting Ambassadors, other public Ministers and Consuls;—to all Cases of admiralty and maritime Jurisdiction;—to Controversies to which the United States shall be a Party;—to Controversies between two or more States;—between a State and Citizens of another State;[6]—between Citizens of different States;—between Citizens of the same State claiming Lands under Grants of different States, and between a State, or the Citizens thereof, and foreign States, Citizens or Subjects.

In all Cases affecting Ambassadors, other public ministers and Consuls, and those in which a State shall be Party, the supreme Court shall have original jurisdiction. In all the other Cases before mentioned, the supreme Court shall have appelate Jurisdiction, both as to Law and Fact, with such Exceptions, and under such Regulations as the Congress shall make.

---

[6]See Eleventh Amendment.

The Trial of all Crimes, except in Cases of Impeachment, shall be by Jury; and such Trial shall be held in the State where the said Crimes shall have been committed; but when not committed within any State, the Trial shall be at such Place or Places as the Congress may by Law have directed.

Section 3. Treason against the United States, shall consist only in levying War against them, or in adhering to their Enemies, giving them Aid and Comfort. No Person shall be convicted of Treason unless on the Testimony of two Witnesses to the same Overt Act, or on Confession in open Court.

The Congress shall have Power to declare the Punishment of Treason, but no Attainder of Treason shall work Corruption of Blood, or Forfeiture except during the Life of the Person attainted.

ARTICLE IV

Section 1. Full Faith and Credit shall be given in each State to the public Acts, Records, and judicial Proceedings of every other State. And the Congress may by general Laws prescribe the Manner in which such Acts, Records, and Proceedings shall be proved, and the Effect thereof.

Section 2. The Citizens of each State shall be entitled to all Privileges and Immunities of Citizens in the several States.

A Person charged in any State with Treason, Felony, or other Crime, who shall flee from Justice, and be found in another State, shall on Demand of the executive Authority of the State from which he fled, be delivered up to be removed to the State having Jurisdiction of the Crime.

No Person held to Service or Labour in one State, under the Laws thereof, escaping into another, shall, in Consequence of any Law or Regulation therein, be discharged from such Service or Labour, but shall be delivered up on Claim of the Party to whom such Service or Labour may be due.[7]

Section 3. New States may be admitted by the Congress into this Union, but no new State shall be formed or erected within the Jurisdiction of any other State; nor any State be formed by the Junction of two or more States, or Parts of States, without the Consent of the Legislatures of the States concerned as well as of the Congress.

The Congress shall have Power to dispose of and make all need-

[7]See Thirteenth Amendment.

ful Rules and Regulations respecting the Territory or other Property belonging to the United States; and nothing in this Constitution shall be so construed as to Prejudice any Claims of the United States, or of any particular State.

Section 4. The United States shall guarantee to every State in this Union a Republican Form of Government, and shall protect each of them against Invasion; and on Application of the Legislature, or of the Executive (when the Legislature cannot be convened) against domestic Violence.

ARTICLE V

The Congress, whenever two thirds of both Houses shall deem it necessary, shall propose Amendments to this Constitution, or, on the Application of the Legislatures of two thirds of the several States, shall call a Convention for proposing Amendments, which, in either Case, shall be valid to all Intents and Purposes, as Part of this Constitution, when ratified by the Legislatures of three fourths of the several States, or by Conventions in three fourths thereof, as the one or the other Mode of Ratification may be proposed by the Congress; Provided that no Amendment which may be made prior to the Year One thousand eight hundred and eight shall in any Manner affect the first and fourth Clauses in the Ninth Section of the first Article; and that no State, without its Consent, shall be deprived of its equal Suffrage in the Senate.

ARTICLE VI

All Debts contracted and Engagements entered into, before the Adoption of this Constitution, shall be as valid against the United States under this Constitution, as under the Confederation.

This Constitution, and the Laws of the United States which shall be made in Pursuance thereof; and all Treaties made, or which shall be made, under the Authority of the United States, shall be the Supreme Law of the Land; and the Judges in every State shall be bound thereby, any Thing in the Constitution or Laws of any State to the Contrary notwithstanding.

The Senators and Representatives before mentioned, and the Members of the several State Legislatures, and all executive and judicial Officers, both of the United States and of the several States, shall be bound by Oath or Affirmation, to support this Constitution; but no religious Test shall ever be required as a Qualification to any Office or public Trust under the United States.

Article VII

The Ratification of the Conventions of nine States shall be sufficient for the Establishment of this Constitution between the States so ratifying the Same. Done in Convention by the Unanimous Consent of the States Present the Seventeenth Day of September in the Year of our Lord one thousand seven hundred and eighty seven, and of the Independence of the United States of America the Twelfth. In witness whereof We have hereunto subscribed our Names, Attest

William Jackson
Secretary

Go: Washington—
Presidt. and deputy from Virginia

Gouv Morris

New Hampshire
John Langdon
Nicholas Gilman

Massachusetts
Nathaniel Gorham
Rufus King

Connecticut
Wm. Saml. Johnson
Roger Sherman

New York
Alexander Hamilton

New Jersey
Wil: Livingston
David Brearley
Wm. Paterson
Jona: Dayton

Pennsylvania
B. Franklin
Thomas Mifflin
Robt. Morris
Geo. Clymer
Thos. Fitzsimons
Jared Ingersoll
James Wilson

Delaware
Geo: Read
Gunning Bedford Jun
John Dickinson
Richard Bassett
Jaco: Broom

Maryland
James McHenry
Dan of St. Thos Jenifer
Danl. Carroll

Virginia
John Blair—
James Madison Jr.

North Carolina
Wm. Blount
Richd. Dobbs Spaight
Hu Williamson

South Carolina
J. Rutledge
Charles Cotesworth Pinckney
Charles Pinckney
Pierce Butler

Georgia
William Few
Abr Baldwin

83

AMENDMENTS

Articles in Addition to, and Amendment of, the Constitution of the United States of America, Proposed by Congress, and Ratified by the Legislatures of the Several States Pursuant to the Fifth Article of the Original Constitution.

ARTICLE I

Congress shall make no law respecting an establishment of religion, or prohibiting the free exercise thereof; or abridging the freedom of speech, or of the press; or the right of the people peaceably to assemble, and to petition the Government for a redress of grievances.

ARTICLE II

A well regulated Militia, being necessary to the security of a free State, the right of the people to keep and bear Arms, shall not be infringed.

ARTICLE III

No soldier shall, in time of peace, be quartered in any house, without the consent of the Owner, nor in time of war, but in a manner to be prescribed by law.

ARTICLE IV

The right of the people to be secure in their persons, houses, papers, and effects, against unreasonable searches and seizures, shall not be violated, and no Warrants shall issue, but upon probable cause, supported by Oath or affirmation, and particularly describing the place to be searched, and the persons or things to be seized.

ARTICLE V

No person shall be held to answer for a capital, or otherwise infamous crime, unless on a presentment or indictment of a Grand Jury, except in cases arising in the land or naval forces, or in the Militia, when in actual service in time of War or public danger; nor shall any person be subject for the same offense to be twice put in jeopardy of life or limb; nor shall be compelled in any Criminal Case to be a witness against himself, nor be deprived of life, liberty, or property, without due process of law; nor shall private property be taken for public use, without just compensation.

ARTICLE VI

In all criminal prosecutions, the accused shall enjoy the right to a speedy and public trial, by an impartial jury of the State and district wherein the crime shall have been committed, which district shall have been previously ascertained by law, and to be informed of the nature and cause of the accusation; to be confronted with the witnesses against him; to have compulsory process for obtaining Witnesses in his favor, and to have the Assistance of Counsel for his defense.

ARTICLE VII

In suits at common law, where the value in controversy shall exceed twenty dollars, the right of trial by jury shall be preserved, and no fact tried by a jury shall be otherwise re-examined in any Court of the United States than according to the rules of the common law.

ARTICLE VIII

Excessive bail shall not be required, nor excessive fines imposed, nor cruel and unusual punishments inflicted.

ARTICLE IX

The enumeration in the Constitution, of certain rights, shall not be construed to deny or disparage others retained by the people.

ARTICLE X

The powers not delegated to the United States by the Constitution, nor prohibited by it to the States, are reserved to the States respectively, or to the people. (First ten amendments adopted in 1791.)

ARTICLE XI

The Judicial power of the United States shall not be construed to extend to any suit in law or equity, commenced or prosecuted against one of the United States by Citizens of another State, or by Citizens or Subjects of any Foreign State. (1798)

ARTICLE XII

The Electors shall meet in their respective States and vote by ballot for President and Vice President, one of whom, at least, shall not be an inhabitant of the same State with themselves; they shall name in their ballots the person voted for as President, and in distinct ballots the person voted for as Vice President and they shall make distinct lists of all persons voted for as President, and of all persons voted for as Vice President, and of the number of votes for each, which lists they shall sign and certify, and transmit sealed to the seat of the Government of the United States, directed to the President of the Senate. The President of the Senate shall, in the presence of the Senate and House of Representatives, open all the certificates and the votes shall then be counted. The person having the greatest number of votes for President shall be the President, if such number be a majority of the whole number of Electors appointed; and if no person have such majority, then from the persons having the highest numbers not exceeding three on the list of those voted for as President, the House of Representatives shall choose immediately, by ballot, the President. But in choosing the President, the votes shall be taken by States, the representation from each State having one vote; a quorum for this purpose shall consist of a member or members from two-thirds of the States, and a majority of all the States shall be necessary to a choice. And if the House of Representatives shall not choose a President, whenever the right of choice shall devolve upon them, before the fourth day of March next following, then the Vice President shall act as President, as in the case of the death or other constitutional disability of the President. The person having the greatest number of votes as Vice President shall be the Vice President, if such number be a majority of the whole number of Electors appointed, and if no person have a majority, then from the two highest numbers on the list, the Senate shall choose the Vice President; a quorum for the purpose shall consist of two-thirds of the whole number of Senators, and a majority of the whole number shall be necessary to a choice. But no person constitutionally ineligible to the office of President shall be eligible to that of Vice President of the United States. (1804)

Article XIII

Section 1. Neither slavery nor involuntary servitude, except as a punishment for crime whereof the party shall have been duly convicted, shall exist within the United States, or any place subject to their jurisdiction.

Section 2. Congress shall have the power to enforce this article by appropriate legislation. (1865)

Article XIV

Section 1. All persons born or naturalized in the United States and subject to the jurisdiction thereof, are citizens of the United States and of the State wherein they reside. No State shall make or enforce any law which shall abridge the privileges or immunities of citizens of the United States; nor shall any State deprive any person of life, liberty, or property, without due process of law; nor deny to any person within its jurisdiction the equal protection of the laws.

Section 2. Representatives shall be apportioned among the several States according to their respective numbers, counting the whole number of persons in each State, excluding Indians not taxed. But when the right to vote at any election for the choice of electors for President and Vice President of the United States, Representatives in Congress, the Executive and Judicial officers of a State, or the members of the Legislature thereof, is denied to any of the male inhabitants of such State, being twenty-one years of age, and citizens of the United States, or in any way abridged except for participation in rebellion, or other crime, the basis of representation therein shall be reduced in the proportion which the number of such male citizens shall bear to the whole number of male citizens twenty-one years of age in such State.

Section 3. No person shall be a Senator or Representative in Congress, or elector of President and Vice President or hold any office, civil or military, under the United States, or under any State, who, having previously taken an oath, as a member of Congress, or as an officer of the United States, or as a member of any State legislature, or as an executive or judicial officer of any State, to support the Constitution of the United States, shall have engaged in insurrection or rebellion against the same, or given aid or comfort to the enemies thereof. But Congress may, by a vote of two-thirds of each House, remove such disability.

Section 4. The validity of the public debt of the United States, authorized by law, including debts incurred for payment of pensions and bounties for services in suppressing insurrection or rebellion, shall not be questioned. But neither the United States nor any State shall assume or pay any debt or obligation incurred in aid of insurrection or rebellion against the United States, or any claim for the loss of emancipation of any slave; but all such debts, obligations and claims shall be held illegal and void.

Section 5. The Congress shall have power to enforce, by appropriate legislation, the provisions of this article. (1868)

Article XV

Section 1. The right of citizens of the United States to vote shall not be denied or abridged by the United States or by any State on account of race, color, or previous condition of servitude.

Section 2. The Congress shall have power to enforce this article by appropriate legislation. (1870)

ARTICLE XVI

The Congress shall have power to lay and collect taxes on incomes, from whatever source derived, without apportionment among the several States, and without regard to any census or enumeration. (1913)

ARTICLE XVII

The Senate of the United States shall be composed of two Senators from each State, elected by the people thereof, for six years and each Senator shall have one vote. The electors in each State shall have the qualifications requisite for electors of the most numerous branch of the State legislatures.

When vacancies happen in the representation of any State in the Senate, the executive authority of such State shall issue writs of election to fill such vacancies: *Provided,* That the legislature of any State may empower the executive thereof to make temporary appointments until the people fill the vacancies by election as the legislature may direct.

This amendment shall not be so construed as to affect the election or term of any Senator chosen before it becomes valid as a part of the Constitution. (1913)

ARTICLE XVIII

[8][*Section* 1. After one year from ratification of this article the manufacture, sale, or transportation of intoxicating liquors within, the importation thereof into, or the exportation thereof from the United States and all territory subject to the jurisdiction thereof for beverage purposes is hereby prohibited.

[*Section* 2. The Congress and the several States shall have concurrent power to enforce this article by appropriate legislation.

[*Section* 3. This article shall be inoperative unless it shall have been ratified as an amendment to the Constitution by the legislatures of the several States, as provided in the Constitution, within seven years from the date of submission hereof to the States by the Congress.] (1919)

---

[8]This amendment has been replaced by the Twenty-first Amendment.

Article XIX

The right of citizens of the United States to vote shall not be denied or abridged by the United States or by any State on account of sex.

Congress shall have power to enforce this article by appropriate legislation. (1920)

Article XX

Section 1. The terms of the President and Vice President shall end at noon on the 20th day of January, and the terms of Senators and Representatives at noon on the 3d day of January, of the years in which such terms would have ended if this article had not been ratified; and the terms of their successors shall then begin.

Section 2. The Congress shall assemble at least once in every year, and such meeting shall begin at noon on the 3d day of January, unless they shall by law appoint a different day.

Section 3. If, at the time fixed for the beginning of the term of the President, the President elect shall have died, the Vice President elect shall become President. If a President shall not have been chosen before the time fixed for the beginning of his term, or if the President elect shall have failed to qualify, then the Vice President elect shall act as President until a President shall have qualified; and the Congress may by law provide for the case wherein neither a President elect nor a Vice President elect shall have qualified, declaring who shall then act as President, or the manner in which one who is to act shall be selected, and such person shall act accordingly until a President or Vice President shall have qualified.

Section 4. The Congress may by law provide for the case of the death of any of the persons from whom the House of Representatives may choose a President whenever the right of choice shall have devolved upon them, and for the case of the death of any of the persons from whom the Senate may choose a Vice President whenever the the right of choice shall have devolved upon them.

Section 5. Sections 1 and 2 shall take effect on the 15th day of October following the ratification of this article.

Section 6. This article shall be inoperative unless it shall have been ratified as an amendment to the Constitution by the legislatures of three-fourths of the several States within seven years from the date of its submission. (1933)

Article XXI

Section 1. The eighteenth article of amendment to the Constitution of the United States is hereby repealed.

Section 2. The transportation or importation into any State, Territory, or possession of the United States for delivery or use therein of intoxicating liquors, in violation of the laws thereof, is hereby prohibited.

Section 3. The article shall be inoperative unless it shall have been ratified as an amendment to the Constitution by conventions in the several States, as provided in the Constitution, within seven years from the date of the submission hereof to the States by the Congress. (1933)

Constitutional Union Party—A political party organized in Baltimore in 1860 and composed mostly of Southern Whigs who, on the dissolution of their party, had joined neither the Republican nor Democratic party. In the election of 1856 they had formed part of the American party. Delegates from twenty states present at the Baltimore convention in May 1860 nominated John Bell of Tennessee for President and Edward Everett of Massachusetts for Vice-President. The platform denounced the platforms of the other parties as tending "to widen political divisions" and "fostering geographical parties." The party urged Republicans and Democrats to unite in dropping slavery as a political issue and "to recognize no political principle other than the Constitution, and the enforcement of the laws." In the election of 1860 the party polled a popular vote of 589,581, carrying the states of Virginia, Kentucky, and Tennessee, with a total electoral vote of 39. The outbreak of the Civil War put an end to the party.

Coolidge, Calvin—On August 3, 1923, the day after Warren Harding died, Calvin Coolidge, in one of the most unusual inaugural ceremonies ever performed, was sworn into office at the age of fifty-one to become the thirtieth President of the United States and the sixth Vice-President to be elevated to that position by the death of a President.

The first news of Harding's death reached Coolidge while he was vacationing at the old family homestead in Plymouth, Vermont, and at early dawn by kerosene lamp he took the oath of office administered by his father, who was a justice of the peace.

It was on this same farm, on July 4, 1872, that Mr. Coolidge was born. He was destined to become the first President to hold office from New England since Franklin Pierce, a time lapse of more than two thirds of a century. His long Yankee heritage and Puritan upbringing were to account for his shy, quiet, and conservative reputation in the White House. "Calvin the Silent" and "Cautious Cal" he was nicknamed.

After graduating from Amherst in 1895 and being admitted to the Massachusetts bar in 1897, his career was largely devoted to serving in public office. Starting at the bottom of the political ladder as city councilman at Northampton in 1899, he advanced to city solicitor in 1900 and to clerk of the courts in 1904. From 1910 to 1911 he was mayor of Northampton, and in 1912 was elected a member of the State Senate. From 1916 to 1918 he filled the office of lieutenant governor, then in 1919 he became governor of Massachusetts for a two-year term. It was at this time that he issued his often-quoted answer to Samuel Gompers's plea for support of the police force out on strike in Boston in 1919. He said, "There is no right to strike against the public safety by anybody, anywhere, any time."

In the fall of 1920 Coolidge was elected Vice-President. In 1924, after completing Harding's unexpired term of office, he defeated John W. Davis, his Democratic opponent, and Senator Robert LaFollette, a Progressive candidate for the presidency, by a tremendous majority.

During his administration there was an era of good feeling and general prosperity, and though he executed his duties capably he was not considered an outstanding President.

On retirement from the White House, he returned to Northampton, where he died unexpectedly at The Beeches, his home, on January 5, 1933.

Copperhead—Northern sympathizers with the South at the time of the Civil War were called Copperheads, from the venomous snake of that name. One notorious Copperhead organization opposed to Lincoln's administration wore as a symbol a copper cent on which was the head of the Goddess of Liberty. The name was revived just before World War II to stigmatize persons who disapproved of the foreign policy of the government.

Corrupt Practices Act—See *Campaign Expenditures.*

Cornerstone Speech—Alexander H. Stephens, Vice-President of the Confederacy, made a speech in Savannah, Georgia, that came to be known as the "cornerstone speech." After remarking that the United States Government had been founded on the "fundamentally wrong assumption of the equality of races," he asserted that the Confederate government was "founded upon exactly opposite ideas. Its foundations are laid, its cornerstone rests, upon the great truth that the Negro is not equal to the white man; that slavery, subordination to the superior race, is his natural and normal condition."

Coughlinites—Followers of the Reverend Charles E. Coughlin, a Canadian-born Detroit priest, who preached against the "money-changers" who should be "driven from the temple." A bitter enemy of President Franklin D. Roosevelt, he launched, in 1934, the National Union of Social Justice, to save the nation from "disaster" and "dictatorship." In 1936 the followers of Father Coughlin, Senator Huey Long, and Dr. Townsend organized a third-party movement. They placed Congressman William Lemke of North Dakota in the field as their presidential candidate, but he received little support.

Counting in the Alternative is a method employed by Congress in counting the electoral votes of a state when objection is made to their reception. The first case seems to have arisen in 1821, when, objection having been made to receiving the votes of Missouri, the houses directed the president of the Senate to declare, "If the votes of Missouri were to be counted the result would be for A. B. —— votes; if not counted, for A. B. —— votes; but in either event A. B. was elected." Other instances occurred when the votes of Michigan were counted in the alternative in 1827 and those of Georgia in 1869 and 1881.

Courtesy of the Senate—In confirming or rejecting presidential appointments to Federal office in a state, the Senate customarily acts in accordance with the wishes of the senators from that state. If only one of the senators belongs to the majority party, his desire alone is followed. Because of the practical control which the Senate exercises over appointments, the President usually consults the senators who are most interested in an appointment.

A famous political quarrel over this practice of senatorial courtesy arose during President Garfield's administration. In 1881 the President ignored the two Republican senators from New York, Roscoe Conkling and Thomas C. Platt, in appointing a collector of the Port of New York. Both senators resigned and immediately sought re-election in order to show the President that they, rather than he, had the approval of the party. After a protracted struggle in the State Legislature, both senators were defeated. This terminated Conkling's political career, but Platt was eventually returned to the Senate.

Other long-standing usages of the Senate are also considered matters of so-called senatorial courtesy.

Cradle of Liberty—Faneuil Hall in Boston is known as the Cradle of Liberty because within its walls some of the most stirring scenes of the American Revolution were enacted. Town meetings were held here, and the eloquence of the old patriots greatly influenced the action of the colonies. Protests were voted in Faneuil Hall against the Stamp Act. On Friday, November 5, 1773, the first of a series of tea meetings was held in the hall. Most of the statesmen and orators of America have stood upon its rostrum. This old market house, the gift of Peter Faneuil to the town of Boston, was commenced in 1740 and completed in 1742. It was burned in 1761, rebuilt in 1762, and enlarged in 1805.

Crédit Mobilier—This was the name of a corporation formed for the purpose of building the Union Pacific Railroad. One of the most extensive scandals in the history of this country centered around this corporation and took its name from it.

The Crédit Mobilier of America was a corporation chartered by the state of Pennsylvania, originally under the name of the Pennsylvania Fiscal Agency. The control of this corporation passed to parties interested in the building of the Union Pacific, among whom were Oakes Ames and Oliver Ames of Massachusetts.

In August 1867, the Crédit Mobilier, through Oakes Ames, contracted with the Union Pacific Railroad to build for it 637 miles of road at prices aggregating $47,000,000. The value of the Crédit Mobilier shares, estimated on the advantages to be derived from this contract, was 200 per cent in December 1867 and 300 or 400 per cent in February 1868. Oakes Ames was at that time a member of Congress and, fearing legislation adverse to the Union Pacific, he undertook to place the stock "where it will do most good to us," as he put it.

Accordingly, in December 1867, he entered into contracts with various members of the House of Representatives to sell to them stock of the Crédit Mobilier at par, merely stating that it was a good investment, and in some cases, in answer to a direct question, asserting that no embarrassment to them could flow from it, as the Union Pacific had received all the aid that it wanted from the government. Some of the members who thus bought stock paid for it; for others Ames advanced the money, agreeing to apply the dividends of the stock to the payment of the indebtedness. Two dividends received in 1868 sufficed to pay for the entire stock of the latter class of members and left a small balance due to them.

Among these members was James A. Garfield of Ohio, and in the presidential campaign of 1880 his connection with this matter was brought up against him. The amount of money he had thus received was $329, and the cry of "329" was a common one on the part of the Democrats in that campaign.

Charges based on the Crédit Mobilier affair had been circulated during the campaign of 1872, and on the assembling of Congress a committee of investigation was ordered by the House on the motion of the Speaker, James G. Blaine. The committee was appointed by a Democrat temporarily acting as Speaker and consisted of two Democrats, two Republicans, and one Liberal Republican. The committee recommended the expulsion of Oakes Ames of Massachusetts and of James Brooks of New York, the former for having attempted to bribe members by sales of stock below its value, the latter for having received stock from the Crédit Mobilier much below its value, knowing that it was intended to influence his action as a congressman and as government director in the Union Pacific. Moreover, as a director he must have known that the Crédit Mobilier was to receive payments in securities of the Union Pacific, a fact of which the other members, so the committee found, were in ignorance. The House did not expel Ames and Brooks but subjected them to the "absolute condemnation of the House." Though these were the only members punished, the innocence of some of the others was at least open to doubt.

Cross-of-Gold Speech—A famous political speech on the money question delivered by William Jennings Bryan, "the boy orator of the Platte," at the Democratic National Convention in Chicago, June 8, 1896.

"We do not come as aggressors. Our war is not a war of conquest; we are fighting in the defense of our homes, our families, and posterity. We have petitioned, and our petitions have been scorned; we have entreated, and our entreaties have been disregarded; we have begged, and they have mocked when our calamity came. We beg no longer; we entreat no more; we petition no more. We defy them!"

Bryan, with his magnificent voice, spoke with the force of a tropical hurricane, whipping his hearers up to such a pitch of excitement that at the close of his peroration his nomination for the presidency by the convention was assured.

"If they dare to come out in the open field and defend the gold standard as a good thing, we will fight them to the uttermost. Having behind us the producing masses of the nation and the world, supported by the commercial interests, the laboring interests, and the toilers everywhere, we will answer their demand for a gold standard by saying to them: 'You will not press down upon the brow of labor this crown of thorns, you shall not crucify mankind upon a cross of gold.'"

Dark Horse, which is a race-track term for an unexpected winner, is used in political circles to describe a candidate who is not considered a serious contender but who suddenly forges to the front in a surprise showing of strength. Dark horses are sometimes named as compromise candidates by rival political factions at nominating conventions. James K. Polk was called the first dark-horse President.

Dartmouth College Case—A controversy arose in 1815 and 1816 between the legislature of New Hampshire and the corporation of Dartmouth College, which was caused chiefly by the removal of the president of that institution by the trustees in consequence of a local religious dispute. The legislature in 1816 passed acts changing the name of Dartmouth College to Dartmouth University and creating a new corporation, to which its property was transferred.

The old trustees began suit for the recovery of the property and were defeated in the highest court of the state. The case (The Trustees of Dartmouth College *vs.* Woodward) was then taken on writ of error to the United States Supreme Court. Daniel Webster made a great argument, claiming that the acts of the legislature violated Article I, Section 10, Clause 1, of the Constitution of the United States, which provides that "no State shall . . . pass any . . . law impairing the obligation of contracts" and that these acts were therefore unconstitutional and void. The decision of the Supreme Court rendered in 1819 upheld this view. It settled the law that a charter granted to a private corporation was a contract which could not be altered in a material point without the consent of those who held it, unless the power of revision is reserved to the legislature by a clause in the charter or a general law of the state. This decision is one of the most important ever rendered by the Supreme Court.

Deadlock is the state of affairs in which the business of a legislative assembly is blocked through the obstructions of a minority, or where in an election of officers by a legislative assembly neither party has sufficient votes to elect its candidate and neither will yield or compromise: as where more than a majority vote is required to elect, or there is a tie, or a majority of the members (present or not present) is requisite and all cannot be induced to attend. The term is also applied to a stoppage of legislative business by reason of the refusal of either of the houses to yield on a question on which there is a difference of opinion between them.

Declaration of Independence—The revolt of the American colonies against Great Britain was begun without any general idea of pushing the matter to complete separation from the mother country. Although the idea of forming an independent government was favored in New England, it was so distasteful to most of the other colonies that Congress formally disavowed it on July 6, 1775. The idea, however, gained ground rapidly during the following year, and no one thing aided more in its spread than the publication of Thomas Paine's pamphlet, *Common Sense.* This struck the keynote of the situation by advocating with forcible logic an assertion of independence on the part of the colonies and the formation of a republican government. The Pennsylvania Legislature so well appreciated the value of Paine's pamphlet that it gave him a grant of $2,500 in consideration of it.

In May 1776, the Virginia Convention instructed its delegates to propose a resolution for independence. This was done on June 7 by Richard Henry Lee. It was the first official statement that the colonies were politically united. On June 10 the Colonial Congress, assembled in Philadelphia, resolved that a committee should be appointed to prepare a declaration "that the United Colonies are, and of right ought to be, free and independent States." Such action was taken, the committee appointed consisting of Thomas Jefferson, John Adams, Benjamin Franklin, Roger Sherman, and Robert R. Livingston. A draft was reported by this committee on June 28. On July 2 a resolution was adopted declaring the colonies free and independent states. Finally, on July 4, the Declaration of Independence was agreed to, engrossed on paper and signed by John Hancock as president and by Charles Thomson as secretary. It was afterward engrossed on parchment and signed.

The document is almost entirely from the pen of Thomas Jefferson, few changes having been made in his original draft.

DECLARATION OF INDEPENDENCE

In Congress, July 4, 1776

THE UNANIMOUS DECLARATION OF THE THIRTEEN
UNITED STATES OF AMERICA

When, in the Course of human events, it becomes necessary for one people to dissolve the political bands which have connected them with another, and to assume among the powers of the earth, the separate and equal station to which the Laws of Nature and of Nature's God entitle them, a decent respect to the opinions of mankind requires that they should declare the causes which impel them to the separation.

We hold these truths to be self-evident, that all men are created equal, that they are endowed by their Creator with certain unalienable Rights, that among these are Life, Liberty and the pursuit of Happiness. That to secure these rights, Governments are instituted among Men, deriving their just powers from the consent of the governed. That whenever any Form of Government becomes destructive of these ends, it is the Right of the People to alter or to abolish it, and to institute new Government, laying its foundation on such principles and organizing its powers in such form, as to them shall seem most likely to effect their Safety and Happiness. Prudence, indeed, will dictate that Governments long established should not be changed for light and transient causes; and accordingly all experience hath shewn, that mankind are more disposed to suffer, while evils are sufferable, than to right themselves by abolishing the forms to which they are accustomed. But when a long train of abuses and usurpations, pursuing invariably the same object, evidence a design to reduce them under absolute Despotism, it is their right, it is their duty, to throw off such Government, and to provide new Guards for their future security. Such has been the patient sufferance of these Colonies; and such is now the necessity which constrains them to alter their former Systems of Government. The history of the present King of Great Britain is a history of repeated injuries and usurpations, all having in direct object the establishment of an absolute Tyranny over these States. To prove this, let Facts be submitted to a candid world.

He has refused his Assent to Laws, the most wholesome and necessary for the public good.

He has forbidden his Governors to pass Laws of immediate and pressing importance, unless suspended in their operation till his Assent should be obtained, and when so suspended, he has utterly neglected to attend to them.

He has refused to pass other Laws for the accommodation of large districts of people, unless those people would relinquish the right of Representation in the Legislature, a right inestimable to them and formidable to tyrants only.

He has called together legislative bodies at places, unusual, uncomfortable, and distant from the depository of their public Records, for the sole purpose of fatiguing them into compliance with his measures.

He has dissolved Representative Houses repeatedly, for opposing with manly firmness his invasions on the rights of the people.

He has refused for a long time, after such dissolutions, to cause others to be elected; whereby the Legislative powers, incapable of Annihilation, have returned to the People at large for their exercise; the State remaining in the meantime exposed to all the dangers of invasion from without, and convulsions within.

He has endeavored to prevent the population of these States; for that purpose obstructing the Laws for Naturalization of Foreigners; refusing to pass others to encourage their migrations hither, and raising the conditions of new Appropriations of Lands.

He has obstructed the Administration of Justice, by refusing his Assent to Laws for establishing Judiciary powers.

He has made Judges dependent on his Will alone, for the tenure of their offices, and the amount and payment of their salaries.

He has erected a multitude of New Offices, and sent hither swarms of Officers to harass our people, and eat out their substance.

He has kept among us, in times of peace, Standing Armies, without the Consent of our legislatures.

He has affected to render the Military independent of and superior to the Civil power.

He has combined with others to subject us to a jurisdiction foreign to our constitution and unacknowledged by our laws; giving his Assent to their Acts of pretended Legislation: For quartering large bodies of armed troops among us: For protecting them by a mock Trial from punishment for any Murders which they should commit on the Inhabitants of these States: For cutting off our Trade with all parts of the world: For imposing Taxes on us without our Consent: For depriving us in many cases of the benefits of Trial by Jury:

For transporting us beyond Seas to be tried for pretended offenses: For abolishing the free System of English Laws in a neighbouring Province, establishing therein an Arbitrary government, and enlarging its Boundaries so as to render it at once an example and fit instrument for introducing the same absolute rule into these Colonies: For taking away our Charters, abolishing our most valuable Laws and altering fundamentally the Forms of our Governments: For suspending our own Legislatures and declaring themselves invested with power to legislate for us in all cases whatsoever.

He has abdicated Government here by declaring us out of his Protection and waging War against us.

He has plundered our seas, ravished our Coasts, burnt our towns, and destroyed the lives of our people.

He is at this time transporting large Armies of foreign Mercenaries to complete the works of death, desolation and tyranny, already begun with circumstances of cruelty and perfidy scarcely paralleled in the most barbarous ages, and totally unworthy the Head of a civilized nation.

He has constrained our fellow Citizens taken Captive on the high Seas to bear Arms against their Country, to become the executioners of their friends and Brethren, or to fall themselves by their Hands.

He has excited domestic insurrections amongst us, and has endeavoured to bring on the inhabitants of our frontiers, the merciless Indian Savages, whose known rule of warfare is an undistinguished destruction of all ages, sexes and conditions. In every stage of these Oppressions We have Petitioned for Redress in the most humble terms. Our repeated Petitions have been answered only by repeated injury. A Prince, whose character is thus marked by every act which may define a Tyrant, is unfit to be the ruler of a free people. Nor have We been wanting in attention to our British brethren. We have warned them from time to time of attempts by their legislature to extend an unwarrantable jurisdiction over us. We have reminded them of the circumstances of our emigration and settlement here. We have appealed to their native justice and magnanimity, and we have conjured them by the ties of our common kindred to disavow these usurpations, which would inevitably interrupt our connections and correspondence. They too have been deaf to the voice of justice and of consanguinity. We must, therefore, acquiesce in the necessity, which denounces our Separation, and hold them, as we hold the rest of mankind, Enemies in War, in Peace Friends.

WE, THEREFORE, the Representatives of the United States of America, in General Congress, Assembled, appealing to the Supreme Judge of the world for the rectitude of our intentions do, in the Name, and by authority of the good People of these Colonies, solemnly publish and declare, That these United Colonies are, and of Right ought to be, Free and Independent States: that they are Absolved from all Allegiance to the British Crown, and that all political connection between them and the State of Great Britain is and ought to be totally dissolved: and that as Free and Independent States, they have full Power to levy War, conclude Peace, contract Alliances, establish Commerce, and to do all other Acts and Things which Independent States may of right do. And for the support of this Declaration, with a firm reliance on the protection of Divine Providence, we mutually pledge to each other our Lives, our Fortunes, and our sacred Honor.

SIGNERS OF THE DECLARATION OF INDEPENDENCE

Arranged according to states, not in the order in which they signed the original document.

NEW HAMPSHIRE
Josiah Bartlett
Wm. Whipple
Matthew Thornton

MASSACHUSETTS
John Hancock
Saml. Adams
John Adams
Robt. Treat Paine
Elbridge Gerry

RHODE ISLAND
Step. Hopkins
William Ellery
Fras. Hopkinson
John Hart
Abra. Clark

PENNSYLVANIA
Robt. Morris
Benjamin Rush
Benja. Franklin

John Morton
Geo. Clymer
Jas. Smith
Geo. Taylor
James Wilson
Geo. Ross

DELAWARE
Cæsar Rodney
Geo. Read
Tho. M'Kean

MARYLAND
Samuel Chase
Wm. Paca
Thos. Stone
Charles Carroll of Carrollton

CONNECTICUT
Roger Sherman
Sam'el Huntington
Wm. Williams
Oliver Wolcott

NEW YORK
Wm. Floyd
Phil. Livingston
Frans. Lewis
Lewis Morris

NEW JERSEY
Richd. Stockton
Jno. Witherspoon

VIRGINIA
George Wythe
Richard Henry Lee
Th. Jefferson
Benja. Harrison
Thos. Nelson, jr.
Francis Lightfoot Lee
Carter Braxton

NORTH CAROLINA
Wm. Hooper
Joseph Hewes
John Penn

SOUTH CAROLINA
Edward Rutledge
Thos. Heyward, Junr.
Thomas Lynch, Junr.
Arthur Middleton

GEORGIA
Button Gwinnett
Lyman Hall
Geo. Walton

Delaware—Bears the nickname "Diamond State" and is sometimes referred to as the "Blue Hen State." State flower, peach blossom. Population, 266,505. Area, 2,057 square miles. Capital, Dover. Delaware is an original state of the Union and the first state to ratify the Constitution—December 1787. The state has been generally Republican for the past fifty years, but it went Democratic in 1936, 1940, and 1944. It has one representative in Congress.

Delegates—The territories of the United States—Alaska and Hawaii—elect delegates to Congress, while a resident commissioner is elected from Puerto Rico. They have seats in the House, where they have the right of debate but not the right to vote. Their compensation is the same as the representatives.

Democracy is government of the people by themselves, either directly, or indirectly through chosen representatives. In a broader sense it is the people with whom the sovereign power of a state rests.

"Democracy Is Not Dying"—Thus said President Franklin D. Roosevelt in his third inaugural address, January 20, 1941.

102

Democratic-Republican Party—This party, known first as the Republican, then as the Democratic-Republican, and in our own time merely as the Democratic party, had as its fundamental principles the limitation of the powers of the Federal Government to those granted by the letter of the Constitution and the increase of the direct influence of the people in the affairs of the government. Though the party from time to time swerved from these principles, when the exigencies of the political situation seemed to demand it (and the slavery question caused very violent fluctuations of this nature), it returned again and again to these principles.

The adoption of the Constitution left the Anti-Federal party without a cause; there was no organized opposition to the Federal party, to which most of the prominent men of the time belonged, and from it the Republican party, as the Democratic-Republican party was first called, was but gradually differentiated.

The financial measures of Hamilton clearly showed his purpose of applying to the Constitution loose principles of construction, and his proposals to assume the state debts and later to incorporate the United States Bank and to levy a tax on distilled spirits were the first measures that marked a divergence in the Federal party. Madison, Jefferson, and Randolph opposed these measures as unconstitutional. As was natural, Hamilton's following consisted largely of the commercial interests, while the agricultural interests as naturally favored a view tending to localize political power. It was not until 1792 that the party thus segregated was known by the name of Republican.

Those who were then known as Democrats, agitating, loud-mouthed, and abusive partisans of France in the war she was then engaged in, were not acknowledged by the Republicans as of their party, though the two were frequently united in action; in the third House, the Republicans elected their candidate for Speaker, and the merging of the two factions was hastened by this event, though for some time thereafter the line between the two was plainly visible within the party; thereafter it was known as the Democratic-Republican party.

John Adams succeeded Washington as President, defeating Jefferson by a majority of but three electoral votes. The Alien and Sedition Laws aided in rendering Adams's administration extremely unpopular, and in the next presidential contest the small Federalist majority was overcome and Jefferson was elected President by the House of Representatives, into which the election had been thrown by a tie in the Electoral College.

The party as now constituted aimed at strict construction, an elective judiciary, reduction of expenditure (on this ground they opposed a navy) and, as a consequence thereof, a reduction of taxation, and the extension of the suffrage. The party was so successful that before 1805 the state governments of all but two of the states (Vermont and Connecticut) were in their hands, and they controlled the Senate and House of Representatives. The purchase of Louisiana by Jefferson, though enthusiastically commended everywhere, was a palpable deviation from strict construction, as was also the embargo; to this latter step the party was forced by its previous policy of refusing to establish a navy. The failure of the embargo occasioned a change in party feeling, and as a result war against England was declared in 1812. The war increased the national feeling; the restriction of trade preceding the war and incident to it had fostered manufactures, to maintain which the party was forced to adopt a slightly protective tariff; and the financial difficulties raised by the war led to the establishment of a national bank in 1816.

Thus the party had been forced into a position closely resembling that of its former antagonists. These were now politically dead, the few who remained calling themselves Federal-Republicans. It was an "era of good feeling," but it was not destined to continue long. The party was soon divided into two wings, again on the general lines of strict and loose construction. John Quincy Adams was an advocate of the latter, and the opposition to him culminated in the election of Andrew Jackson as his successor.

During the presidency of Adams, his followers gradually came to be known as National Republicans, while the others, first known as Jackson Men, ultimately took the name of Democrats. The former were the precursors of the Whigs. Jackson undertook to give form to his party, using the Federal patronage as a means, and he was eminently successful; his own leanings were to strict construction, and the party was once more placed on that basis. A distinctively Southern and slavery faction of the party, under Calhoun, carried its opposition to the length of threatening secession, but Jackson firmly repressed the movement.

In practice Jackson was not uniformly consistent, but he enforced his strict construction theories in the case of the United States Bank, and the adoption of the subtreasury system under Van Buren still more firmly entrenched the theory. The panic during Van Buren's administration was effectively used against him in the next campaign, and Harrison, a Whig, was elected. It was about this time that the name Locofoco was applied to the Democratic party.

Harrison died within a month after his inauguration and was succeeded by the Vice-President, Tyler, a Calhoun Democrat. The ascendancy of the Calhoun faction committed the party, in its convention of 1844, to the annexation of Texas. From this time forward it vibrated between strict and loose construction, as suited its purpose, using the latter for the purpose of spreading slavery, and the former to secure it where thus established; the Calhoun faction was first and foremost a pro-slavery party.

The election of Polk was in great part due to the Liberty party. His successor, Taylor, was a Whig, but his election was due to local dissensions among the Democrats; and Fillmore, who became President on Taylor's death, was succeeded by Pierce, a Democrat. Northern Democrats were not in favor of slavery, but they regarded it as the policy of their party to ignore the question; Southern Whigs were pro-slavery, and to them the question of slavery was paramount to any party ties.

Buchanan, another Democrat, succeeded Pierce, but the power of the party was diminishing, especially in the West. When it appeared that the Kansas-Nebraska Bill would fail to make Kansas a slave state, the Southern section of the party took refuge in the Calhoun doctrine of the duty of government to protect slavery, and the split thus occasioned ended in dissension at the party convention in Charleston in 1860. Douglas led the Northern Democrats, who upheld popular sovereignty; the Southern members had adopted the Calhoun view. Douglas triumphed in the convention. On this the

Southern wing withdrew, to meet in Richmond; the Douglas wing adjourned to Baltimore, where further dissensions caused the withdrawal of many of the border states. These states, aided by the original seceders, nominated John C. Breckenridge; Douglas was named by his party. These conflicts in the party resulted in the election of Lincoln, the Republican candidate.

The Civil War followed. During that struggle the party was uniformly opposed to the government measures rendered necessary by the anomalous condition of the country. The secession of the Southern states had deprived them of most of their members in Congress, and in the North only New York and New Jersey had Democratic governors. Their convention of 1864 denounced the war measures of the Republicans, declared the war a failure, and demanded the cessation of hostilities. On this issue they were overwhelmingly defeated. The reconstruction measures of the Republicans, notably the Civil Rights Bill, were strenuously opposed by the Democrats, and opposition to this was made the most prominent feature of the party creed, and in its desire to repress the Negroes the party swerved from its old principle of the extension of suffrage.

In 1872 the action of the Liberal Republicans helped in clearing away these dogmas, which had greatly hampered the party; and, aided by the financial depression of 1873 and by the disfavor with which Grant's second term was regarded, the party made large gains, carrying the state elections in many of the Northern states and getting a majority in the House.

Tilden, the Democratic candidate for President in 1876, had a popular majority over Hayes, the Republican, but the result of the electoral vote was in doubt, and the election was finally awarded to Hayes. Their next candidate, Hancock, was likewise defeated. The action of the party after the war in opposing Negro suffrage had tended to consolidate Southern whites in its favor, while the memories of the war were a strong rallying point for the Republicans in the North, so that, generally speaking, the latter has been Republican, the former Democratic.

Since the Civil War the Democratic party has had four Presidents in office—Grover Cleveland, Woodrow Wilson, Franklin D. Roosevelt, and Harry S. Truman.

Disability of the President—Disability signifies lack of qualification, inability, lack of power. A man who is not a natural-born citizen of this country is disabled from occupying the presidential chair. A President stricken with insanity is unable to act as President. The word "disability" is commonly used when "inability" is meant. The Constitution, Article II, Section 1, Clause 6, provides for the succession in case of the removal, death, resignation, or inability of the President. (See *Presidential Succession.*) There is, however, no provision, nor can there be any, to indicate what degree of inability shall shift the office to the Vice-President. In the case, for example, of the insanity of the President, in which it is not probable that he himself will realize his condition or give notice of it, it must be left to the Vice-President to assume the office at his discretion, leaving the determination of the question, in case of a contest, to the courts.

Disputed Presidential and Vice-Presidential Elections—The original method of choosing the President and Vice-President is prescribed in Article II, Section 1, Clause 3, of the Constitution; the Twelfth Amendment, ratified September 25, 1804, altered that method to its present form. There have been three controversies in regard to the presidency and one in regard to the vice-presidency.

I   When the electoral votes were counted in 1801 it was found that Jefferson and Burr had each received 73, being a majority of all the electors, each elector having two votes. On the House of Representatives was therefore thrown the task of deciding between them. All but two of the members were present; one had died and one was ill; another, though ill, was carried to the House in his bed.

Rules were adopted as follows: The public was to be excluded, the Senate to be admitted; there was to be no adjournment, and no other business was to be considered until a choice had been arrived at; states were to sit together; duplicate statements of the vote of each state were to be prepared and to be cast into two different ballot boxes, to be passed around by the sergeant at arms. The word "divided" was to be used in the cases of states that could not agree. The contents of the two ballot boxes were then to be counted by tellers, of whom one was to be appointed by each state. The agreement of the boxes was to be the test of the correctness of the vote.

The Federalists, obliged to choose between two Republicans, at first supported Burr, though not unanimously. The balloting continued for seven days with no choice. At length, on February 17, the Federalists' chief, James A. Bayard of Delaware, having obtained from Jefferson assurance that he would maintain the Navy and the public credit and that he would not remove Federalist officeholders for party causes, decided to end the struggle, and on the thirty-seventh ballot three members in Vermont and Maryland, by voting blank, gave these states to Jefferson, who was thus elected.

II   There was practically but one party in 1824, and the contest in that year was between John Quincy Adams, Andrew Jackson, William Crawford, and Henry Clay, all Republicans. Their electoral votes were respectively 84, 99, 41, and 37. None having a majority, the election went to the House, which was obliged to choose from the highest three; Clay was thus excluded, and his strength went to Adams, between whose views and those of Clay there was marked agreement; and Adams, carrying thirteen states, was elected. Jackson carried seven states and Crawford four. The House had adopted the rules of 1801. Adams made Clay his Secretary of State, the price, it was alleged, of Clay's support and influence in the House.

III   The third presidential dispute differed from the others. In 1876 four states had each sent in several disagreeing returns. The question arose as to which was to be recognized. The Democratic nominees, Tilden and Hindricks, had indisputably received 184 votes, one less than a majority. The votes of South Carolina, Florida, and Louisiana, and one vote from Oregon, being twenty in all, were in doubt, differing returns having been made, owing, in the first three states, to the rejection by the Returning Boards of votes alleged to be fraudulent.

To settle the matter the Electoral Commission was created. It decided in favor of the Republican, Hayes, and as only the concurrent vote of both houses could overthrow the result, its decision stood, the Republican Senate voting to sustain, the Democratic House to reject. One elector in each of five states was objected to as ineligible because holding Federal office, but both houses consented to admit these votes.

IV   The only distinctively vice-presidential contest was in 1837, when Richard M. Johnson received 147 votes, to 147 for all the other candidates. The Senate, thus compelled to choose between the highest two, gave 33 votes to Johnson and 16 to Francis Granger; Johnson was thus elected.

District of Columbia, The, originally included sixty-four square miles ceded to the national government by Maryland in 1788 and thirty-six square miles ceded by Virginia in 1789. The District was organized by acts of July 16, 1790, and March 3, 1791. In 1800 the national seat of government was removed to Washington. (See *Capital of the United States.*) In 1801 Congress took complete control of the District, and the inhabitants had no representation in that body till 1871, when it was organized as the other territories of the United States. By act of June 20, 1874, however, a government by three commissioners, appointed by the President, was established. In 1846 the portion west of the Potomac was retroceded to Virginia.

Dollar Diplomacy was an imperialistic foreign policy instituted by President Theodore Roosevelt in dealing with our Caribbean neighbors and extended by his successor, President Taft, to China. President Roosevelt said of this policy, "If a nation shows that it knows how to act with reasonable efficiency and decency in social and political matters; if it keeps order and pays its obligations, it need fear no interference from the United States. Chronic wrongdoing, or an impotence which results in a general loosening of the ties of civilized society, may in America, as elsewhere, ultimately require intervention by some civilized nation, and in the Western hemisphere the adherence of the United States to the Monroe Doctrine may force the United States, however reluctantly, in flagrant cases of such wrongdoing or impotence, to the exercise of an international police power."

In describing the foreign policy of his administration President Taft said, "The diplomacy of the present administration has sought to respond to modern ideas of commercial intercourse. This policy has been characterized as substituting dollars for bullets. . . . It is an effort frankly directed to the increase of American trade upon the axiomatic principle that the government of the United States shall extend all proper support to every legitimate and beneficial American enterprise abroad."

"Don't Badger Them"—Blondin, the tightrope walker, was at the peak of his fame when Abraham Lincoln was elected President in 1860. Blondin's greatest feat was wheeling his wife in a wheelbarrow on a rope stretched across the Niagara River near the Falls. Lincoln used the incident to illustrate a point in a speech.

"Gentlemen, suppose all the property you were worth was in gold and you put it in the hands of Blondin to carry across the Niagara River on a rope. Would you shake the cable or keep shouting at him, 'Blondin, stand up a little straighter—Blondin, stoop a little more—go a little faster—lean a little more to the North—lean a little more to the South'? No, you would hold your breath as well as your tongue and keep your hands off till he was safe over. The government is carrying an enormous weight. Untold treasures are in their hands; they are doing the very best they can. Don't badger them. Keep silence, and we will get you safe across."

Dorr Rebellion—In 1840 Connecticut and Rhode Island were the only states that were still governed by their colonial charters. The charter of the latter state, imposing, as it did, a property qualification so high as to disfranchise two thirds of the citizens, was extremely unpopular. A proposition of Thomas W. Dorr, of Providence, to extend the franchise was voted down. Dorr then took to agitation, and finally a convention prepared a constitution and submitted it to a popular vote. Its supporters claimed a majority for it, which its opponents, known as the Law-and-Order party, denied.

Nevertheless, in 1842 the constitution was proclaimed to be in force. An election was held under it, only the suffrage party participating. Dorr was elected governor. The suffrage legislature assembled at Providence with Thomas W. Dorr as governor; the charter legislature at Newport, with Samuel W. King as governor.

After transacting some business the suffrage legislature adjourned. The charter legislature authorized the governor to take energetic steps, and an appeal for aid was made to the national government.

The suffragists attempted armed resistance but were dispersed. Dorr fled but soon returned and gave himself up. He was convicted of high treason in 1844 and sentenced to imprisonment for life, but was pardoned in 1847 and in 1852 was restored to his civil rights. The charter party, soon after the rebellion, proposed a new constitution, largely extending the suffrage, which was carried and went into effect in May 1843.

Doughfaces—In the debate over the Missouri Bill in 1820, eighteen Northern members of the House of Representatives voted with the Southern members in what John Randolph called a "dirty bargain." He denounced the Northern men as "doughfaces," meaning that they were easily molded and led to forsake their principles from unworthy motives. The epithet came to be applied to Northerners who favored slavery, and more broadly to persons who were like dough in the hands of professional politicians.

Dred Scott Case—Dred Scott was a Negro slave of Dr. Emerson of the United States Army. In 1834 Dr. Emerson was ordered from Missouri to Rock Island, Illinois, where slavery was prohibited by statute, and in 1836 to Fort Snelling, in what is now Minnesota, but then a territory. Scott went with him, and at Fort Snelling married Harriet, another of his master's slaves. In 1838, after a child had been born to them, they returned with their master to St. Louis.

In 1848 Scott brought a suit in the state courts involving the question of his freedom and obtained a verdict in his favor, which was, however, reversed by the Supreme Court of Missouri. Shortly afterward he was sold to J. F. A. Sandford of New York, against whom he at once began a similar suit in the United States courts. The case was carried to the United States Supreme Court, and on March 6, 1857, Chief Justice Roger Brooke Taney of Maryland announced the decision.

The court held that Scott had no right to sue because, even if he were free, no colored person was regarded by the Constitution as a citizen. He says "they had for more than a century before been regarded as . . . so far inferior that they had no rights which the white man was bound to respect."

111

After deciding this, the question at issue, the court went out of its way to declare the Missouri Compromise void and to deny the right of Congress to exclude slavery from any territory. Of the associate justices, six supported the Chief Justice, and two, McLean of Ohio and Curtis of Massachusetts, dissented. The opinion was for a time withheld from publication in order not to increase the excitement of the then pending presidential election.

Eagle—The eagle as the national emblem of the United States did not meet with the approval of Benjamin Franklin, who preferred the turkey. "I wish," he wrote in 1784, "the Bald Eagle had not been chosen as the Representative of our Country; he is a Bird of bad moral Character; like those among Men who live by Sharping and Robbing, he is generally poor, and often very lousy. The Turkey is a much more respectable Bird, and withal a true original Native of America."

A blue eagle was the symbol of the NRA during President Franklin D. Roosevelt's first term. It was killed by the Supreme Court when it declared the National Industrial Recovery Act unconstitutional in May 1935.

Economic Royalists—A Rooseveltian term for the captains of industry who were unsympathetic to reform and fought much of the New Deal legislation. President Roosevelt used the term in his speech accepting renomination, June 27, 1936. (See *Bourbons.*)

Election Bets are against public policy and void because they have a tendency to corrupt elections. In one or two states a voter who has made a wager on the outcome of an election is disqualified and may be challenged at the polls.

Electoral College—By analogy to the College of Cardinals which elects the Pope at Rome, the term Electoral College is applied in this country to the presidential electors chosen every four years to vote for President and Vice-President. The term has no official meaning, as it does not occur in the Constitution, nor in any Federal law.

Although the President of the United States is chosen by the people, they do not vote directly for him, but for a group of party electors, equal in each state to the sum of the senators and representatives to which it is entitled, who in turn meet at their state capitals and vote for the presidential candidates as provided by the Twelfth Amendment to the Constitution. A few states require electors to vote for their party candidates, but in most states they are not bound to do so. No case has arisen, however, in which an elector voted for the candidate of another party. Members of Congress cannot be presidential electors.

The total number of votes in the Electoral College is at present 531, and therefore 226 votes are necessary to elect a President and Vice-President.

STATE-BY-STATE ELECTORAL VOTES AS OF 1944

Alabama	11	Nevada	3
Arizona	4	New Hampshire	4
Arkansas	9	New Jersey	16
California	25	New Mexico	4
Colorado	6	New York	47
Connecticut	8	North Carolina	14
Delaware	3	North Dakota	4
Florida	8	Ohio	25
Georgia	12	Oklahoma	10
Idaho	4	Oregon	6
Illinois	28	Pennsylvania	35
Indiana	13	Rhode Island	4
Iowa	10	South Carolina	8
Kansas	8	South Dakota	4
Kentucky	11	Tennessee	12
Louisiana	10	Texas	23
Maine	5	Utah	4
Maryland	8	Vermont	3
Massachusetts	16	Virginia	11
Michigan	19	Washington	8
Minnesota	11	West Virginia	8
Mississippi	9	Wisconsin	12
Missouri	15	Wyoming	3
Montana	4		
Nebraska	6	Total	531

113

Electoral Commission, The—In the presidential election in 1876 four states each sent in different and differing returns, each set having some claims to be considered regular. Aside from the doubtful votes, the Democratic nominees, Tilden and Hendricks, lacked only one vote for a majority. The twenty-second joint rule of the houses, ordering the rejection of any electoral votes to which objection should be made, unless accepted by the concurrent vote of both houses, had been repealed by the Republican Senate in January 1876; its application would have elected Tilden.

To pass upon the conflicting returns, the Electoral Commission was created by an act of Congress approved on January 29, 1877. Four justices of the Supreme Court (those assigned to certain circuits specified in the bill) were made members of the commission; these four were to select a fifth justice; with these five were to sit five members of the Senate and five of the House, each house to elect its own representatives. To this commission was delegated the power in the premises of "the two houses acting separately or together," and its decisions were to be reversed only by the concurrent action of both Houses. The commission was constituted as follows (Democrats in *italics*): Senators—George F. Edmunds, Vermont; Oliver P. Morton, Indiana; Frederick T. Frelinghuysen, New Jersey; *Thomas F. Bayard,* Delaware; *Allen G. Thurman,* Ohio (the latter having become ill, *Francis Kernan,* New York, was substituted). Representatives—*Henry B. Payne,* Ohio; *Eppa Hunton,* Virginia; *Josiah G. Abbott,* Massachusetts; James A. Garfield, Ohio; George F. Hoar, Massachusetts. Supreme Court—*Nathan Clifford,* president of the commission; William Strong, Samuel F. Miller, *Stephen J. Field.* These had been designated by the act; the fifth selected by them was Joseph P. Bradley.

The commission first considered the Florida returns. There were three sets: 1. The votes of the Hayes electors, with the certificate of Governor Stearns attached, according to the decision of the State Returning Board in throwing out certain returns. 2. The votes of the Tilden electors, with the certificate of the attorney general of the state attached, according to the actual vote cast. 3. Same as second, with the certificate of the new Governor Drew, according to a recanvass of the votes as ordered by the state law of January 17, 1877.

The Democratic counsel maintained that the Returning Board had improperly and illegally thrown out votes and that the State Supreme Court had so decided, and also that one of the Hayes electors, Humphreys, when elected, held an office under the United States and was thus disqualified. The Republicans, on the contrary, declared that the commission had no power to examine into returns made in due form; that the first return was in due form; that the second had attached to it the certificate of an officer officially unknown to the United States in the capacity of certifying officer, and that the third set was also irregular, having been prepared after the Electoral College had ceased in law to exist. In Humphreys's case the Republicans maintained that he had, previous to his election, sent a letter of resignation to the officer who had appointed him and that the absence of that officer was the cause of its not having been received in time. The commission in each case sustained the Republican view by a vote of 8 to 7, a strictly party vote, on February 9, 1877.

Louisiana sent three returns; the first and third were identical, being the votes of the Hayes electors as canvassed by the Returning Board, with the certificate of Governor Kellogg; the second contained the votes of the Tilden electors based on the votes as actually cast, with the certificate of John McEnery, who claimed to be governor.

The Democrats maintained that the Returning Board had illegally cast out votes; that two Hayes electors were United States officers; that McEnery was the rightful governor, and various violations of state election laws, all of which they offered to prove. The Republican claims, similar to those in the case of Florida, were again upheld by a vote of 8 to 7 on February 16, 1877.

In Oregon one of the three electors, Watts, was, when elected, a United States officer, being thus disqualified; the Democratic governor, Grover, had given a certificate to the other two Hayes electors and to Cronin, the highest Tilden elector. The popular vote was not called in question. The Hayes electors refused to serve with Cronin and elected a third Hayes elector, as they were by the law entitled to do, while Cronin, by reason of their refusal to serve with him, appointed two other electors; these voted for Hayes. There were thus two returns, one consisting of three Hayes votes, attached to

115

which was a statement of the popular vote of the state, certified by the Secretary of the state, and one consisting of two Hayes votes and one Tilden vote, with the certificate of the governor and the Secretary of the state attached.

The Democrats contended that the governor's certificate must be considered final, to which the Republicans replied that it was the duty of the commission to see that the governor had correctly certified the return of the canvassers of the state, and that behind these returns the commission could not go; the governor's certificate they could and should review. On February 23 the commission sustained this view 8 to 7.

From South Carolina there were two returns: one, the votes of Hayes electors based on the canvass of the Returning Board, having Governor Chamberlain's certificate attached; the other, the vote of the Tilden electors, with the mere claim of a popular election. The claim was made of military influence in the election, but the Republican return was accepted on February 27 by a vote of 8 to 7. The commission adjourned sine die on March 2, 1877. The House voted to reject, the Senate to accept, the findings of the commission, and a concurrent vote being required to reject, its decision was enforced and Hayes became President.

Elephant—The elephant as a symbol of the Republican party was originated by the political cartoonist Thomas Nast (1840–1902), who was also responsible for introducing and establishing the donkey as the Democratic party symbol. Nast tagged the two parties with these zoological emblems in 1874. The Tammany tiger was another product of his pen.

Emancipation—Slavery was abolished by the constitution of Vermont in 1777, but Vermont was not admitted as a state until 1791. In 1780 Massachusetts did away with slavery, and that same year Pennsylvania adopted an act of gradual emancipation, as did New Hampshire in 1783, Rhode Island and Connecticut in 1784, and New Jersey in 1804. New York followed suit in 1799, afterward passing a law of complete emancipation to take effect July 4, 1827. The rest of the thirteen states allowed slavery, and in the case of new states the question was settled at the time of admission.

116

Emancipation Proclamation—Abraham Lincoln abhorred slavery, but he was not an Abolitionist. In a letter written to Horace Greeley, August 22, 1862, he said, "My paramount object in this struggle is to save the Union, and is not either to save or destroy slavery. If I could save the Union without freeing any slave, I would do it; and if I could do it by freeing all the slaves, I would do it; and if I could save it by freeing some and leaving others alone, I would also do that."

One month later, on September 22, 1862, he issued a proclamation giving notice to the inhabitants of the Southern states that unless they returned to their allegiance by January 1, 1863, he would declare their slaves forever free. This he did the following New Year's Day by issuing the Emancipation Proclamation. He issued it, he said, as Commander in Chief of the Army and Navy as an act of "military necessity." It enjoined on the free slaves to abstain from violence unless in necessary self-defense, and recommended to them that in all cases where allowed they labor faithfully for reasonable wages. It also offered to receive them into the armed services. Approximately 4,300,000 slaves were freed in the Southern states by the Emancipation Proclamation, which was acclaimed throughout the North. The ratification of the Thirteenth Amendment in 1865 abolished slavery throughout the United States.

Embargo Act—In May 1806, Great Britain, which was at that time engaged in a bitter war with France, proclaimed a blockade of the territory bordering on the English Channel and the German Ocean from Brest to the Elbe. Napoleon retaliated in November by his Berlin Decree, declaring a blockade of English ports. A year later England issued her famous Orders in Council, prohibiting commerce with almost every country of Europe. The next month, December 1807, Napoleon replied with the Milan Decree, forbidding commerce with England or her colonies. These and similar acts, although in violation of the laws of nations, were enforced by France and England so far as they were able, and many American vessels were seized. Moreover, Great Britain revived an old rule prohibiting neutral vessels from trading with the dependencies of any nation with which she was at war. She also claimed and exercised the right of searching American vessels for those whom she claimed to be her subjects and impressing them into her service.

In maintaining this position, the British man-of-war *Leopard,* in June 1807, fired on the American frigate *Chesapeake.* It was in consequence of these events, although news of the Milan Decree had not yet been received, that Congress, on December 22, 1807, passed an Embargo Act prohibiting exportations from the United States, hoping to force France and England to recede from their position by showing the importance of our commercial relations. It had some effect on these nations, but a far more ruinous result on our own commerce, the exports for 1808 shrinking to one fifth of the sum they had reached in the preceding year.

It was a measure of the Democratic party and was approved by the agricultural portions of the United States. The New England states, deeply interested in foreign commerce, and the Federalists loudly condemned it. Its opponents, spelling the name backward, called it the "O Grab Me" Act, and threats of secession were heard from New England. As a result, Congress fixed March 4, 1809, for the termination of the embargo. The first embargo in our history was laid in 1794 for a period of sixty days, and other minor acts of a similar nature were passed during the War of 1812. The plan of limiting commercial intercourse by embargo, non-importation, and non-intercourse acts was called the "restrictive system."

Eminent Domain—The right of eminent domain is the right to take private property for public uses. In the United States its justification is the common welfare, and the Fifth Amendment to the Constitution provides that just compensation must be made. The right is usually exercised in order to secure land for the construction of railroads and highways.

Era of Good Feeling—The period between 1817 and 1825, when James Monroe was President. The Federalist party having become extinct, there was practically no opposition to his administration.

Essex Junto—President John Adams caused a rift in the Federal party when he unceremoniously dropped two members from his

Cabinet whom he thought were unpopular in the Southern states, whence he expected to draw his greatest strength in winning re-nomination and re-election. Several of the party leaders who were opposed to him were residents of Essex County, Massachusetts, and Adams called these and other Federalists who were against him the "Essex Junto." He charged them with being slaves to British influence, some because of their monarchical tendencies, others because of British gold. He even denounced Hamilton as a "British sympathizer." A pamphlet by Hamilton weakened Adams's political position.

The charge of British influence delighted the Republicans, who sang:

> "The *Federalists* are down at last,
> The *Monarchists* completely cast!
> The *Aristocrats* are stripped of power—
> Storms o'er the *British faction* lower.
> Soon we *Republicans* shall see
> Columbia's sons from bondage free.
> Lord how the Federalists will stare—
> A *Jefferson* in *Adams's* chair!"

There was a great falling off in the Federalist vote as the result of Adams's course, and Jefferson was elected President.

Ex Post Facto Laws—Strictly speaking, an *ex post facto* law is one that takes effect retroactively; that is, on transactions which took place before its passage. The provision in the Constitution of the United States (Article I, Section 9, Clause 3) that "no . . . *ex post facto* law shall be passed" has been interpreted to refer only to crimes, and in that sense the words are commonly used.

The following have been decided to come within the scope of the phrase: every law that makes an action done before its passage, and innocent when done, criminal, and punishes such action; every law that aggravates a crime or makes it greater than when committed; every law that changes the nature of the punishment or makes it greater than at the time the act was committed; every law that alters the rules of evidence so as to make it easier to convict the

119

offender; every law that, while not avowedly relating to crimes, in effect imposes a penalty or the deprivation of a right; every law that deprives persons accused of crime of some lawful protection to which they have become entitled, as a former acquittal. Such laws are unconstitutional so far as they apply to acts committed before their passage.

Executive, The—At the head of the executive department of the Federal Government is the President, who holds office for a term of four years but may be re-elected any number of times. (See *Third Term.*) He must be a natural-born citizen of the United States, at least thirty-five years old, and a resident of the United States not less than fourteen years.

It is the duty of the President to administer the national government and to see that the laws are faithfully executed. He does this through instructions to the heads of the various government departments and agencies. He has the power, subject to the approval of the Senate, to appoint ambassadors, Cabinet members, Federal judges, and other high officers of the government, and also minor officials if Congress vests the power in him. When Congress is in recess he may make appointments which expire at the end of its next session. He can negotiate treaties with foreign powers (subject to confirmation by two thirds of the Senate), receive and send envoys, and make executive agreements. He acts as Commander in Chief of the Army and Navy and the militia of the several states when it is called into the service of the United States. He commissions all officers, and in time of war exercises extraordinary powers. He has the power to grant pardons, reprieves (stays of punishment), commutations (diminishments of punishment), and amnesties (pardons to a group of persons), except in the cases of impeachment. From time to time he gives Congress information on the state of the Union and recommends measures for their consideration. The President has limited control over Congress, the veto power enabling him to kill bills which he disapproves, unless two thirds of each house concur in overriding his veto. (See *Veto; Presidents of the United States.*)

For the various executive departments of the government, see

Commerce, Department of; Agriculture, Department of; Interior, Department of; Justice, Department of; Labor, Department of; Navy, Department of the; Post Office Department; State Department of; Treasury Department; War Department.

Executive Session—When the Senate meets to transact business outside the usual legislative routine, such as the confirmation of appointments or the ratification of treaties, it is said to be in executive session.

Expatriation means the act or state of banishment from one's native country, and it also means the voluntary renunciation of the rights and liabilities of citizenship in one country to become the citizen or subject of another. It is in this latter sense that it is used here.

In the early part of the Nineteenth century the United States was almost the only nation that claimed for individuals the right of expatriation without the consent of the government of which they were citizens or subjects. The European nations, as a rule, maintained that the permission of the sovereign was necessary; and the enforcement by England of this claim was one of the causes of the War of 1812. Fortunately England did not carry into practice the theoretical extreme of her doctrine, which would have permitted her to hang as traitors all prisoners captured in that war who had once been British subjects.

It must be said, however, that, notwithstanding the position of the United States in regard to citizens or subjects of foreign powers, the right of voluntary renunciation of allegiance to the United States by one of our citizens was unsettled, so far as legislation was concerned, until the act of Congress of July 27, 1868, asserted that expatriation "is a natural and inherent right of all people," but the action of the Department of State had previously seemed practically to admit the right. So far as foreign states are concerned, however, the United States has steadily maintained its original position. The first formal recognition of its claims was secured in an expatriation treaty with the North German Confederation, signed February 22, 1868. England first recognized the right of voluntary expatriation by

121

act of Parliament in 1870 and immediately concluded an expatriation treaty with the United States. All the leading nations now recognize the right.

Exterritoriality—By a fiction of international law a sovereign, though temporarily in a foreign country, is considered as being on his own territory. By an extension of this principle, diplomatic agents who represent the sovereign, and also those who represent the state (as ambassadors of republics), are said to enjoy the privilege of exterritoriality, the privilege of living under their own laws while accredited to a foreign nation. They preserve their domiciles as if at home. Their persons, families, attendants, and property are inviolable except in extreme cases. In case of a crime committed by a diplomatic representative, unless imperative necessity demands his seizure, the government to which he is accredited merely asks his recall.

Extra Sessions—Under Article II, Section 3, of the Constitution the President may, on "extraordinary occasions," convene both houses of Congress, or either one of them, and in case of disagreement between them with respect to the time of adjournment, he may adjourn them until such time as he thinks proper.

Farewell Addresses—George Washington, on September 17, 1796, issued a farewell address to the people of the United States in anticipation of his retirement from public life in March of the next year. The document is chiefly the work of Washington and Hamilton, though portions of it were taken from a draft prepared by Madison at Washington's request when the latter had expected to retire to private life after his first term. A farewell address was also issued by Andrew Jackson on March 3, 1837, the last day of his official life, rehearsing the principles on which he had acted. The following is Washington's address:

FRIENDS AND FELLOW-CITIZENS:

The period for a new election of a citizen to administer the executive government of the United States being not far distant, and the time actually arrived when your thoughts must be employed in

122

designating the person who is to be clothed with that important trust, it appears to me proper, especially as it may conduce to a more distinct expression of the public voice, that I should now apprize you of the resolution I have formed, to decline being considered among the number of those out of whom a choice is to be made.

I beg you at the same time to do me the justice to be assured, that this resolution has not been taken without a strict regard to all the considerations appertaining to the relation which binds a dutiful citizen to his country; and that in withdrawing the tender of service, which silence in my situation might imply, I am influenced by no diminution of zeal for your future interest; no deficiency of grateful respect for your past kindness; but am supported by a full conviction that the step is compatible with both.

The acceptance of, and continuance hitherto in, the office to which your suffrages have twice called me, have been a uniform sacrifice of inclination to the opinion of duty, and to a deference for what appeared to be your desire. I constantly hoped that it would have been much earlier in my power, consistently with motives which I was not at liberty to disregard, to return to that retirement from which I had been reluctantly drawn. The strength of my inclination to do this, previous to the last election, had even led to the preparation of an address to declare it to you; but mature reflection on the then perplexed and critical posture of our affairs with foreign nations, and the unanimous advice of persons entitled to my confidence, impelled me to abandon the idea.

I rejoice that the state of your concerns, external as well as internal, no longer renders the pursuit of inclination incompatible with the sentiment of duty or propriety; and am persuaded, whatever partiality may be retained for my services, that, in the present circumstances of our country, you will not disapprove my determination to retire.

The impressions with which I first undertook the arduous trust were explained on the proper occasion. In the discharge of this trust, I will only say, that I have with good intentions contributed toward the organization and administration of the government the best exertions of which a very fallible judgment was capable. Not unconscious, in the outset, of the inferiority of any qualifications, experience in my own eyes, perhaps still more in the eyes of others, has strengthened the motives to diffidence of myself; and every day the

123

increasing weight of years admonishes me more and more, that the shade of retirement is as necessary to me as it will be welcome. Satisfied that if any circumstances have given peculiar value to my services, they were temporary, I have the consolation to believe, that while choice and prudence invite me to quit the political scene, patriotism does not forbid it.

In looking forward to the moment which is intended to terminate the career of my public life, my feelings do not permit me to suspend the deep acknowledgment of that debt of gratitude which I owe to my beloved country, for the many honors it has conferred upon me; still more for the steadfast confidence with which it has supported me; and for the opportunities I have thence enjoyed of manifesting my inviolable attachment, by services faithful and persevering, though in usefulness unequal to my zeal. If benefits have resulted to our country from these services, let it always be remembered to your praise, and as an instructive example in our annals, that under circumstances in which the passions, agitated in every direction, were liable to mislead, amidst appearances sometimes dubious—vicissitudes of fortune often discouraging—in situations in which not unfrequently want of success has countenanced the spirit of criticism—the constancy of your support was the essential prop of the efforts, and a guaranty of the plans by which they were effected. Profoundly penetrated with this idea, I shall carry it with me to my grave, as a strong incitement to unceasing wishes that Heaven may continue to you the choicest tokens of its beneficence— that your union and brotherly affection may be perpetual—that the free constitution which is the work of your hands may be sacredly maintained—that its administration in every department may be stamped with wisdom and virtue—that, in fine, the happiness of the people of these States, under the auspices of liberty, may be made complete, by so careful a preservation, and so prudent a use of this blessing, as will acquire to them the glory of recommending it to the applause, the affection, and adoption of every nation which is yet a stranger to it.

Here, perhaps, I ought to stop. But a solicitude for your welfare, which cannot end but with my life, and the apprehension of danger, natural to that solicitude, urge me, on an occasion like the present, to offer to your solemn contemplation, and to recommend to your frequent review, some sentiments, which are the result of much reflection, of no inconsiderable observation, and which appear to me all-important to the permanency of your felicity as a people. These will be offered to you with the more freedom, as you can only see in them the disinterested warnings of a parting friend, who can possibly have no personal motive to bias his counsel. Nor can I forget, as an encouragement to it, your indulgent reception of my sentiments on a former and not dissimilar occasion.

Interwoven as is the love of liberty with every ligament of your hearts, no recommendation of mine is necessary to fortify or confirm the attachment.

The unity of government which constitutes you one people, is also now dear to you. It is justly so; for it is a main pillar in the edifice of your real independence, the support of your tranquility at home, your peace abroad; of your safety; of your prosperity; of that very liberty which you so highly prize. But as it is easy to foresee that from different causes and from different quarters, much pains will be taken, many artifices employed, to weaken in your minds the conviction of this truth; as this is the point in your political fortress against which the batteries of internal and external enemies will be most constantly and actively (though often covertly and insidiously) directed, it is of infinite moment that you should properly estimate the immense value of your national Union, to your collective and individual happiness; that you should cherish a cordial, habitual and immovable attachment to it; accustoming yourselves to think and speak of it as of the palladium of your political safety and prosperity; watching for its preservation with jealous anxiety; discountenancing whatever might suggest even a suspicion that it can in any event be abandoned; and indignantly frowning upon the first dawning of every attempt to alienate any portion of our country from the rest, or to enfeeble the sacred ties which now link together the various parts.

For this you have every inducement of sympathy and interest. Citizens by birth or choice, of a common country, that country has a right to concentrate your affections. The name of AMERICAN, which belongs to you, in your national capacity, must always exalt the just pride of patriotism, more than any appellation derived from local discriminations. With slight shades of difference, you have the same religion, manners, habits and political principles. You have in a common cause fought and triumphed together; the Independence and Liberty you possess are the work of joint councils and joint efforts, of common dangers, sufferings and successes.

But these considerations, however powerfully they address themselves to your sensibility, are greatly outweighed by those which apply more immediately to your interest. Here every portion of our country finds the most commanding motives for carefully guarding and preserving the union of the whole.

The *North,* in an unrestrained intercourse with the *South,* protected by the equal laws of a common government, finds in the productions of the latter great additional resources of maritime and commercial enterprise and precious materials of manufacturing industry. The *South,* in the same intercourse, benefiting by the agency of the *North,* sees its agriculture grow and its commerce expand. Turning partly into its own channels the seamen of the *North,* it finds its particular navigation invigorated; and while it contributes, in different ways, to nourish and increase the general mass of the national navigation, it looks forward to the protection of a maritime strength, to which itself is unequally adapted. The *East,* in a like intercourse with the *West,* already finds, and in the progressive improvement of interior communications, by land and water, will more and more find a valuable vent for the commodities which it brings from abroad or manufactures at home. The *West* derives from the *East* supplies requisite to its growth and comfort—and what is perhaps of still greater consequence, it must of necessity owe the *secure* enjoyment of indispensable *outlets* for its own productions to the weight, influence and the future maritime strength of the Atlantic side of the Union, directed by an indissoluble community of interest as one nation. Any other tenure by which the *West* can hold this essential advantage, whether derived from its own separate strength, or from an apostate and unnatural connection with any foreign power, must be intrinsically precarious.

While then every part of our country thus feels the immediate and particular interest in union, all the parts combined cannot fail to find in the united mass of means and efforts, greater strength, greater resource, proportionably greater security from external danger, a less frequent interruption of their peace by foreign nations; and what is of inestimable value, they must derive from union an exemption from those broils and wars between themselves, which so frequently afflict neighboring countries, not tied together by the same government; which their own rivalship alone would be sufficient to produce, but which opposite foreign alliances, attachments and intrigues would stimulate and embitter. Hence likewise they will avoid the necessity of those overgrown military establishments, which under any form of government are inauspicious to liberty, and which are to be regarded as particularly hostile to Republican Liberty. In this sense it is, that your Union ought to be considered as the main prop of your liberty, and that the love of the one ought to endear to you the preservation of the other.

These considerations speak a persuasive language to every reflecting and virtuous mind, and exhibit the continuance of the Union as a primary object of patriotic desire. Is there a doubt whether a common government can embrace so large a sphere? Let experience solve it. To listen to mere speculation in such a case were criminal. We are authorized to hope that a proper organization of the whole, with the auxiliary agency of governments for the respective subdivisions, will afford a happy issue to the experiment. It is well worth a fair and full experiment. With such powerful and obvious motives to union, affecting all parts of our country, while experience shall not have demonstrated its impractibility, there will always be reason to distrust the patriotism of those who in any quarter may endeavor to weaken its bands.

In contemplating the causes which may disturb our union, it occurs as matter of serious concern, that any ground should have been furnished for characterizing parties by *geographical* discriminations—*Northern* and *Southern*—*Atlantic* and *Western;* whence designing men may endeavor to excite a belief that there is a real difference of local interests and views. One of the expedients of party to acquire influence, within particular districts, is to misrepresent the opinions and aims of other districts. You cannot shield yourselves too much against the jealousies and heart-burnings which spring from these misrepresentations; they tend to render alien to each other those who ought to be bound together by fraternal affection. The inhabitants of our western country have lately had a useful lesson on this head; they have seen, in the negotiation by the Executive, and in the unanimous ratification by the Senate, of the treaty with Spain, and the universal satisfaction at the event throughout the United States, a decisive proof how unfounded were the suspicions propagated among them of a policy in the general government, and in the Atlantic States, unfriendly to their interests in regard to the Mississippi: they have been witnesses to the formation of two treaties, that with Great Britain and that with Spain, which secure to them everything they could desire, in respect to our foreign relations, toward confirming their prosperity. Will it not be their wisdom to rely for the preservation of these advantages on the UNION by which they were procured? Will they not henceforth be deaf to those advisers, if such they are, who would sever them from their brethren, and connect them with aliens?

To the efficacy and permanency of your Union, a Government for the whole is indispensable. No alliances, however strict, between the parts can be an adequate substitute; they must inevitably experience the infractions and interruptions which all alliances in all times have experienced. Sensible of this momentous truth, you have improved upon your first essay, by the adoption of a Constitution of Government better calculated than your former for an intimate Union, and for the efficacious management of your common concerns. This Government, the offspring of your own choice, uninfluenced and unawed, adopted upon full investigation and mature deliberation, completely free in its principles, in the distribution of its powers, uniting security with energy, and containing within itself a provision for its own amendment, has a just claim to your confidence and your support. Respect for its authority, compliance with its laws, acquiescence in its measures, are duties enjoined by the fundamental maxims of true liberty. The basis of our political systems is the right of the people to make, and to alter their Constitutions of Government. But the Constitution which at any time exists, until changed by an explicit and authentic act of the whole people, is sacredly obligatory upon all. The very idea of the power and the right of the people to establish Government, presupposes the duty of every individual to obey the established Government.

All obstructions to the execution of the laws, all combinations and associations, under whatever plausible character, with the real design to direct, control, counteract or awe the regular deliberation and action of the constituted authorities, are destructive of this fundamental principle, and of fatal tendency. They serve to organize faction, to give it an artificial and extraordinary force—to put in the place of the delegated will of the nation, the will of a party, often a small but artful and enterprising minority of the community; and, according to the alternate triumphs of different parties, to make the public administration the mirror of the ill-concerted and incongruous projects of faction, rather than the organ of consistent and wholesome plans digested by common councils and modified by mutual interests.

However combinations or associations of the above description may now and then answer popular ends, they are likely, in the course of time and things, to become potent engines, by which cunning, ambitious, and unprincipled men will be enabled to subvert the power of the people, and to usurp for themselves the reins of government; destroying afterward the very engines which have lifted them to unjust dominion.

Toward the preservation of your government, and the permanency of your present happy state, it is requisite, not only that you steadily discountenance irregular oppositions to its acknowledged authority, but also that you resist with care the spirit of innovation upon its principles, however specious the pretexts. One method of assault may be to effect in the form of the Constitution alterations which will impair the energy of the system, and thus to undermine what cannot be directly overthrown. In all the changes to which you may be invited, remember that time and habit are at least as necessary to fix the true character of governments, as of other human institutions; that experience is the surest standard by which to test the real tendency of the existing constitution of a country—that facility in changes upon the credit of mere hypothesis and opinion, exposes to perpetual change from the endless variety of hypothesis and opinion; and remember, especially, that for the efficient management of your common interests, in a country so extensive as ours, a government of as much vigor as is consistent with the perfect security of liberty, is indispensable. Liberty itself will find in such a government, with powers properly distributed and adjusted, its surest guardian. It is, indeed, little else than a name, where the government is too feeble to withstand the enterprises of faction, to confine each member of the society within the limits prescribed by the laws, and to maintain all in the secure and tranquil enjoyment of the rights of person and property.

I have already intimated to you the danger of parties in the state, with particular reference to the founding of them on geographical discriminations. Let me now take a more comprehensive view, and warn you in the most solemn manner against the baneful effects of the spirit of party, generally.

This spirit, unfortunately, is inseparable from our nature, having its root in the strongest passions of the human mind. It exists under different shapes in all governments, more or less stifled, controlled, or repressed; but in those of the popular form it is seen in greatest rankness, and it is truly their worst enemy.

129

The alternate domination of one faction over another, sharpened by the spirit of revenge, natural to party dissension, which in different ages and countries has perpetrated the most horrid enormities, is itself a frightful despotism. But this leads at length to a more formal and permanent despotism. The disorders and miseries which result, gradually incline the minds of men to seek security and repose in the absolute power of an individual, and sooner or later the chief of some prevailing faction, more able or more fortunate than his competitors, turns this disposition to the purposes of his own elevation on the ruins of public liberty.

Without looking forward to an extremity of this kind (which nevertheless ought not to be entirely out of sight), the common and continual mischiefs of the spirit of party are sufficient to make it the interest and duty of a wise people to discourage and restrain it.

It serves always to distract the public councils, and enfeeble the public administration. It agitates the community with ill-founded jealousies and false alarms; kindles the animosity of one part against another, foments occasionally riot and insurrection. It opens the door to foreign influence and corruption, which find a facilitated access to the government itself through the channels of party passions. Thus the policy and the will of one country are subjected to the policy and will of another. There is an opinion that parties in free countries are useful checks upon the administration of government, and serve to keep alive the spirit of liberty. This within certain limits is probably true; and in governments of a monarchial cast, patriotism may look with indulgence, if not with favor, upon the spirit of party. But in those of the popular character, in governments purely elective, it is a spirit not to be encouraged. From their natural tendency it is certain there will always be enough of that spirit for every salutary purpose. And there being constant danger of excess, the effort ought to be, by force of public opinion, to mitigate and assuage it. A fire not to be quenched, it demands uniform vigilance to prevent its bursting into a flame, lest, instead of warming, it should consume.

It is important, likewise, that the habits of thinking, in a free country, should inspire caution in those intrusted with its administration, to confine themselves within their respective constitutional spheres, avoiding in the exercise of the powers of one department to encroach upon another. The spirit of encroachment tends to consolidate the powers of all departments in one, and thus to create, whatever the form of government, a real despotism. A just estimate of that love of power, and proneness to abuse it, which predominates in the human heart, is sufficient to satisfy us of the truth of this position. The necessity of reciprocal checks in the exercise of political power, by dividing and distributing it into different depositories, and constituting each the guardian of the public weal against invasions by the others, has been evinced by experiments ancient and modern; some of them in our country and under our own eyes. To preserve them must be as necessary as to institute them. If, in the opinion of the people, the distribution or modification of the constitutional powers be in any particular wrong, let it be corrected by an amendment in the way which the Constitution designates. But let there be no change by usurpation; for though this, in one instance, may be the instrument of good, it is the customary weapon by which free governments are destroyed. The precedent must always greatly overbalance in permanent evil any partial or transient benefit which the use can at any time yield.

Of all the dispositions and habits which lead to political prosperity, RELIGION and MORALITY are indispensable supports. In vain would that man claim the tributes of PATRIOTISM, who should labor to subvert these great pillars of human happiness, these firmest props of the duties of men and citizens. The mere politician, equally with the pious man, ought to respect and to cherish them. A volume could not trace all their connections with private and public felicity. Let it simply be asked, where is the security for property, for reputation, for life, if the sense of religious obligation desert the oaths, which are the instruments of investigation in courts of justice? And let us with caution indulge the supposition that morality can be maintained without religion. Whatever may be conceded to the influence or refined education on minds of peculiar structure, reason and experience both forbid us to expect that national morality can prevail in exclusion of religious principle.

It is substantially true that virtue or morality is a necessary spring of popular government. The rule indeed extends with more or less force to every species of free government. Who, that is a sincere friend to it, can look with indifference upon attempts to shake the foundation of the fabric?

Promote, then, as an object of primary importance, institutions for the general diffusion of knowledge. In proportion as the structure of a government gives force to public opinion, it is essential that public opinion should be enlightened.

As a very important source of strength and security, cherish public credit. One method of preserving it, is to use it as sparingly as possible—avoiding occasions of expense by cultivating peace; but remember also that timely disbursements to prepare for danger frequently prevent much greater disbursements to repel it; avoiding likewise the accumulation of debt, not only by shunning occasions of expense, but by vigorous exertions in time of peace to discharge the debts which unavoidable wars may have occasioned, not ungenerously throwing upon posterity the burden which we ourselves ought to bear. The execution of these maxims belongs to your Representatives, but it is necessary that public opinion should cooperate. To facilitate to them the performance of their duty, it is essential that you should practically bear in mind, that toward the payment of debts there must be revenue; that to have revenue there must be taxes; that no taxes can be devised which are not more or less inconvenient and unpleasant; that the intrinsic embarrassment inseparable from the selection of the proper objects (which is always a choice of difficulties) ought to be a decisive motive for a candid construction of the conduct of the government in making it, and for a spirit of acquiescence in the measures for obtaining revenue which the public exigencies may at any time dictate.

Observe good faith and justice toward all nations, cultivate peace and harmony with all: religion and morality enjoin this conduct; and can it be, that good policy does not equally enjoin it? It will be worthy of a free, enlightened, and, at no distant period, a great nation, to give to mankind the magnanimous and too novel example of a people always guided by an exalted justice and benevolence. Who can doubt but in the course of time and things, the fruits of such a plan would richly repay any temporary advantage which might be lost by a steady adherence to it? Can it be that Providence has not connected the permanent felicity of a nation with its virtue? The experiment, at least, is recommended by every sentiment which ennobles human nature. Alas! is it rendered impossible by its vices?

In the execution of such a plan, nothing is more essential than that permanent, inveterate antipathies against particular nations, and passionate attachments for others, should be excluded; and that in place of them just and amicable feelings toward all should be cultivated. The nation which indulges toward another an habitual hatred or an habitual fondness, is in some degree a slave. It is a slave to its animosity or to its affection, either of which is sufficient to lead it astray from its duty and its interest. Antipathy in one nation against another disposes each more readily to offer insult and injury, to lay hold of slight causes of umbrage, and to be haughty and intractable, when accidental or trifling occasions of dispute occur. Hence frequent collisions, obstinate, envenomed and bloody contests. The nation, prompted by ill-will and resentment, sometimes impels to war the government, contrary to the best calculations of policy. The government sometimes participates in the national propensity, and adopts through passion what reason would reject; at other times, it makes the animosity of the nation subservient to projects of hostility instigated by pride, ambition and other sinister and pernicious motives. The peace often, sometimes perhaps the liberty, of nations has been the victim.

So, likewise, a passionate attachment of one nation for another produces a variety of evils. Sympathy for the favorite nation, facilitating the illusion of an imaginary common interest in cases where no real common interest exists, and infusing into one the enmities of the other, betrays the former into a participation in the quarrels and wars of the latter, without adequate inducement or justification. It leads also to concessions to the favorite nation of privileges denied to others, which is apt doubly to injure the nation making the concessions, by unnecessarily parting with what ought to have been retained; and by exciting jealousy, ill-will and a disposition to retaliate, in the parties from whom equal privileges are withheld. And it gives to ambitious, corrupted or deluded citizens (who devote themselves to the favorite nation) facility to betray or sacrifice the interests of their own country, without odium, sometimes even with popularity; gilding with the appearance of a virtuous sense of obligation a commendable deference for public opinion, or a laudable zeal for public good, the base or foolish compliances of ambition, corruption, or infatuation.

As avenues to foreign influence in innumerable ways, such attachments are particularly alarming to the truly enlightened and independent patriot. How many opportunities do they afford to tamper with domestic factions; to practice the arts of sedition, to mislead public opinion, to influence or awe the public councils! Such an attachment of a small or weak, toward a great and powerful nation, dooms the former to be the satellite of the latter. Against the insidious wiles of foreign influence (I conjure you to believe me, fellow-citizens) the jealousy of a free people ought to be *constantly*

133

awake; since history and experience prove that foreign influence is one of the most baneful foes of Republican Government. But that jealousy to be useful must be impartial; else it becomes the instrument of the very influence to be avoided, instead of a defense against it. Excessive partiality for one foreign nation, and excessive dislike of another, cause those whom they actuate to see danger only on one side, and serve to veil and even second the arts of influence on the other. Real patriots, who may resist the intrigues of the favorite, are liable to become suspected and odious; while its tools and dupes usurp the applause and confidence of the people, to surrender their interest.

The great rule of conduct for us, in regard to foreign nations, is, in extending our commercial relations, to have with them as little political connection as possible. So far as we have already formed engagements, let them be fulfilled with perfect good faith. Here let us stop.

Europe has a set of primary interests, which to us have none, or a very remote relation. Hence she must be engaged in frequent controversies, the causes of which are essentially foreign to our concerns. Hence, therefore, it must be unwise in us to implicate ourselves, by artificial ties, in the ordinary vicissitudes of her politics, or the ordinary combinations and collisions of her friendships or enmities.

Our detached and distant situation invites and enables us to pursue a different course. If we remain one people, under an efficient government, the period is not far off when we may defy material injury from external annoyance; when we may take such an attitude as will cause the neutrality we may at any time resolve upon to be scrupulously respected; when belligerent nations, under the impossibility of making acquisitions upon us, will not lightly hazard the giving us provocation; when we may choose peace or war, as our interest, guided by justice, shall counsel.

Why forego the advantages of so peculiar a situation? Why quit our own to stand upon foreign ground? Why, by interweaving our destiny with that of any part of Europe, entangle our peace and prosperity in the toils of European ambition, rivalship, interest, humor or caprice?

It is our true policy to steer clear of permanent alliances with any portion of the foreign world; so far, I mean, as we are now at liberty to do it; for let me not be understood as capable of patronizing infidelity to existing engagements. I hold the maxim no less applicable to public than to private affairs, that honesty is always the best policy. I repeat it, therefore, let those engagements be observed in their genuine sense. But, in my opinion, it is unnecessary, and would be unwise to extend them.

Taking care always to keep ourselves, by suitable establishments, on a respectable defensive posture, we may safely trust to temporary alliances for extraordinary emergencies.

Harmony, and a liberal intercourse with all nations, are recommended by policy, humanity and interest.

But even our commercial policy should hold an equal and impartial hand; neither seeking nor granting exclusive favors or preferences; consulting the natural course of things; diffusing and diversifying by gentle means the streams of commerce, but forcing nothing; establishing, with powers so disposed, in order to give trade a stable course, to define the rights of our merchants, and to enable the government to support them, conventional rules of intercourse, the best that present circumstances and mutual opinion will permit, but temporary, and liable to be from time to time abandoned or varied, as experience and circumstances shall dictate; constantly keeping in view, that it is folly in one nation to look for disinterested favors from another; that it must pay with a portion of its independence for whatever it may accept under that character; that by such acceptance it may place itself in the condition of having given equivalents for nominal favors, and yet of being reproached with ingratitude for not giving more. There can be no greater error than to expect, or calculate upon, real favors from nation to nation. It is an illusion, which experience must cure, which a just pride ought to discard.

In offering to you, my countrymen, these counsels of an old and affectionate friend, I dare not hope they will make the strong and lasting expression I could wish—that they will control the usual current of the passions, or prevent our nation from running the course which has hitherto marked the destiny of nations. But if I may even flatter myself that they may be productive of some partial benefit, some occasional good; but they may now and then recur to moderate the fury of party spirit, to warn against the mischiefs of foreign intrigue, to guard against the impostures of pretended patriotism; this hope will be a full recompense for the solicitude for your welfare, by which they have been dictated.

How far in the discharge of my official duties I have been guided by the principles which have been delineated, the public records and other evidences of my conduct must witness to you and to the world. To myself, the assurance of my own conscience is, that I have at last believed myself to be guided by them.

In relation to the still subsisting war in Europe, my proclamation of the 22d of April, 1793, is the index to my plan. Sanctioned by your approving voice, and by that of your Representatives in both Houses of Congress, the spirit of that measure has continually governed me, uninfluenced by any attempts to deter or divert me from it.

After deliberate examination, with the aid of the best lights I could obtain, I was well satisfied that our country, under all the circumstances of the case, had a right to take, and was bound in duty and interest to take, a neutral position. Having taken it, I determined, as far as should depend upon me, to maintain it with moderation, perseverance and firmness.

The considerations which respect the right to hold this conduct, it is not necessary on this occasion to detail. I will only observe, that, according to my understanding of the matter, that right, so far from being denied by any of the Belligerent-Powers, has been virtually admitted by all.

The duty of holding a neutral conduct may be inferred, without any thing more, from the obligation which justice and humanity impose on every nation, in cases in which it is free to act, to maintain inviolate the relations of peace and amity toward other nations.

The inducements of interest for observing that conduct will best be referred to your own reflections and experience. With me, a predominant motive has been to endeavor to gain time to our country to settle and mature its yet recent institutions, and to progress, without interruption, to that degree of strength and consistency which is necessary to give it, humanely speaking, the command of its own fortunes.

Though, in reviewing the incidents of my administration, I am unconscious of intentional error, I am nevertheless too sensible of my own defects, not to think it probable that I may have committed many errors. Whatever they may be, I fervently beseech the Almighty to avert or mitigate the evils to which they may tend. I shall also carry with me the hope that my country will never cease to view them with indulgence; and that after forty-five years of my life dedicated to its service, with an upright zeal, the faults of incompetent abilities will be consigned to oblivion, as myself must soon be to the mansions of rest.

Relying on its kindness in this as in other things, and actuated by that fervent love toward it, which is so natural to a man who views it in the native soil of himself and his progenitors for several generations; I anticipate with pleasing expectation, that retreat in which I promise myself to realize, without alloy, the sweet enjoyment of partaking, in the midst of my fellow-citizens, the benign influence of good laws under a free government—the ever favorite object of my heart, and the happy reward, as I trust, of our mutual cares, labors and dangers.

G. Washington

United States,
17th September, 1796.

Father of His Country—A popular name given to George Washington on account of the part he played in the birth of the nation. Those who were opposed to him while he was President called him "Stepfather of His Country."

Father of the Constitution—Because he was the author of the resolution issued by the Virginia Legislature which led to the Constitutional Convention of 1787, James Madison received the name Father of the Constitution.

Favorite Son—A person who is popular with the voters in any given area, large or small, but usually of a state. At national presidential nominating conventions favorite sons have the support of the delegates from their states.

Federal Party—This name was given to those who were in favor of the adoption of the United States Constitution. The looseness of the Union under the Articles of Confederation had unsettled business, and all citizens who were injured by this state of affairs were in favor of a stronger government. Moreover, the feeling that thus only could we become a nation among nations had much weight in inclining the more thoughtful to favor the Constitution. Washington, Jefferson, Madison, and Randolph were all Federalists in the earlier and wider meaning of the term.

The adoption of the Constitution left the anti-Federalists without a cause, and the Federal party went into power with Washington at

137

its head practically unopposed. During the first session of Congress the departments of the government were organized. At the second session Alexander Hamilton introduced his financial measures. The foreign debt was to be paid in full, the continental debt was to be paid at par, and the debts of the several states were to be assumed. To the second of these propositions Madison dissented, but it was nevertheless carried. The third aroused enormous opposition, and it was hotly debated both in and out of Congress. After one defeat it was reintroduced and carried by means of a bargain. At the third session a bill taxing distilled spirits was passed, and the Bank of the United States was incorporated. These measures Jefferson and Randolph opposed.

The party had thus gradually strengthened the broad construction view of the Constitution and had attained real principles and party life. It stood committed to the protection of manufactures by import duties, to building up a navy and an army, and to strengthening the Federal Government. The opposition raised by these centralizing tendencies gradually took shape and, headed by Jefferson, Madison, and Randolph, formed the Republican party, from which sprang the Democratic-Republican party. The work of the Federalists was carried on in the Second Congress. In the Third, the Senate was theirs by but a small majority, while in the House there was a small majority against them.

The assumption of the state debts had rendered the prompt establishment of a navy impossible, and its want now forbade the energetic assertion of our commercial rights. As a consequence, Jay's Treaty was negotiated. In 1798 the party favored war with France, and the popularity of this measure tended to give it temporary prestige, but trouble was brewing.

John Adams and his wing of the party were strongly opposed by Hamilton and his followers. The Alien and Sedition Laws had made the administration of the former thoroughly unpopular. Jefferson and Burr had completely organized the opposition, and the election of 1800 bore heavily against the Federalists and elected Jefferson. The Federalists, now in the minority, resorted to obstruction and offered opposition even to measures that were in line with those previously advocated by themselves. Their opposition to the Louisi-

138

ana Purchase, certainly an instance of broad construction, is a fair example of these tactics. To the opposition of this last measure they were not, however, able to bring their full strength.

In 1804 Federalist electors were chosen from but three states. The party opposed the embargo and other restrictive measures, and in this they were joined by Randolph. Attempts to secure a navy and opposition to the War of 1812 and to the policy of protection of home manufactures now constituted its program. It had, in fact, gone so far as to adopt the strict construction theory. In the presidential election of 1812 it showed a decided increase in strength, but this soon fell off again, and although it still had influence in some of the New England states, its national importance was over. Its supporters became National Republicans and were of the elements that subsequently formed the Whig party. One of the most serious defects of the party was that it never made any attempt to gain the confidence of the people—its leaders stood aloof. Among the prominent members of the party, besides those mentioned, were John Jay, Fisher Ames, John Marshall, Roger Sherman, Rufus King, and James A. Bayard.

Federalist, The—Beginning in October 1787 and continuing until March 1788, a series of eighty-five essays on the Constitution appeared in the *Independent Gazeteer* of New York. This collection of essays is known as *The Federalist*. Written by Hamilton, Madison, Jay, and William Duer for the purpose of rallying public opinion in support of the Constitution, which was then before the people for adoption, *The Federalist* ranks high as an authority on questions of constitutional interpretation. The essays which played an influential part in the fight for ratification were mostly the work of Alexander Hamilton, who quite properly has received the major share of the credit for them. Only three were written by Duer. The earlier Federalist papers were signed "A Citizen of New York," the later ones "Publius."

Fellow Traveler—A person who, though not actually a member of the Communist party, is in sympathy with its principles and is willing to co-operate with it.

139

"Few Die and None Resign"—Thomas Jefferson was the first President to advocate a system of removals from and appointments to public office for political reasons, although the spoils system did not become fully established until Jackson's time. In a letter written to a committee of New Haven merchants in 1801 Jefferson said, "If a due participation of office is a matter of right, how are vacancies to be obtained? Those by death are few; by resignation none." This is usually misquoted, "Few die and none resign."

"Fifty-Four Forty or Fight"—This was a campaign slogan used by the Democrats in the 1844 presidential race. It referred to the northern boundary line of Oregon which had long been a subject of dispute between the United States and Great Britain. We claimed all the territory as far north as the southern boundary of Russian Alaska, namely, to the line of 54° 40′ north latitude. The Democrats were opposed to yielding our claims to the territory short of that line and declared their willingness to fight for it. Their candidate, James K. Polk, was elected President, and shortly afterward he settled for the forty-ninth parallel. (See *Northwest Boundary*.)

Filibuster—In the vocabulary of American politics, to filibuster is to employ delaying parliamentary tactics to hold up or defeat legislation. Taking advantage of the freedom of debate, the minority members of a legislative assembly who are opposed to the passage of a bill will talk in relays for days. Continuous quorum calls and moves to correct the record, accompanied by appeals from the decisions of the chair, are also among the dilatory tactics employed. In the closing hours of a session one member alone may by talking succeed in preventing the passage of a bill. But whether a filibuster succeeds or not, those resorting to it have at least made a good show of their opposition.

Senator Robert M. La Follette, Sr., of Wisconsin holds the record for the longest individual filibuster in the Senate. In 1908 he talked for eighteen hours and twenty-three minutes against the Aldrich-Vreeland Currency Bill. Senator Huey Long of Louisiana became runner-up when in 1935 he succeeded in killing the extension of the NRA by talking for fifteen hours and thirty-five minutes.

140

Under the rules of the House of Representatives it is now practically impossible to filibuster. Action on a bill may be delayed for a while by forcing roll calls, but even this procedure fails when the Rules Committee brings in a drastic rule which prohibits the offering of amendments and limits the time for considering a bill.

It is still possible to filibuster in the Senate unless the Cloture Rule is invoked to put a stop to it. Numerous attempts have been made to apply the rule since it was adopted in 1917, but this has been done only four times. If sixteen senators petition to end debate, the petition must be voted on two days later. If two thirds of those present then vote for cloture, debate is limited to one hour for each senator. (See *Cloture.*)

Fillmore, Millard, thirteenth President of the United States, was born in Cayuga County, New York, January 7, 1800, and died in Buffalo on March 8, 1874. He had few early advantages, and his education was obtained solely by his own efforts. At twenty-three he was admitted to the bar. From 1829 to 1831 he served in the legislature as a member of the Anti-Masonic party. He was elected to Congress as a Whig, serving from 1833 to 1835 and from 1837 to 1843. In 1844 he was the Whig candidate for governor of New York but was defeated. In 1848 he was state comptroller. In the national elections of that year he was chosen Vice-President under General Zachary Taylor, on whose death he succeeded to the presidency, taking the oath of office on July 10, 1850. In 1852 he was defeated for the Whig nomination for President by General Winfield Scott. In 1856 he made another bid for the presidency, this time as nominee of the American party, the members of which were called Know-Nothings. It was a three-cornered contest between Buchanan, the Democratic candidate, Frémont, the Republican nominee, and Fillmore. Buchanan won. The electoral vote was Buchanan 174, Frémont 114, Fillmore 8. The latter put up a good fight but only succeeded in carrying Maryland.

The outstanding event of his administration was the passage of the Compromise of 1850. Thousands of adventurers had flocked to California in the gold rush. Desirous of forming a state government, the inhabitants had adopted a constitution which excluded slavery

141

forever from its limits. This clause caused violent debates in Congress and created bitter feeling between the North and South. To meet the difficulty, Henry Clay offered in the Senate his famous Compromise Bill, which after months of discussion became a law in September 1850, and California was admitted as a free state.

Fireside Chats—In March 1934 President Franklin D. Roosevelt inaugurated a series of reports to the people by radio which became known as fireside chats. He used the radio quite extensively in his formal addresses and during political campaigns. Compilations made by CBS and NBC showed he did more than three hundred all-network broadcasts during the twelve years he was in office. His distinctive voice and the drama which he put into the delivery of his talks made him an outstanding personality on the air waves.

"First in War, First in Peace, and First in the Hearts of his Countrymen"—Washington was thus alluded to by General Henry Lee in his funeral oration on our first President.

First Lady of the Land—By virtue of the fact that her husband holds the highest position in the country, the wife of the President takes social precedence over all other women and is known as the First Lady of the Land.

Flag, Pledge to the—The following pledge to the United States flag is taught in many schools throughout the country, and the pupils recite it daily:

"I pledge allegiance to the flag of the United States of America, and to the republic for which it stands; one nation, indivisible, with liberty and justice for all."

This pledge, says a report issued by the Historical Committee of the United States Flag Association, was written by Francis Bellamy in August 1892. Mr. Bellamy was a member of the editorial staff of the *Youth's Companion*.

Flag, Presidential—The colors of the President's flag consist of a blue field with the seal of the President in bronze in the center and in each of the four corners a white five-pointed star with one point upward. The flag was suggested by President Arthur in 1882, and the suggestion being approved by his Cabinet, the flag was first used by him the following year. The Navy Department ordered the flag to be flown from the mainmast of any United States vessel bearing the President. His colors are broken out the instant he steps on deck and kept flying as long as he remains on board.

Flag of the United States—During the early days of the Revolution flags of various designs, depending on the taste of different commanders, were in use. In December 1775, on the recommendation of a committee of Congress, what was known as the "Grand Union" flag came into use. It consisted of a field of seven red and six white stripes like the present national flag, but its union, or corner, was the same as that of the British flag, allegiance to Great Britain not having as yet been renounced by the signing of the Declaration of Independence.

In June 1776, when the issue of some such declaration appeared almost inevitable, Washington and a committee of Congress informally substituted for the British union a union consisting of a five-pointed star. On June 14, 1777, Congress formally established a field of thirteen stripes and a union of thirteen white stars on a blue field, and this new flag was probably first used at the battle of Brandywine, September 11, 1777.

On January 13, 1794, Congress ordered two more stripes and two more stars to be added to the flag to represent the states of Vermont and Kentucky, admitted in the meanwhile. Notwithstanding the admission of several more states, the flag was then left unchanged until the act of April 4, 1818, changed the number of stripes to thirteen, which number has remained fixed. The number of stars was thereafter to be equal to the number of states. The arrangement of the stars in the union was not provided for. Thus the stripes typify the original states, the stars the present states.

Flag Day—June 14 is observed in the United States as Flag Day in commemoration of the adoption of the Stars and Stripes by the Continental Congress on June 14, 1777. The flag is displayed generally throughout the country on this day.

Florida—Known as the "Peninsula State." State flower, orange blossom. Population, 1,897,414. Area, 58,560 square miles. Capital, Tallahassee. Admitted as a state in 1845. The Australian ballot, with tickets of a non-partisan nature, is provided for in the state constitution and enables control over the Negro vote. The state has six representatives in Congress.

Forgotten Man—During a radio speech delivered April 7, 1932, President Franklin D. Roosevelt declared: "These unhappy times call for the building of plans that rest upon the forgotten, the unorganized but indispensable units of economic power, for plans like those of 1917 that build from the bottom up, and not from the top down, that put their faith once more in the forgotten man at the foot of the economic pyramid."

Four Freedoms—President Franklin D. Roosevelt, in his annual message to Congress in January 1941, said: "In future days, which we seek to make secure, we look forward to a world founded upon four essential human freedoms.

"The first is freedom of speech and expression—everywhere in the world.

"The second is freedom of every person to worship God in his own way—everywhere in the world.

"The third is freedom from want—which, translated into world terms, means economic understandings which will secure to every nation a healthy peaceful life for its inhabitants—everywhere in the world.

"The fourth is freedom from fear—which, translated into world terms, means a world-wide reduction of armaments to such a point and in such a thorough fashion that no nation will be in a position to commit an act of aggression against any neighbor—anywhere in the world."

Four More Years of the Full Dinner Pail—Republican campaign slogan of the McKinley-Bryan presidential race in 1900. Workers formerly carried their dinners in pails, and during the campaign Republicans paraded with dinner pails to give the impression that labor was for McKinley.

Fourteen Points—During World War I President Wilson, in an address delivered before a joint session of Congress on January 8, 1918, outlined his program for world peace, a program, he said, for which we were willing to fight and would continue to fight until it was achieved. As a basis for a general settlement he laid down the following Fourteen Points:

I Open covenants of peace must be openly arrived at, after which there shall be no private international understandings of any kind, but diplomacy shall proceed always frankly and in the public view.

II Absolute freedom of navigation upon the seas, outside territorial waters, alike in peace and in war, except as the seas may be closed in whole or in part by international action for the enforcement of international covenants.

III The removal, so far as possible, of all economic barriers and the establishment of an equality of trade conditions among all the nations consenting to the peace and associating themselves for its maintenance.

IV Adequate guarantees given and taken that national armaments will be reduced to the lowest point consistent with domestic safety.

V Free, open-minded, and absolutely impartial adjustment of all colonial claims, based upon a strict observance of the principle that in determining all such questions of sovereignty the interests of the populations concerned must have equal weight with the equitable claims of the government whose title is to be determined.

VI The evacuation of all Russian territory and such a settlement of all questions affecting Russia as will secure the best and freest co-operation of the other nations of the world in obtaining for her an unhampered and unembarrassed opportunity for the independent determination of her own political development and national policy, and assure her of a sincere welcome into the society of free nations under institutions of her own choosing; and, more than a welcome, assistance also of every kind that she may need and may herself desire. The treatment accorded Russia by her sister nations in the months to come will be the acid test of their good-will, of their comprehension of her needs as distinguished from their own interests, and of their intelligent and unselfish sympathy.

VII Belgium, the whole world will agree, must be evacuated and restored, without any attempt to limit the sovereignty which she enjoys in common with all other free nations. No other single act will serve as this will serve to restore confidence among the nations in the laws which they have themselves set and determined for the government of their relations with one another. Without this healing act the whole structure and validity of international law is forever impaired.

VIII All French territory should be freed and the invaded portions restored, and the wrong done to France by Prussia in 1871 in the matter of Alsace-Lorraine, which has unsettled the peace of the world for nearly fifty years, should be righted, in order that peace may once more be made secure in the interest of all.

IX A readjustment of the frontiers of Italy should be effected along clearly recognizable lines of nationality.

X The peoples of Austria-Hungary, whose place among the nations we wish to see safeguarded and assured, should be accorded the freest opportunity of autonomous development.

XI Rumania, Serbia, and Montenegro should be evacuated, occupied territories restored, Serbia accorded free and secure access to the sea, and the relations of the several Balkan States to one another determined by friendly counsel along historically established lines of allegiance and nationality, and international guarantees of the political and economic independence and territorial integrity of the several Balkan States should be entered into.

XII The Turkish portions of the present Ottoman Empire should be assured a secure sovereignty, but the other nationalities which are now under Turkish rule should be assured an undoubted security of life and an absolutely unmolested opportunity of autonomous development, and the Dardanelles should be permanently opened as a free passage to the ships and commerce of all nations under international guarantees.

XIII An independent Polish state should be erected which should include the territories inhabited by indisputably Polish populations, which should be assured a free and secure access to the sea, and whose political and economic independence and territorial integrity should be guaranteed by international covenant.

XIV A general association of nations must be formed under specific covenants for the purpose of affording mutual guarantees of political independence and territorial integrity to great and small states alike.

"Free Soil, Free Men, Free Speech, and Fre-mont"—Rallying cry of the supporters of John C. Frémont when he ran for President in 1856. He was defeated by his Democratic opponent, James Buchanan.

Free Soil Party—The Southern leaders of the Democratic party had determined to prevent the nomination of Martin Van Buren for the presidency in the convention of 1844. This was accomplished by declaring the vote of two thirds of the convention necessary to nominate. This rule once adopted, Van Buren's defeat followed naturally.

These tactics caused a split in the Democratic ranks, especially in Van Buren's state, New York. Van Buren's faction was there known as the Barnburners, the other as the Hunkers. In 1848 both factions sent delegations to the national convention, which determined to give one half of the state vote to each. Both sections withdrew dissatisfied.

Van Buren's faction, joining with the remnants of the Liberty party, formed the Free Soil party, by which Van Buren and Charles Francis Adams were nominated. Their platform was a strong and frank protest against the extension of slavery and contained such ringing phrases as "a free soil to a free people," and "Congress has no more power to make a slave than to make a king." Van Buren and Adams received no electoral votes, but their popular vote was 291,342 against 1,219,962 for Cass and 1,360,752 for Taylor. In 1852 the party nominated John P. Hale of New York and again received no electoral votes. During its existence it always had from fifteen to twenty representatives in Congress, among them Charles Sumner, Salmon P. Chase, and David Wilmot. It opposed the Kansas-Nebraska Bill and was finally swallowed up by the Republican party.

Fusion—Where two or more political parties agree on the same candidates on a general ticket, the joint ticket is called a fusion ticket. Such tickets are to be met with in national, state, and municipal elections. One of the most conspicuous modern examples was the fusion that kept Fiorello H. La Guardia in office as mayor of New York for twelve years.

Gallup Poll—See *Straw Vote*.

Garfield, James A., who was to become our twentieth President, was born in a log cabin on his father's farm in Orange, Ohio, November 19, 1831. He was an industrious youth and in his early days contributed to the family income by chopping wood, doing carpentry work, and working aboard boats on the Ohio canals.

He was an avid reader and student and because of his persistent ambition for an education succeeded in graduating from Williams College in 1856. He then returned to Ohio to teach and to study law. He was elected to the State Senate in 1859. His political career was interrupted for two years by the Civil War, in which he served as a major general of the Union Army. In 1863 Garfield resigned his command to take a seat in the United States House of Representatives. He remained a member of Congress for seventeen years, serving actively on many important committees.

Garfield was elected to the United States Senate in 1880, and in that same year he was nominated by the Republicans to run for President against Winfield Scott Hancock, the Democratic candidate. He won by a comfortable margin, although the electoral count of 215 to 155 showed that it was by no means a landslide victory.

On July 2, 1881, four months after his inauguration, he was shot in the Baltimore and Potomac Railway Depot by Charles Guiteau, a disappointed office seeker. Although there was some question as to Guiteau's sanity, he was convicted and hanged in Washington on June 30, 1882. Garfield lingered for seventy-nine days before he succumbed on September 19, 1881, in Elberon, New Jersey.

Because of the short time he served as President, no reliable account of his ability as Chief Executive is possible. As a politician he was inclined to be vacillating and conciliatory in making decisions. His judgment was good, but he did not always follow it, and many say that his opinions, private and personal and those in office, were not always in agreement. This may have been due to the man's amiable nature, his sensitiveness, and eagerness for approval.

In looks Garfield could never have been taken for an ordinary man. He was tall, broad-shouldered, and presented an imposing figure both in manner and physical appearance.

Georgia—This is the "Cracker State" but is ofttimes called the "Empire State of the South." State flower, Cherokee rose. Population, 3,123,723. Area, 58,876 square miles. Capital, Atlanta. Georgia was one of the original states of the Union. When the Declaration of Independence was signed a convention was held which ratified the state's first constitution. When the military government was abolished after the Civil War conditions were in an unsettled state, and it was found necessary for the protection of the Negro population to reinstitute a military regime. The state, however, was finally readmitted to the Union in July 1871. Georgia has ten representatives in Congress.

Gerrymander—Gerrymandering is an American political term for arranging electoral districts in such a way as to give an undue advantage to a political party. By manipulating districts a party having only a minority of votes out of the total popular vote may elect a majority of the representatives in a legislative body. This is done by taking part of a district having a large majority in favor of the gerrymandering party and annexing it to a neighboring district controlled by the other party in order to gain a majority there too. In this way control of a majority of districts may be gained.

The term originated in 1812, following the election the preceding year of Elbridge Gerry as governor of Massachusetts. In the election the Democrats gained a majority over the Federalists in both houses of the legislature. In an attempt to perpetuate their control of the State Senate, they proceeded to divide the senatorial districts so as to give themselves a distinct advantage. Governor Gerry approved the action of his party.

Gilbert Stuart, the artist, was looking over the divided map with Benjamin Russell, editor of the Boston *Centinel*. Taking a pencil, Stuart added a head, claws, and tail to one of the districts, saying, "There, that will do for a salamander."

"Salamander!" Russell cried. "Call it Gerrymander!"

Stuart's cartoon, which was printed all over the country, gave currency to the newly coined word.

Gettysburg Address—A speech delivered by President Lincoln on the battlefield of Gettysburg, November 19, 1863, on the occa-

149

sion of the dedication of a cemetery there for the soldiers who fell in that battle. Lincoln spoke as follows:

"Fourscore and seven years ago our fathers brought forth on this continent a new nation, conceived in liberty and dedicated to the proposition that all men are created equal. Now we are engaged in a great civil war, testing whether that nation, or any nation so conceived and so dedicated, can long endure. We are met on a great battlefield of that war. We have come to dedicate a portion of that field as a final resting place for those who here gave their lives that that nation might live. It is altogether fitting and proper that we should do this. But, in a larger sense, we cannot dedicate—we cannot consecrate—we cannot hallow—this ground. The brave men, living and dead, who struggled here have consecrated it far above our poor power to add or to detract. The world will little note nor long remember what we say here, but it can never forget what they did here. It is for us, the living, rather to be dedicated here to the unfinished work which they who fought here have thus far so nobly advanced. It is rather for us to be here dedicated to the great task remaining before us—that from these honored dead we take increased devotion to that cause for which they gave the last full measure of devotion; that we here highly resolve that these dead shall not have died in vain; that this nation, under God, shall have a new birth of freedom; and that government of the people, by the people, for the people, shall not perish from the earth."

Ghost Writers—Political ghost writers have been active in the field of American politics since the earliest days of the Republic. Washington made no bones about enlisting the help of his colleagues in preparing his most important state papers, which abound in the ideas and phrases of his friends. His famous Farewell Address is a political cocktail composed, perhaps, of one-third Madison, one-third Hamilton, and only one-third Washington. His rough drafts came back to him, said Woodrow Wilson, "in great part rephrased and rewritten, in many passages reconceived and given a new color." Probably no President since Washington has worked entirely without the aid of phantom penmen, about whom lately there has come to be little or no mystery. During political campaigns newspapers like to give the local habitations and names of the ghost writers employed by the more prominent candidates. Women as well as men have engaged successfully in this kind of writing.

Gilded Trap—When the Constitution was before the people for ratification it was called the Gilded Trap. Other nicknames were New Roof and New Breeches.

"Give Me Liberty, or Give Me Death"—Patrick Henry, speaking before the Virginia Convention in March 1775, in support of a resolution "that the colony be immediately put in a state of defense," said: "Is life so dear or peace so sweet as to be purchased at the price of chains and slavery? Forbid it, Almighty God! I know not what course others may take, but as for me, give me liberty, or give me death!"

"God Reigns, and the Government at Washington Still Lives!"—On April 15, 1865, the morning following the assassination of Abraham Lincoln, an angry crowd was assembled in Wall Street, New York, bent on attacking the office of the New York *World*, which had been strongly opposed to Lincoln. The mob was about to move off to the attack when it was diverted and its passions calmed by the following brief address by James A. Garfield, then a young congressman: "Fellow citizens! Clouds and darkness are round about Him. His pavilion is dark waters and thick clouds of the skies. Justice and judgment are the establishment of His throne. Mercy and truth shall go before His face. Fellow citizens! God reigns, and the Government at Washington still lives!"

Sixteen years later Garfield was himself assassinated by a disappointed office seeker.

Good Enough Morgan Till after Election—The disappearance in 1826 of William Morgan of Batavia, New York, who revealed the secrets of Freemasonry, and the finding of what was supposed to be his dead body below Niagara Falls, caused intense excitement. One of the leading anti-Masonic agitators in New York State was Thurlow Weed, who took full advantage of the feeling that prevailed against Masons. When doubt was cast on the identity of the

151

body found in the Niagara River, Weed is said to have remarked privately that it was a "good enough Morgan till after election." (See *Anti-Masonic Party*.)

Good-Neighbor Policy—"In the field of world policy," said Franklin D. Roosevelt in his first inaugural address, March 4, 1933, "I would dedicate this nation to the policy of the good neighbor— the neighbor who resolutely respects himself and, because he does so, respects the rights of others—the neighbor who respects his obligations and respects the sanctity of his agreements in and with a world of neighbors."

Grand Old Party, or more briefly G.O.P., has been the nickname of the Republican party since 1880.

Grangers—In 1867 a secret society known as the Patrons of Husbandry was formed in Washington. Its object was to aid the farmers by enabling them to co-operate and purchase their supplies at first hand, and by offering opportunities for social and educational improvement. Lodges called Granges were established in several Western states.

The association received a setback through the financial reverses of many of its lodges, which had, without proper training, engaged in business enterprises. Nevertheless, they succeeded in carrying the legislatures of Illinois and Wisconsin in 1873 and 1874; these legislatures passed stringent laws directed against "extortion and unjust discrimination in the rates charged for the transportation of passengers and freights." These acts were subsequently repealed but while they were in force had a very unfavorable effect on the railroads. In Congress their efforts led to considerable discussion regarding the regulation of interstate commerce, since consummated by the act of February 4, 1887, which established the Interstate Commerce Commission.

Grant, Ulysses Simpson, or Hiram Ulysses Grant, was born at Point Pleasant, Clermont County, Ohio, on April 27, 1822, and died at Mt. McGregor, near Saratoga, New York, on July 23, 1885. His name was Hiram Ulysses, but an error on the part of the congressman who named him for West Point caused his name to be entered there as Ulysses S., and by that name he has since gone; Simpson he adopted, it being a name in his mother's family.

He graduated from West Point in 1843 and remained in the Army until 1854, serving in the Mexican War. In 1854 he resigned his commission and engaged in business. At the outbreak of the Civil War he raised a company; he was rapidly promoted and in 1862 had risen to the rank of major general of volunteers. He was made major general in the Regular Army on July 4, 1863, lieutenant general on March 2, 1864, and finally general of the Army on July 25, 1866. He was for a short time Secretary of War, ad interim, under Johnson. The crowning event of his military career was the surrender of Lee to him at Appomattox on April 9, 1865.

In 1868 he was nominated for the presidency by the Republican party and elected. In 1872 he was again elected. In 1880, one term having intervened, a strong effort to renominate him was made, but it failed. His second term was marked by various scandals like the Whisky Ring, but no one ever connected the President's name with them.

Among the principal events of his administration are the completion of the Pacific railways and the settlement of the Alabama claims. He was a plain man, possessed of much common sense. Unskilled in public affairs and unfortunate in the choice of his civil subordinates, he clung to these latter even when their guilt was clear to other minds and so made himself the target for much abuse.

Great Commoner—A popular title borne by at least three leading political personages in the United States, namely, Thaddeus Stevens, Henry Clay, and William Jennings Bryan. It originally referred to William Pitt, the great eighteenth-century leader in the British House of Commons.

Great Engineer—President Herbert Hoover was often spoken of as the Great Engineer.

Greenback-Labor Party—The demand for agricultural products on the part of the government during the Civil War tended to

153

render farmers prosperous; their prosperity was increased by the payment in greenbacks of debts previously contracted, and these concurrent circumstances tended to make agricultural sections look on the unlimited issue of paper money as the cure for all economic evils.

A convention of Greenbackers was held in 1874, and it was resolved that it was desirable to have all bank currency withdrawn and only national currency issued and, moreover, to have the principal of that portion of the national debt not in terms made payable in gold paid in currency. As early as 1868 this plan had been known as the Ohio Idea. The Democratic party in 1875 showed some leaning toward these views, but it soon fell away from them.

In 1876 the Greenbackers held a national convention and, adopting the name of Independent party, nominated Peter Cooper of New York for the presidency. The party polled a total of about 80,000 votes. Its strength lay mainly in the agricultural regions, in Illinois, Indiana, Iowa, Kansas, and Michigan. In 1877 the party's vote in the state elections was about 185,000. About this time the labor-reform parties assumed greater prominence, and in several states the labor and Greenback parties united.

In 1878 a national convention adopted the name of National party. In that year its vote rose to 1,000,000, and a number of national representatives were elected, usually by fusions with whichever party happened to be in the minority in any district. In 1880 James B. Weaver of Iowa was nominated for President, polling about 300,000 votes; in 1884 the nominee was Benjamin F. Butler of Massachusetts, who was also the Anti-Monopoly candidate, the joint ticket being known as the People's party, and the vote about 130,000. Not long afterward the party faded away.

Hard Cider Campaign—Log cabins and cider barrels figured as political emblems of the Whig party in the presidential campaign of 1840, when General William Henry Harrison, the Whig candidate, defeated the Democratic nominee, Martin Van Buren. Harrison had lived in a log cabin at North Bend, Ohio, where, it was said, he loved to roll out a barrel of hard cider to treat his friends. His supporters, taking this to be to their candidate's credit, adopted the log cabin as symbolical of Harrison's simple, homely virtues, and used a barrel of cider to represent his hospitality. Log cabins were built in villages, towns, and cities throughout the country by Harrison's adherents as local party headquarters, and at these meeting places hard cider was freely dispensed to all comers. Log cabins were carried in political parades, and Horace Greeley edited a Whig campaign paper called the *Log-Cabin,* which reached a circulation of 80,000. But it was the enormous amount of hard cider consumed that made the campaign memorable. Drunkenness was rife, and for years afterward drunkards were fond of attributing their first downfall to the Hard Cider Campaign.

The campaign was also notable for a slick political slogan. General Harrison had won an important victory over the Indians at Tippecanoe in 1811. His running mate for Vice-President was John Tyler. And the Whig campaign cry of "Tippecanoe and Tyler too!" undoubtedly helped the Whigs win the election.

The Hard Cider Campaign set a new pattern for conducting presidential contests. (See *Tippecanoe and Tyler Too.*)

Harding, Warren G.—Warren Harding was tall, genial, attractive, and a social favorite. He was not a leader, and his election as President in 1920 was an unfortunate episode in American history. By fellow members of the Senate and friends from his native state of Ohio, he unwillingly was pressed to pursue the Republican nomination.

His Democratic opponent was Governor James M. Cox of Ohio, whose running mate was Franklin D. Roosevelt, then Assistant Secretary of the Navy. Notable in this election was the polling of a million votes by the Socialists, who ran Eugene V. Debs, at that time in prison for denouncing the war. Mr. Harding received almost twice the popular vote recorded for the other two candidates combined, but the people were not voting for him or against Cox. It was a protest vote against the Democratic regime of Wilson.

Harding was one of only half a dozen presidents who were not lawyers. Born in Corsica, Ohio, on November 2, 1865, he studied from 1879 to 1882 at the Ohio Central College and left at an early age to become established in Marion. In 1884 he became connected with a local newspaper, the *Daily Star,* as reporter and printer. Later he came to own and edit it—the only editor ever to be elected President.

From 1900 to 1904 he was in the Ohio State Senate, and he served as lieutenant governor from 1904 to 1906. Although defeated for governor in 1910, Harding entered the United States Senate in 1915. He was one of the few senators ever to become Chief Executive.

During his administration the Limitation of Armament Conference was held in Washington. About this time the Tomb of the Unknown Soldier was erected at Arlington, and Harding took part in the first memorial service held there.

In the summer of 1923 he made a tour of Alaska to investigate confused conditions there. The exertion of this extensive trip gravely affected his health. On his way back, at San Francisco, he suffered an attack of pneumonia and died there while in office on August 2, 1923.

Harrison, Benjamin—Short, austere, and aloof, Benjamin Harrison lacked the ability to attract or inspire. Intellectually, however, he ranks among our foremost presidents, and he showed marked ability in making excellent extemporaneous speeches.

He was the grandson of President William Henry Harrison and was born in North Bend, Ohio, on August 20, 1833. In his early years he worked on his father's four-hundred-acre farm, the scene of his birthplace. Harrison graduated from Miami University in Ohio in 1852 and was admitted to practice law in Cincinnati the following year.

Shortly afterward he moved to Indiana and in 1860 was elected reporter of the Indiana Supreme Court. Then followed a four-year period in the Civil War where he made a splendid record, serving as an officer in the Union Army.

In 1876 he was defeated as the Republican candidate for governor of Indiana, but in 1879 he was elected to the United States Senate from that state.

Harrison defeated Grover Cleveland in 1888 to become our twenty-third Chief Executive. No events of unusual importance are

156

connected with his administration. Of some note was the passing of the Silver Act, the McKinley Tariff Act, and the admission of North and South Dakota, Montana, Idaho, and Washington to the Union.

In 1892 he was renominated for President, but Cleveland was returned to office in a sweeping victory.

Harrison died in Indianapolis on March 13, 1901.

Harrison, William Henry, ninth President of the United States, was born in Berkeley, Virginia, on February 9, 1773, and died in the White House in Washington on April 4, 1841. His father was a signer of the Declaration of Independence.

Young Harrison abandoned the study of medicine to become a Regular Army officer. He fought against the Indians under General Wayne. In 1801 he was appointed governor of the Indiana Territory, after he had served as secretary. As governor he defeated the Indians under Tecumseh in the Battle of Tippecanoe in 1811. After the defeat of Hull in the War of 1812, he was made commander of the American forces in the Northwest, with the rank of major general. He was a congressman from Ohio from 1816 to 1819, and senator from 1825 to 1828. He resigned to become Minister to Colombia from 1828 to 1829. He was defeated for the presidency in 1836 by Martin Van Buren, but in the election of 1840—the famous Hard Cider Campaign (*q.v.*)—he beat Van Buren. The popular vote was 1,275,017 for Harrison and 1,128,702 for Van Buren. Out of a total of 294 electoral votes, Harrison received 234, Van Buren 60.

President Harrison died just one month after he had taken the oath of office and was succeeded by John Tyler. In that year the United States had three presidents. Harrison's grandson became the twenty-third President.

Hartford Convention—The War of 1812 against England had been entered into in the face of the protest of the New England and northern middle states. These, being commercial in their pursuits, had everything to lose by war; what they demanded was a strong navy to protect commerce. In politics they were Federalists.

When the Democratic majority in Congress had forced the war

on the Democratic President, Madison, and hostilities had actually commenced, these states took no active part in the struggle; they opposed the war; finally, in October 1814, Massachusetts passed a resolution inviting the other New England states to a convention having in view an ultimate convention of all the states for the purpose of a revision of the Constitution. Connecticut and Rhode Island and some counties of New Hampshire and Vermont signified their approval of this course, but these resolutions explicitly declared that the proposed action was to be within the limits of the Constitution.

The reverses of the war had put the Democratic party into no humor for these proceedings; they were denounced; it was charged that there was a conspiracy to establish a grand duchy under an English prince; government agents were sent all over New England to find proofs of these facts.

As a matter of fact, the convention of representatives from Massachusetts, Connecticut, Rhode Island, New Hampshire, and Vermont met in Hartford, Connecticut, December 15, 1814; this convention disclaimed any intention to dissolve the Union at that time; such dissolution, it declared, must "be the work of peaceable times and deliberate consent." Among the grievances it recited were the "easy admission of naturalized foreigners to places of trust, honor, and profit," and the easy formation of new Western states; it desired the defense of every state to be entrusted to the state itself, and declared it to be "as much the duty of the state authorities to watch over the rights *reserved,* as of the United States to exercise the powers which are *delegated.*" It desired changes in the Constitution as follows: abrogation of the right of Southern states to representation for three fifths of their slaves; requirement of a two-thirds vote of both houses for the admission of new states or the prohibition of commercial intercourse or to declare war or to authorize hostilities except in cases of invasion; embargoes to be limited to sixty days; foreigners to be disqualified from all civil offices under the United States; presidents to be ineligible for a second term, and no two successive presidents to be from the same state.

Massachusetts and Connecticut sent commissioners to Washington to attempt to carry out the suggestions of the report, but the war had in the meantime ended and the commissioners were ignored. The convention did not meet again; but the odium attaching to it was so great that its president placed a copy of the proceedings in the hands of the Massachusetts Secretary of State in order thus to disprove charges of treason.

"Have Faith in Massachusetts"—In his address to the Massachusetts Senate on being made the presiding officer of that body in January 1914, Calvin Coolidge said, "Have faith in Massachusetts. In some unimportant detail some other states may surpass her, but in the general results, there is no place on earth where the people secure, in larger measures, the blessings of organized government, and nowhere can those functions more properly be termed self-government."

Hawaii—The Territory of Hawaii consists of twenty islands in the Pacific which were annexed to the United States during the Spanish American War in 1898. They had been a constitutional monarchy, but a revolution in 1893 had deposed Queen Liliuokalani. Population, 423,330. Area, 6,454 square miles. Capital, Honolulu. Pearl Harbor, where the Japanese made their sneak attack on December 7, 1941, is situated on Oahu Island. One delegate represents the territory in Washington.

Hayes, Rutherford B.—Shortly before Rutherford Hayes was born in Delaware, Ohio, on October 4, 1822, his father died, leaving the family in comfortable circumstances. His childhood was free from worry and care, and as a youth few advantages were denied him in his pursuit of a successful career. He graduated from Kenyon College in 1842, and from Harvard Law School in 1845. Upon completing his studies Hayes started practicing law in Fremont, Ohio, and in 1858 was made city solicitor of Cincinnati.

In the Civil War he served from 1861 to 1865, attaining the rank of brevet major general of the Union Army. His splendid record as a soldier helped elect him to the House of Representatives from 1865 to 1867. The people of Ohio elected him governor in 1867 and re-elected him two years later. In 1872 he was defeated for Congress, but in 1875 was re-elected governor of his home state.

Originally a member of the Whig party, Hayes joined the Republican party when it was first organized, and in 1876 he was made Republican candidate for President to run against Samuel J. Tilden, the Democratic choice. The election was so close that contradictory returns from Louisiana, South Carolina, and Florida left the outcome in doubt. Congress elected a commission consisting of five senators, five representatives, and five justices of the Supreme Court to decide who was the victor. They voted 8 to 7 in favor of Hayes, and a perilous crisis in American history was averted.

The issues that received the most attention during the administration of our nineteenth Chief Executive were civil-service reform, a sound money system, and reuniting the North and South. Hayes worked tirelessly to remove the spoils system and to improve civil service. "He serves his party best who serves his country best," he once said, and the lines have become famous.

Although in his effort to establish finance on a stable basis he strongly opposed the Free Silver Bill, it was passed over his veto in both houses. His order for the withdrawal of Federal troops from the capitals of the South paved the way for the beginning of an era of good feeling between the North and South.

Hayes was not a candidate for a second term and retired from office with dignity and the respect of the people. His ability as a President has been underestimated. He was a man of courage and deep understanding. His best efforts were constantly thwarted by a small powerful group of spoilsmen whom he offended by his independent views.

He died in Fremont, Ohio, on January 17, 1893.

He Kept Us Out of War—Democratic campaign slogan in the Wilson-Hughes presidential contest in 1916.

Hell-Bent for Election—Why a person should go to perdition at a faster clip than to other places is a question, but that he does so is the suggestion conveyed by the common American expression "hell-bent." In Maine's election for governor in 1840, the Whigs, who hadn't won an election for years, surprised themselves by electing Edward Kent, the Whig candidate. This was taken as an indication that in the November presidential election the country would go the same way. The Whigs celebrated the victory with a song:

> "Oh have you heard how old Maine went?
> She went hell-bent for Governor Kent,
> And Tippecanoe and Tyler, too!"

The phrase "hell-bent for election" has since then become a common saying which is applied not only to political contests, but to anything done with a great show of activity.

It was also about this time that the political maxim, "As Maine goes, so goes the nation," had its origin.

Henry Documents—Sir James H. Craig, the governor of British North America, in January 1809, sent an adventurer, John Henry by name, into the New England states to report the feeling of that section of the country on the question of secession from the Union and possibly to increase the discontent already caused among these people of commercial interests by the Embargo Act and the non-intercourse system of the government. Failing of the reward he sought from the British Ministry, Henry sold to President Madison for $50,000 his correspondence with the English officials, and these papers became known as the Henry documents. Madison submitted the letters to Congress and claimed that they proved a design on the part of England to annex the New England states. They did not make certain, however, that the Eastern states entertained seriously the idea of secession. This whole episode is often referred to as the Henry affair.

Hermitage, The—The name of Andrew Jackson's home near Nashville, Tennessee.

His Accidency was the nickname given to John Tyler when, on the death of President William Henry Harrison only a month after his inauguration, Tyler succeeded him to the presidency.

His Superfluous Excellency—In 1791 some of the Federalists wanted the title of the President to be "His Highness, the President

of the United States, and Protector of their Liberties." The Democrats mockingly suggested that the Vice-President should be called
"His Superfluous Excellency."

Home Department—The name the Department of the Interior
is called in the title of the act of 1849 creating the department.

Hoover, Herbert—Herbert Clark Hoover, a Republican and our
thirty-first President, was born of humble Quaker ancestry in West
Branch, Ohio, on August 10, 1874. He was left an orphan at nine
and spent the early years of his life with relatives in Ohio and Oregon, where he attended public schools.

Hoover entered Leland Stanford Junior University in 1891 and
graduated in 1895. He worked his way through college, specializing
in engineering, and as an undergraduate was employed in the
mines of California and by the Arkansas and United States Geological Surveys.

Bewick, Moreing and Company of London, in 1897, hired Mr.
Hoover as consulting mining engineer. At the time he was only
twenty-three and had already gained considerable reputation in
that field. Until 1914 he was thus engaged, his work taking him to
Australia, Africa, Europe, and Asia.

When war was declared in 1914, Hoover was made chairman of
the American Relief Committee at London and later headed the
Commission for Relief in Belgium; he carried out his duties as
relief administrator with great success.

Mr. Hoover served as Secretary of Commerce from 1921 to
1928. In 1928 he ran with Charles Curtis against Alfred E. Smith
for President and was elected by an unprecedented majority.

Six months after Hoover took office the postwar boom collapsed.
Banks failed, stocks fell, on an average, nearly forty points a day;
and governments abroad were on the verge of collapse. Unemployment became a problem of major concern, and the country was
further plagued by floods and droughts. Though he was not a
dramatic leader, Hoover made frantic efforts to keep the boom
going. It was at his insistence that we remained on the gold standard.
Large-scale public works were organized under his administration to

put labor and capital back to work. The Federal Home Loan Bank, the Reconstruction Finance Corporation, and the Farm Board were created to aid the suffering farmers, businessmen, and homeowners.

Although intelligent Americans appreciated his difficulties and recognized the honesty of his struggles, the devastating depression left the people disillusioned and in a state of economic and political distrust. Hoover made such blunders as coining the phrase "Rugged Individualism"; he was strongly opposed to anything in the nature of a "dole" and therefore delayed in organizing public relief. Hoover was the man who had promised "two cars in every garage and two chickens in every pot," but within a few months knots of packing-case huts were springing up on city dumps and wastelands, to be bitterly christened "Hoovervilles" by their pauper inhabitants.

In 1933 Franklin D. Roosevelt defeated Hoover by landslide proportions and succeeded him as President.

Horse-and-Buggy Days—President Franklin D. Roosevelt, at a White House press conference on May 31, 1935, remarked: "The whole tendency over many years has been to view the interstate commerce clause in the light of present-day civilization, although it was written into the Constitution in the horse-and-buggy days of the eighteenth century."

Hot-Water War—Soon after the Whisky Insurrection had been overcome a fresh trouble arose from a tax laid by the Federal Government on houses, which were classified according to their dimensions, the size and number of the windows, and so forth. The people objected to these direct taxes, though they bore more lightly on the poor than on the rich, and Pennsylvania was again the scene of the chief resistance.

When the officers went to make the necessary measurements the women deluged them with hot water, and hence the disturbance was known as the Hot-Water War. But further violence was offered, and when the United States marshal, in March 1799, arrested some offenders, they were rescued in the town of Bethlehem by an armed band led by one John Fries. The militia was called out and succeeded in restoring order. Fries was convicted of treason and sentenced to death, and a number of his followers were condemned to imprisonment. President Adams, however, soon pardoned them all, and two or three years later, under Jefferson, the house tax was abolished.

House of Representatives—This is the lower house of the United States Congress over which a Speaker elected by the members presides. The number of representatives is fixed by the House itself. They are apportioned among the states in proportion to the population as determined by the last Federal decennial census, but each state is entitled to at least one representative. The states are divided into congressional districts, from each of which one congressman is elected. Should a state be entitled to more representatives than it has apportioned districts, the additional representatives are elected at large from the whole state. At present the House of Representatives has 435 members.

To qualify, a representative must be at least twenty-five years old, a citizen of the United States for at least seven years, and resident of the state from which he is chosen. He cannot hold any other office under the United States. The House, like the Senate, is by the Constitution "the judge of the elections, the returns, and qualifications of its own members."

The term of office is two years. In November of even-numbered years a new House is elected, the newly elected members taking their seats on the following third of January, the day on which Congress meets regularly each year. Before the adoption of the Twentieth Amendment to the Constitution on October 15, 1933, Congress met in a "lame-duck session" on the first Monday of December. The members who had lost their seats in the November elections were called "lame ducks" and were notorious for their recklessness in legislation for which their constituents could no longer call them to account.

The House, like the Senate, is empowered by the Constitution to determine the rules of its proceedings, punish its members for disorderly behavior, and, with the concurrence of two thirds of the House, expel a member. Except in cases of felony, treason, and breach of the peace, members are exempt from arrest during attendance at a session and in going to and returning from the same. For any speech or debate in the House they cannot be questioned at any other place.

A bill introduced in Congress must pass both houses and be approved by the President before it becomes a law. If the President vetoes it a two-thirds vote of each house is required to pass the bill. (See *Congress* and *Senate.*)

Hyphenated Americans—"Some Americans," said Woodrow Wilson, "need hyphens in their names because only part of them has come over; but when the whole man has come over, heart and thought and all, the hyphen drops of its own weight out of his name."

"I Choose to Be Found Doing My Duty"—New England's most effective black-out was the famous Dark Day of May 19, 1780, when a remarkable dimness settled over all the Northern states. At midday it was as black as midnight, and people thought the day of judgment was at hand. The legislature of Connecticut was in session in Hartford at the time. The House of Representatives, being unable to transact any business, adjourned. A proposal to adjourn the Council was under consideration. When the opinion of Colonel Davenport was asked he said, "I am against an adjournment. The day of judgment is either approaching, or it is not. If it is not, there is no cause for an adjournment; if it is, I choose to be found doing my duty. I wish, therefore, that candles may be brought."

Idaho—"Gem of the Mountain State." State flower, syringa. Population, 524,873. Area, 83,577 square miles. Capital, Boise. Admitted as a state in 1890. Republicans generally have control in state elections, but in national elections the state, as a general rule, goes Democratic. Idaho extended the suffrage to women as far back as 1896. It has two representatives in Washington.

Illinois—The "Prairie State." State flower, violet. Population, 7,897,241. Area, 56,400 square miles. Capital, Springfield. Admitted to the Union in December 1818. Politically Illinois has been a doubtful state, particularly in presidential years, swaying this way and that. The same holds true in its state politics. The state adopted the Australian ballot system for all elections in 1891. It has twenty-six representatives in Congress.

Impeachment is the arraignment before a legislative body of an officer charged with an offense against the state. The President, Vice-President, and all civil officers of the United States are liable to impeachment for treason, bribery, or other high crimes and misdemeanors. The House of Representatives has the sole right of impeachment, drawing up the accusations and appointing persons to conduct the prosecution before the Senate, which has the sole right of trying such cases.

When the President is impeached the Chief Justice of the Supreme Court presides. A two-thirds vote of the senators present is necessary for conviction. Punishment extends only to removal from and disqualification to hold office under the United States, but the convicted person is still liable to an ordinary trial in the law courts. The President's pardoning power cannot be exercised in impeachment cases.

The sections of the Constitution relating to impeachment are Article I, Section 2, Clause 5; Article I, Section 3, Clauses 6 and 7; and Article II, Section 4. Provision for the impeachment of state officers is made in the constitutions of the various states.

There have been only thirteen impeachments of Federal officers since the adoption of the Constitution, and four convictions, though several resignations may have been in anticipation of conviction. Those convicted were all Federal judges, as have been most of those who have been impeached.

The only President to be impeached was Andrew Johnson, who succeeded Lincoln to the presidency. He began almost immediately to quarrel with Congress over questions connected with the reconstruction in the Southern states. Bill after bill was vetoed by Johnson, only to be passed over his veto by Congress, which sought every means to hamper the President. The rift between the executive and legislative departments widened until it resulted in impeachment proceedings.

On March 2, 1867, Congress passed the so-called Tenure of Office Act, which provided that no officer subject to confirmation by the Senate should be removed without the consent of that body, but during a recess of the Senate the President might remove such officer and appoint a successor till the end of the next session of the Senate.

Johnson vetoed the bill, and it was promptly passed over his veto. Edwin M. Stanton, Secretary of War, refused to co-operate with Johnson in his plans for restoring the Southern states to the Union, and on August 12, 1867, Johnson suspended him and appointed General Grant in his place ad interim. When the Senate met, Johnson gave his reasons for suspending Stanton, but in January the Senate refused to sanction the suspension and Stanton resumed his office. Johnson again removed Stanton on February 21, 1868, appointing General Lorenzo Thomas in his place, but Stanton, backed by a Senate resolution, refused to vacate. On February 24 the House of Representatives passed a resolution to impeach the President by a vote of 126 to 47, with seventeen not voting, and the following day a committee of the House appeared before the Senate and impeached Johnson.

The following committee was appointed by the House to conduct the prosecution: John A. Bingham of Ohio, George S. Boutwell and Benjamin F. Butler of Massachusetts, James F. Wilson of Iowa, Thomas Wilson and Thaddeus Stevens of Pennsylvania, and John A. Logan of Illinois. The President was represented by the following counsel: Henry Stanbery and W. S. Groesbeck of Ohio, William M. Evarts of New York, Thomas A. R. Nelson of Tennessee, and Benjamin R. Curtis of Massachusetts.

On the fifth of March eleven articles of impeachment were presented to the Senate, which was organized as a court for the trial of the President, with Chief Justice Salmon P. Chase presiding. The articles charged that the President, in violation of the Tenure of Office Act, had removed Stanton and appointed Thomas; that he had been guilty of intimidation of the former and of an attempt to seize unlawfully the property and money of the War Department; that he had declared that the Thirty-ninth Congress was not a legally constituted body; and that he had failed in the proper execution of its acts.

To this the President's counsel replied that the removal of Stanton and the appointment of Thomas did not come within the provisions of the Tenure of Office Act but were legal according to the laws of 1789 and 1795, which were the only controlling ones in the case; that he was not guilty of the other charges, except those in regard to statements concerning Congress, and that as to these he was protected by the rights of freedom of opinion and freedom of speech.

The taking of evidence began on March 30 and was finished by April 20. Arguments of counsel were finished May 6, and on May 16 a vote was taken on the article covering the President's declarations about the Thirty-ninth Congress. The vote was 35 for conviction and 19 for acquittal, one vote less than a sufficient number to convict. Seven Republicans voted in the minority with the twelve Democratic senators. The same result occurred when the vote was taken on the legality of Thomas's appointment. No vote was taken on the other articles; the court adjourned sine die, and at the direction of Chief Justice Chase a verdict of acquittal was entered.

In the Line of Succession—Thomas Jefferson was Secretary of State under Washington; James Madison held the office under Jefferson; James Monroe under Madison; John Quincy Adams under Monroe. All these secretaries subsequently became President, in every case except that of Jefferson, immediately after the President under whom they had served. Henry Clay was Secretary of State under John Quincy Adams, and when in 1832 he ran for the presidency against Andrew Jackson, he was said to be in the line of succession, but Jackson won and the line was broken.

Inauguration Day was changed from March 4 to January 20 by the Twentieth Amendment to the Constitution, which was proclaimed in effect on February 3, 1933. The terms of the President and Vice-President end at noon on that day, and immediately thereafter the President-elect and the Vice-President-elect are sworn into office. (See *Oaths.*)

The retiring President and the President-elect ride together to the Capitol, where the inaugural ceremony takes place out of doors on a temporary platform. If the weather is unfavorable the President-elect takes the special oath prescribed by the Constitution in the Senate Chamber.

When it was suggested to President Franklin D. Roosevelt at his second inauguration, January 20, 1937, that because of the bad weather the ceremony be held inside the Capitol, he said, referring to the throngs outside, "If they can take it, I can."

As soon as he is sworn in the President delivers his inaugural address, in which he usually pours oil on the troubled waters stirred up by the political campaign, outlines his policies, asks all good citizens to aid him in the task ahead, and closes with an appeal for divine help and guidance. The Constitution does not require the President to give an inaugural address, but the precedent set by Washington has been followed ever since.

Inauguration Day also refers to the day on which governors of states and mayors of cities assume office.

Independence Hall—By an agreement signed by the city of Philadelphia and the Federal Government in 1943, Independence Hall and the other historic buildings in Independence Square were made a national shrine. The old State House or main building, which was begun in 1732 and completed in 1759, was the scene of the adoption of the Declaration of Independence by the Continental Congress in 1776, and it was here that the Constitutional Convention of 1787 met. Congress Hall, one of the detached buildings in the group which was erected in 1787, housed the United States Congress from 1790 to 1800. In the courthouse, built in 1790, the early sessions of the United States Supreme Court were held. The Liberty Bell was hung in the tower of the State House (now Independence Hall) in 1753.

Independents—Independent voters are those without any party affiliations or those whose party feality is not strong enough to hold them if they personally disapprove of their party candidate. The name is also applied to the members of a legislative assembly who are laws unto themselves. (See *Mugwumps.*)

169

Indiana—The "Hoosier State." State flower, zinnia. Population, 3,427,796. Area, 36,291 square miles. Capital, Indianapolis. In 1800 the Northwest Territory was divided, Ohio being separated and the remainder being called Indiana Territory. From this, in 1805, Michigan Territory was severed, and in 1809 Illinois Territory. The remnant was admitted to the Union in 1816. Like Illinois, Indiana is in the doubtful column in both national and state elections. Benjamin Harrison, twenty-third President of the United States, was elected to the Senate from Indiana and in 1888 was elected President. The state has eleven representatives in Congress.

Indispensable Man—President Franklin D. Roosevelt's third and fourth term bids led the opposition to cry "indispensable man," "one-man government," and "dictatorship."

Innocuous Desuetude—This phrase was used by President Cleveland in a special message to Congress on March 1, 1886, on the subject of removals from office. He used the words in referring to certain laws which had become dead letters. He said, "After an existence of nearly twenty years of innocuous desuetude these laws are brought forth." Later he said he used the words because he thought they would please the Western taxpayers, who were fond of such things.

Insurgent—A political insurgent is one who rebels against his party, refusing to conform to its policies and decisions. (See *Mugwumps.*)

Insurrection—The Constitution (Article I, Section 8, Clause 15) gives Congress the power to call forth the militia to suppress insurrections. Acts were passed in 1792, 1795, and 1807, giving the President power to call forth the militia when notified by an associate justice of the Supreme Court or a district judge that the execution of the laws is obstructed, and on application of a legislature or a governor when the legislature could not be convened, and to employ also the land and naval forces of the United States.

The Whisky Insurrection was directed against the Federal authority, and the President employed force to suppress it on notification by the Federal judge. During the Buckshot War the governor of Pennsylvania asked for assistance, but it was refused. The governor of Rhode Island made a similar application during the Dorr Rebellion, and the Regulars were held ready for action, but their aid proved unnecessary. These last two cases came under Article IV, Section 4, of the Constitution, which provides that "the United States shall protect" each state "on application of the legislature, or of the executive (when the legislature cannot be convened), against domestic violence." When the Civil War broke out the President was obliged to take prompt steps in calling out the militia, though no application had been made to him as required by the acts of 1792 and 1795. His action was justified by Article II, Section 3, of the Constitution, providing that "he shall take care that the laws be faithfully executed," but Congress on August 6, 1861, formally validated and made legal all Lincoln's previous acts, proclamations, and orders.

The Force Bill of April 20, 1871, gave the President power to call forth the militia and to employ the forces of the United States to suppress disorders intended to deprive any portion of the people of their constitutional rights, even if the state authorities should be unwilling to restore order. During the reconstruction period Federal troops were called for in all the states that had seceded, except Georgia and Florida, to preserve the peace which had been disturbed by attempts to overthrow the newly established Republican administrations in those states.

Interior, Department of—Created by an act of Congress on March 3, 1849, and its Secretary made a member of the Cabinet, the Department of the Interior is charged with the task of bettering the domestic interests of the people of the United States. The Secretary of the Interior has supervision over the surveying and mapping of the country as well as the improvement and administration of all national parks and the drainage and irrigation of land for reclamation purposes. Large dams and the distribution of power therefrom are part of the Secretary's tasks. Indian affairs, including education and relief, come under his supervision. Insular affairs, fisheries, and biological surveys are handled by his department. Dispensing appropriations for agricultural colleges and mechanical institutions is his responsibility. He also has jurisdiction over petroleum resources, and his staff collects data on minerals and mining.

Included among the chief bureaus, divisions, and offices of the department are the Bonneville Power Administration, the Bureau of Mines, Coal Mines Administration, Bureau of Reclamation, Division of Power, Division of Territories and Island Possessions, Fish and Wildlife Service, General Land Office, Geological Survey, Grazing Service, National Park Service, Office of Indian Affairs, Office of Land Utilization, Office of Fishery Co-ordination, Solid Fuels Administration, Petroleum Conservation Division, Southwestern Power Administration, United States Board on Geographical Names, and War Relocation Authority.

International Bank—See *Bretton Woods Conference.*

International Court of Justice—This court is "the principal judicial organ on the United Nations." It was created by the San Francisco Charter to function in accordance with a statute annexed to that instrument. All members of the United Nations are parties to this statute, and each member must comply with the decision of the court in any case to which it is a party. A state which is not a member of the United Nations may on certain conditions become a party to the statute, which is based on that of the old Permanent Court of Justice at the Hague created by the Covenant of the League of Nations and often called the World Court. On February 6, 1946, fifteen of the world's leading jurists were elected to the bench of the new court. (See *United Nations.*) The statute under which this international tribunal functions provides as follows:

STATUTE OF THE INTERNATIONAL COURT OF JUSTICE

Article 1

The International Court of Justice established by the Charter of the United Nations as the principal judicial organ of the United Nations shall be constituted and shall function in accordance with the provisions of the present Statute.

172

CHAPTER I ORGANIZATION OF THE COURT

Article 2

The Court shall be composed of a body of independent judges, elected regardless of their nationality from among persons of high moral character, who possess the qualifications required in their respective countries for appointment to the highest judicial offices, or are jurisconsults of recognized competence in international law.

Article 3

1. The Court shall consist of fifteen members, no two of whom may be nationals of the same state.

2. A person who for the purposes of membership in the Court could be regarded as a national of more than one state shall be deemed to be a national of the one in which he ordinarily exercises civil and political rights.

Article 4

1. The members of the Court shall be elected by the General Assembly and by the Security Council from a list of persons nominated by the national groups in the Permanent Court of Arbitration, in accordance with the following provisions.

2. In the case of Members of the United Nations not represented in the Permanent Court of Arbitration, candidates shall be nominated by national groups appointed for this purpose by their governments under the same conditions as those prescribed for members of the Permanent Court of Arbitration by Article 44 of the Convention of The Hague of 1907 for the pacific settlement of international disputes.

3. The conditions under which a state which is a party to the present Statute but is not a Member of the United Nations may participate in electing the members of the Court shall, in the absence of a special agreement, be laid down by the General Assembly upon recommendation of the Security Council.

Article 5

1. At least three months before the date of the election, the Secretary-General of the United Nations shall address a written request to the members of the Permanent Court of Arbitration belonging to the states which are parties to the present Statute, and to the members of the national groups appointed under Article 4, paragraph 2,

inviting them to undertake, within a given time, by national groups, the nomination of persons in a position to accept the duties of a member of the Court.

2. No group may nominate more than four persons, not more than two of whom shall be of their own nationality. In no case may the number of candidates nominated by a group be more than double the number of seats to be filled.

Article 6

Before making these nominations, each national group is recommended to consult its highest court of justice, its legal faculties and schools of law, and its national academies and national sections of international academies devoted to the study of law.

Article 7

1. The Secretary-General shall prepare a list in alphabetical order of all the persons thus nominated. Save as provided in Article 12, paragraph 2, these shall be the only persons eligible.

2. The Secretary-General shall submit this list to the General Assembly and to the Security Council.

Article 8

The General Assembly and the Security Council shall proceed independently of one another to elect the members of the Court.

Article 9

At every election, the electors shall bear in mind not only that the persons to be elected should individually possess the qualifications required, but also that in the body as a whole the representation of the main forms of civilization and of the principal legal systems of the world should be assured.

Article 10

1. Those candidates who obtain an absolute majority of votes in the General Assembly and in the Security Council shall be considered as elected.

2. Any vote of the Security Council, whether for the election of judges or for the appointment of members of the conference envisaged in Article 12, shall be taken without any distinction between permanent and non-permanent members of the Security Council.

3. In the event of more than one national of the same state ob-

taining an absolute majority of the votes both of the General Assembly and of the Security Council, the eldest of these only shall be considered as elected.

Article 11

If, after the first meeting held for the purpose of the election, one or more seats remain to be filled, a second and, if necessary, a third meeting shall take place.

Article 12

1. If, after the third meeting, one or more seats still remain unfilled, a joint conference consisting of six members, three appointed by the General Assembly and three by the Security Council, may be formed at any time at the request of either the General Assembly or the Security Council, for the purpose of choosing by the vote of an absolute majority one name for each seat still vacant, to submit to the General Assembly and the Security Council for their respective acceptance.

2. If the joint conference is unanimously agreed upon any person who fulfils the required conditions, he may be included in its list, even though he was not included in the list of nominations referred to in Article 7.

3. If the joint conference is satisfied that it will not be successful in procuring an election, those members of the Court who have already been elected shall, within a period to be fixed by the Security Council, proceed to fill the vacant seats by selection from among those candidates who have obtained votes either in the General Assembly or in the Security Council.

4. In the event of an equality of votes among the judges, the eldest judge shall have a casting vote.

Article 13

1. The members of the Court shall be elected for nine years and may be re-elected; provided, however, that of the judges elected at the first election, the terms of five judges shall expire at the end of three years and the terms of five more judges shall expire at the end of six years.

2. The judges whose terms are to expire at the end of the above-mentioned initial periods of three and six years shall be chosen by lot to be drawn by the Secretary-General immediately after the first election has been completed.

3. The members of the Court shall continue to discharge their duties until their places have been filled. Though replaced, they shall finish any cases which they may have begun.

4. In the case of the resignation of a member of the Court, the resignation shall be addressed to the President of the Court for transmission to the Secretary-General. This last notification makes the place vacant.

Article 14

Vacancies shall be filled by the same method as that laid down for the first election, subject to the following provision: the Secretary-General shall, within one month of the occurrence of the vacancy, proceed to issue the invitations provided for in Article 5, and the date of the election shall be fixed by the Security Council.

Article 15

A member of the Court elected to replace a member whose term of office has not expired shall hold office for the remainder of his predecessor's term.

Article 16

1. No member of the Court may exercise any political or administrative function, or engage in any other occupation of a professional nature.

2. Any doubt on this point shall be settled by the decision of the Court.

Article 17

1. No member of the Court may act as agent, counsel, or advocate in any case.

2. No member may participate in the decision of any case in which he has previously taken part as agent, counsel, or advocate for one of the parties, or as a member of a national or international court, or of a commission of enquiry, or in any other capacity.

3. Any doubt on this point shall be settled by the decision of the Court.

Article 18

1. No member of the Court can be dismissed unless, in the unanimous opinion of the other members, he has ceased to fulfil the required conditions.

176

2. Formal notification thereof shall be made to the Secretary-General by the Registrar.

3. This notification makes the place vacant.

Article 19

The members of the Court, when engaged on the business of the Court, shall enjoy diplomatic privileges and immunities.

Article 20

Every member of the Court shall, before taking up his duties, make a solemn declaration in open court that he will exercise his powers impartially and conscientiously.

Article 21

1. The Court shall elect its President and Vice-President for three years; they may be re-elected.

2. The Court shall appoint its Registrar and may provide for the appointment of such other officers as may be necessary.

Article 22

1. The seat of the Court shall be established at The Hague. This, however, shall not prevent the Court from sitting and exercising its functions elsewhere whenever the Court considers it desirable.

2. The President and the Registrar shall reside at the seat of the Court.

Article 23

1. The Court shall remain permanently in session, except during the judicial vacations, the dates and duration of which shall be fixed by the Court.

2. Members of the Court are entitled to periodic leave, the dates and duration of which shall be fixed by the Court, having in mind the distance between The Hague and the home of each judge.

3. Members of the Court shall be bound, unless they are on leave or prevented from attending by illness or other serious reasons duly explained to the President, to hold themselves permanently at the disposal of the Court.

Article 24

1. If, for some special reason, a member of the Court considers that he should not take part in the decision of a particular case, he shall so inform the President.

177

2. If the President considers that for some special reason one of the members of the Court should not sit in a particular case, he shall give him notice accordingly.

3. If in any such case the member of the Court and the President disagree, the matter shall be settled by the decision of the Court.

Article 25

1. The full Court shall sit except when it is expressly provided otherwise in the present Statute.

2. Subject to the condition that the number of judges available to constitute the Court is not thereby reduced below eleven, the Rules of the Court may provide for allowing one or more judges, according to circumstances and in rotation, to be dispensed from sitting.

3. A quorum of nine judges shall suffice to constitute the Court.

Article 26

1. The Court may from time to time form one or more chambers, composed of three or more judges as the Court may determine, for dealing with particular categories of cases; for example, labor cases and cases relating to transit and communications.

2. The Court may at any time form a chamber for dealing with a particular case. The number of judges to constitute such a chamber shall be determined by the Court with the approval of the parties.

3. Cases shall be heard and determined by the chambers provided for in this Article if the parties so request.

Article 27

A judgment given by any of the chambers provided for in Articles 26 and 29 shall be considered as rendered by the Court.

Article 28

The chambers provided for in Articles 26 and 29 may, with the consent of the parties, sit and exercise their functions elsewhere than at The Hague.

Article 29

With a view to the speedy despatch of business, the Court shall form annually a chamber composed of five judges which, at the request of the parties, may hear and determine cases by summary procedure. In addition, two judges shall be selected for the purpose of replacing judges who find it impossible to sit.

Article 30

1. The Court shall frame rules for carrying out its functions. In particular, it shall lay down rules of procedure.

2. The Rules of the Court may provide for assessors to sit with the Court or with any of its chambers, without the right to vote.

Article 31

1. Judges of the nationality of each of the parties shall retain their right to sit in the case before the Court.

2. If the Court includes upon the Bench a judge of the nationality of one of the parties, any other party may choose a person to sit as judge. Such person shall be chosen preferably from among those persons who have been nominated as candidates as provided in Articles 4 and 5.

3. If the Court includes upon the Bench no judge of the nationality of the parties, each of these parties may proceed to choose a judge as provided in paragraph 2 of this Article.

4. The provisions of this Article shall apply to the case of Articles 26 and 29. In such cases, the President shall request one or, if necessary, two of the members of the Court forming the chamber to give place to the members of the Court of the nationality of the parties concerned, and, failing such, or if they are unable to be present, to the judges specially chosen by the parties.

5. Should there be several parties in the same interest, they shall, for the purpose of the preceding provisions, be reckoned as one party only. Any doubt upon this point shall be settled by the decision of the Court.

6. Judges chosen as laid down in paragraphs 2, 3, and 4 of this Article shall fulfil the conditions required by Articles 2, 17 (paragraph 2), 20, and 24 of the present Statute. They shall take part in the decision on terms of complete equality with their colleagues.

Article 32

1. Each member of the Court shall receive an annual salary.

2. The President shall receive a special annual allowance.

3. The Vice-President shall receive a special allowance for every day on which he acts as President.

4. The judges chosen under Article 31, other than members of the Court, shall receive compensation for each day on which they exercise their functions.

5. These salaries, allowances, and compensation shall be fixed by the General Assembly. They may not be decreased during the term of office.

6. The salary of the Registrar shall be fixed by the General Assembly on the proposal of the Court.

7. Regulations made by the General Assembly shall fix the conditions under which retirement pensions may be given to members of the Court and to the Registrar, and the conditions under which members of the Court and the Registrar shall have their traveling expenses refunded.

8. The above salaries, allowances, and compensation shall be free of all taxation.

Article 33

The expenses of the Court shall be borne by the United Nations in such a manner as shall be decided by the General Assembly.

Chapter II   Competence of the Court

Article 34

1. Only states may be parties in cases before the Court.

2. The Court, subject to and in conformity with its Rules, may request of public international organizations information relevant to cases before it, and shall receive such information presented by such organizations on their own initiative.

3. Whenever the construction of the constituent instrument of a public international organization or of an international convention adopted thereunder is in question in a case before the Court, the Registrar shall so notify the public international organization concerned and shall communicate to it copies of all the written proceedings.

Article 35

1. The Court shall be open to the states parties to the present Statute.

2. The conditions under which the Court shall be open to other states shall, subject to the special provisions contained in treaties in force, be laid down by the Security Council, but in no case shall

such conditions place the parties in a position of inequality before the Court.

3. When a state which is not a Member of the United Nations is a party to a case, the Court shall fix the amount which that party is to contribute towards the expenses of the Court. This provision shall not apply if such state is bearing a share of the expenses of the Court.

Article 36

1. The jurisdiction of the Court comprises all cases which the parties refer to it and all matters specially provided for in the Charter of the United Nations or in treaties and conventions in force.

2. The states parties to the present Statute may at any time declare that they recognize as compulsory *ipso facto* and without special agreement, in relation to any other state accepting the same obligation, the jurisdiction of the Court in all legal disputes concerning:

a. the interpretation of a treaty;

b. any question of international law;

c. the existence of any fact which, if established, would constitute a breach of an international obligation;

d. the nature or extent of the reparation to be made for the breach of an international obligation.

3. The declarations referred to above may be made unconditionally or on condition of reciprocity on the part of several or certain states, or for a certain time.

4. Such declarations shall be deposited with the Secretary-General of the United Nations, who shall transmit copies thereof to the parties to the Statute and to the Registrar of the Court.

5. Declarations made under Article 36 of the Statute of the Permanent Court of International Justice and which are still in force shall be deemed, as between the parties to the present Statute, to be acceptances of the compulsory jurisdiction of the International Court of Justice for the period which they still have to run and in accordance with their terms.

6. In the event of a dispute as to whether the Court has jurisdiction, the matter shall be settled by the decision of the Court.

Article 37

Whenever a treaty or convention in force provides for reference of a matter to a tribunal to have been instituted by the League of Nations, or to the Permanent Court of International Justice, the matter shall, as between the parties to the present Statute, be referred to the International Court of Justice.

Article 38

1. The Court, whose function is to decide in accordance with international law such disputes as are submitted to it, shall apply:

a. international conventions, whether general or particular, establishing rules expressly recognized by the contesting states;

b. international custom, as evidence of a general practice accepted as law;

c. the general principles of law recognized by civilized nations;

d. subject to the provisions of Article 59, judicial decisions and the teachings of the most highly qualified publicists of the various nations, as subsidiary means for the determination of rules of law.

2. This provision shall not prejudice the power of the Court to decide a case *ex aequo et bono,* if the parties agree thereto.

CHAPTER III PROCEDURE

Article 39

1. The official languages of the Court shall be French and English. If the parties agree that the case shall be conducted in French, the judgment shall be delivered in French. If the parties agree that the case shall be conducted in English, the judgment shall be delivered in English.

2. In the absence of an agreement as to which language shall be employed, each party may, in the pleadings, use the language which it prefers; the decision of the Court shall be given in French and English. In this case the Court shall at the same time determine which of the two texts shall be considered as authoritative.

3. The Court shall, at the request of any party, authorize a language other than French or English to be used by that party.

Article 40

1. Cases are brought before the Court, as the case may be, either by the notification of the special agreement or by a written application addressed to the Registrar. In either case the subject of the dispute and the parties shall be indicated.

2. The Registrar shall forthwith communicate the application to all concerned.

3. He shall also notify the Members of the United Nations through

the Secretary-General, and also any other states entitled to appear before the Court.

Article 41

1. The Court shall have the power to indicate, if it considers that circumstances so require, any provisional measures which ought to be taken to preserve the respective rights of either party.

2. Pending the final decision, notice of the measures suggested shall forthwith be given to the parties and to the Security Council.

Article 42

1. The parties shall be represented by agents.

2. They may have the assistance of counsel or advocates before the Court.

3. The agents, counsel, and advocates of parties before the Court shall enjoy the privileges and immunities necessary to the independent exercise of their duties.

Article 43

1. The procedure shall consist of two parts: written and oral.

2. The written proceedings shall consist of the communication to the Court and to the parties of memorials, counter-memorials and, if necessary, replies; also all papers and documents in support.

3. These communications shall be made through the Registrar, in the order and within the time fixed by the Court.

4. A certified copy of every document produced by one party shall be communicated to the other party.

5. The oral proceedings shall consist of the hearing by the Court of witnesses, experts, agents, counsel, and advocates.

Article 44

1. For the service of all notices upon persons other than the agents, counsel, and advocates, the Court shall apply direct to the government of the state upon whose territory the notice has to be served.

2. The same provision shall apply whenever steps are to be taken to procure evidence on the spot.

Article 45

The hearing shall be under the control of the President or, if he is unable to preside, of the Vice-President; if neither is able to preside, the senior judge present shall preside.

Article 46

The hearing in Court shall be public, unless the Court shall decide otherwise, or unless the parties demand that the public be not admitted.

Article 47

1. Minutes shall be made at each hearing and signed by the Registrar and the President.

2. These minutes alone shall be authentic.

Article 48

The Court shall make orders for the conduct of the case, shall decide the form and time in which each party must conclude its arguments, and make all arrangements connected with the taking of evidence.

Article 49

The Court may, even before the hearing begins, call upon the agents to produce any document or to supply any explanations. Formal note shall be taken of any refusal.

Article 50

The Court may, at any time, entrust any individual, body, bureau, commission, or other organization that it may select, with the task of carrying out an enquiry or giving an expert opinion.

Article 51

During the hearing any relevant questions are to be put to the witnesses and experts under the conditions laid down by the Court in the rules of procedure referred to in Article 30.

Article 52

After the Court has received the proofs and evidence within the time specified for the purpose, it may refuse to accept any further oral or written evidence that one party may desire to present unless the other side consents.

Article 53

1. Whenever one of the parties does not appear before the Court, or fails to defend its case, the other party may call upon the Court to decide in favor of its claim.

2. The Court must, before doing so, satisfy itself, not only that it has jurisdiction in accordance with Articles 36 and 37, but also that the claim is well founded in fact and law.

Article 54

1. When, subject to the control of the Court, the agents, counsel, and advocates have completed their presentation of the case, the President shall declare the hearing closed.

2. The Court shall withdraw to consider the judgment.

3. The deliberations of the Court shall take place in private and remain secret.

Article 55

1. All questions shall be decided by a majority of the judges present.

2. In the event of an equality of votes, the President or the judge who acts in his place shall have a casting vote.

Article 56

1. The judgment shall state the reasons on which it is based.

2. It shall contain the names of the judges who have taken part in the decision.

Article 57

If the judgment does not represent in whole or in part the unanimous opinion of the judges, any judge shall be entitled to deliver a separate opinion.

Article 58

The judgment shall be signed by the President and by the Registrar. It shall be read in open court, due notice having been given to the agents.

Article 59

The decision of the Court has no binding force except between the parties and in respect of that particular case.

Article 60

The judgment is final and without appeal. In the event of dispute as to the meaning or scope of the judgment, the Court shall construe it upon the request of any party.

185

Article 61

1. An application for revision of a judgment may be made only when it is based upon the discovery of some fact of such a nature as to be a decisive factor, which fact was, when the judgment was given, unknown to the Court and also to the party claiming revision, always provided that such ignorance was not due to negligence.

2. The proceedings for revision shall be opened by a judgment of the Court expressly recording the existence of the new fact, recognizing that it has such a character as to lay the case open to revision, and declaring the application admissible on this ground.

3. The Court may require previous compliance with the terms of the judgment before it admits proceedings in revision.

4. The application for revision must be made at latest within six months of the discovery of the new fact.

5. No application for revision may be made after the lapse of ten years from the date of the judgment.

Article 62

1. Should a state consider that it has an interest of a legal nature which may be affected by the decision in the case, it may submit a request to the Court to be permitted to intervene.

2. It shall be for the Court to decide upon this request.

Article 63

1. Whenever the construction of a convention to which states other than those concerned in the case are parties is in question, the Registrar shall notify all such states forthwith.

2. Every state so notified has the right to intervene in the proceedings; but if it uses this right, the construction given by the judgment will be equally binding upon it.

Article 64

Unless otherwise decided by the Court, each party shall bear its own costs.

CHAPTER IV ADVISORY OPINIONS

Article 65

1. The Court may give an advisory opinion on any legal question at the request of whatever body may be authorized by or in accordance with the Charter of the United Nations to make such a request.

2. Questions upon which the advisory opinion of the Court is asked shall be laid before the Court by means of a written request containing an exact statement of the question upon which an opinion is required, and accompanied by all documents likely to throw light upon the question.

Article 66

1. The Registrar shall forthwith give notice of the request for an advisory opinion to all states entitled to appear before the Court.

2. The Registrar shall also, by means of a special and direct communication, notify any state entitled to appear before the Court or international organization considered by the Court, or, should it not be sitting, by the President, as likely to be able to furnish information on the question, that the Court will be prepared to receive, within a time limit to be fixed by the President, written statements, or to hear, at a public sitting to be held for the purpose, oral statements relating to the question.

3. Should any such state entitled to appear before the Court have failed to receive the special communication referred to in paragraph 2 of this Article, such state may express a desire to submit a written statement or to be heard; and the Court will decide.

Article 67

The Court shall deliver its advisory opinions in open court, notice having been given to the Secretary-General and to the representatives of Members of the United Nations, of other states and of international organizations immediately concerned.

Article 68

In the exercise of its advisory functions the Court shall further be guided by the provisions of the present Statute which apply in contentious cases to the extent to which it recognizes them to be applicable.

CHAPTER V AMENDMENT

Article 69

Amendments to the present Statute shall be effected by the same procedure as is provided by the Charter of the United Nations for amendments to that Charter, subject however to any provisions which the General Assembly upon recommendation of the Security

Council may adopt concerning the participation of states which are parties to the present Statute but are not Members of the United Nations.

Article 70

The Court shall have power to propose such amendments to the present Statute as it may deem necessary, through written communications to the Secretary-General, for consideration in conformity with the provisions of Article 69.

International Monetary Fund—See *Bretton Woods Conference.*

Iowa—"Hawkeye State." State flower, wild rose. Population, 2,538,268. Area, 56,280 square miles. Capital, Des Moines. Under the Louisiana Purchase Treaty it was ceded to the United States in April 1803. It formed at one time part of the Territory of Missouri. Following the admission of Missouri to the Union, Iowa was neglected until 1834, when it was placed under the jurisdiction of Michigan. In 1836 it was transferred to Wisconsin and in 1838 was made into the separate Territory of Iowa. Admission to the Union came in 1846. It has eight representatives in Congress.

Isolationism as a national policy dates from the days of Washington, who in his Farewell Address said that "the great rule of conduct for us in regard to foreign nations is, in extending our commercial relations, to have as little political connection as possible." Adams and Jefferson warned against "entangling alliances," a phrase often construed to mean foreign connections of any kind; and for generations isolationism, with occasional lapses, was a salient part of American foreign policy. Blind devotion to this doctrine kept us from joining the League of Nations after World War I.

World War II, however, destroyed our policy of aloofness. The death knell of isolationism was sounded by the Atlantic Charter, and it came to an end when Congress ratified the charter of the United Nations on August 8, 1945. In January 1946, Secretary of State Byrnes made the following declaration of policy to the United Nations Assembly in London:

"Twenty-five years ago we in the United States were not fully aware of our responsibility. But with others we have learned from experience. This time both the United States government and the people are deeply conscious of their responsibility. This time, on their behalf, I pledge full and wholehearted co-operation." (See *America First.*)

Jackson, Andrew, was born at Waxhaw Settlement, South Carolina, on March 15, 1767, and died at The Hermitage, his residence near Nashville, Tennessee, on January 8, 1845. As a boy he fought in the Revolutionary Army. He then studied law and was admitted to the bar. His early education had been neglected, nor was this shortcoming ever thoroughly repaired.

He served in the House of Representatives from 1796 to 1797 and in the Senate from 1797 to 1798. He had made a name for himself in Tennessee as prosecuting attorney. He had won military glory in fights with the Indians, and his services in the Creek War increased his reputation. He was made a major general and in 1815 won the Battle of New Orleans against the British. From 1823 to 1825 he again served as senator and in 1824 was defeated for the presidency by John Quincy Adams. In the next presidential contest he defeated Adams.

As President he served two terms, from 1829 to 1837. The principal events of his administration were Indian wars, controversies about the United States Bank, nullification troubles, tariff agitation and changes, and the removals from office effected by him. At the end of his second term he retired to private life at The Hermitage.

Jackson was a Democrat. From his time dates a new departure in the politics of this country, namely, the principle of rotation in office for the subordinate employees of the government and the distribution of the offices to political retainers as spoils of the campaign.

In character Jackson was stern, bluff, uncompromising, and most determined. It was due to his energy that the nullification troubles were so promptly quelled, and this same trait was well shown in the persistence of his fight against the United States Bank. His comment on a decision by the Supreme Court in the Cherokee case is indicative of the man. He said: "Well, John Marshall has made his

189

decision; now let him enforce it." (See *Cherokee Case; Coffin Hand-bills; United States Bank.*)

Jackson Day—Democrats in the United States observe January 8 in honor of Andrew Jackson. It is the anniversary of the Battle of New Orleans (1815) and a legal holiday in Louisiana. Celebrations commonly take the form of political dinners.

Jefferson, Thomas, was born in Shadwell, Virginia, on April 2, 1743; he died on the same day as John Adams, July 4, 1826, at Monticello, Virginia. He was graduated from William and Mary College and became a member of the bar. He was a member of the House of Burgesses from 1769 to 1774; between 1775 and 1778 he was a member of the Continental Congress; it was he who wrote the Declaration of Independence, only few changes being made in his draft of that document. In 1779 he became governor of Virginia and retained the post until 1781. He represented this country abroad first generally and then in France. He became Secretary of State under Washington and represented in the latter's Cabinet those principles of strict construction that formed at least the theoretical basis of the party founded by him, the Democratic-Republican. Elected Vice-President under Adams in 1797, he was elected in 1800 to succeed the latter and served as President two terms.

The principal events of his administration were the purchase of Louisiana (by far the most important), the war with the Barbary pirates, and the embargo. At the end of his second term he retired to his home in Monticello, where he passed the remainder of his life. He was the founder of the Democratic-Republican party, now called simply the Democratic party, which has existed to the present day.

Though of aristocratic birth, his sympathies were intensely popular; he hated display and pomp and carried his love of simplicity to the extreme of objecting even to so harmless a title as "Mister." His influence on the government was to check the tendency to extreme centralization which, if developed, might have led to a nation too unpliable and unwieldy for long life.

Jeffersonian Simplicity—Although by birth an aristocrat, Thomas Jefferson loathed display of all kinds. He wore pantaloons instead of knee breeches and rode alone on horseback to his inauguration. Presidential levees were abandoned during his administration. He was responsible for a marked change of manners.

At that period all the barbers in Washington were Federalists because the members of that party in Congress wore powder and long queues which they had dressed daily by the barbers. The Democrats, on the other hand, wore short hair, or at least small queues tied up carelessly with a ribbon, and gave little encouragement to the tonsorial art. One day a United States senator, while being shaved by the leading barber of the city, who was, of course, a Federalist, was surprised to hear the barber burst out suddenly and vehemently against the nomination of Madison for the presidency by the Democratic party, which had been announced just that morning.

"Dear me!" cried the barber. "Surely this country is doomed to disgrace and shame. What presidents we might have, sir! Just look at Daggett of Connecticut and Stockton of New Jersey! What queues they have got, sir—as big as your wrist and powdered every day, sir, like the gentlemen they are. Such men, sir, would confer dignity upon the chief magistracy; but this little Jim Madison, with a queue no bigger than a pipestem! Sir, it is enough to make a man forswear his country."

Johnson, Andrew, was born in Raleigh, North Carolina, on December 29, 1808, and died in Carter County, Tennessee, on July 31, 1875. He was mayor of Greenville, Tennessee; member of the State Legislature in 1835 and State Senate in 1841; congressman from Tennessee from 1843 to 1853. He was at this time a Democrat. From 1853 to 1857 he was governor of Tennessee, and United States senator from 1857 to 1862. In 1862 he was appointed military governor of Tennessee, and in 1864 the Republicans nominated him as Vice-President. On Lincoln's assassination he became President. He began almost at once to quarrel with Congress, and his impeachment marked the culmination of that conflict. (See *Impeachments.*)

The most important matter during his administration was Recon-.

191

struction. Johnson's early education had been neglected to such an extent that it was only after his marriage that he learned to read and write. He was persistent and determined but blind to the political signs of the times. In 1875 he was elected United States senator but served only at the extra session, dying in July.

Judiciary—The judiciary is the third great department of the Federal Government. "The judicial power of the United States," says Article III of the Constitution, "shall be vested in one Supreme Court, and in such inferior courts as the Congress may from time to time ordain and establish."

The system adopted by Congress at its first session remains essentially the same today. At the top stands the United States Supreme Court (*q.v.*), under which is the Circuit Court of Appeals, consisting of ten courts and thirty-seven judges, and below that eighty-three district courts with one hundred and twenty-five judges. Alongside the district courts and also under the Circuit Court of Appeals are the territorial courts for Alaska, Hawaii, Puerto Rico, the Canal Zone, and the Virgin Islands. Quite apart from these are the Court of Claims, which has jurisdiction over claims against the United States, the Court of Customs and Patent Appeals, and the Circuit Court of Appeals for the District of Columbia, over all of which the Supreme Court has appellate jurisdiction.

The jurisdiction of the Federal courts is in general distinct from that of the state courts, though in some cases it is concurrent. The Supreme Court has original jurisdiction only of "cases affecting ambassadors, other public ministers and consuls, and those in which a state shall be a party"; that is to say, only such cases can be commenced in the Supreme Court, but cases decided in other Federal courts can, under certain circumstances, be reviewed by the Supreme Court by virtue of its appellate jurisdiction. Cases decided by the highest courts of any state may be reviewed by the Supreme Court when questions concerning the Constitution, the laws, or treaties of the United States are involved.

The judicial power of the Federal courts also extends to all cases of admiralty and maritime jurisdiction; to controversies in which

192

the United States is a party; to controversies between two or more states, between a state and citizens of another state, between citizens of different states, between citizens of the same state claiming lands under grants of different states, and between a state, or the citizens thereof, and foreign states, citizens, or subjects.

In addition to the regular Federal courts, the Senate, when necessary, sits as a court of impeachment.

Federal judges are appointed by the President, confirmed by the Senate, and hold office during good behavior. Removal is by impeachment proceedings.

Justice, Department of—The office of the Attorney General was created by act of Congress on September 24, 1789, and Edmund Randolph of Virginia was appointed the first Attorney General of the United States. Made a member of the Cabinet in 1814, the chief function of the Attorney General is the enforcement of the Federal laws. As the principal law officer of the United States Government he is called upon to furnish legal counsel in Federal cases and act as legal adviser to the President and the heads of the executive departments. The Attorney General conducts suits in the Supreme Court in which the government is concerned and has under his jurisdiction all Federal penal institutions. He has in charge of a sizable staff of attorneys and marshals throughout the eighty-five judicial districts of the United States and territories. A Bureau of Investigation—the FBI—is conducted by the department. It obtains evidence of crimes which are considered violations of Federal laws and renders assistance to states and territories in the enforcement of the laws. This department did not become known as the Department of Justice until June 23, 1870.

The Department of Justice organization includes the Office of the Solicitor General, which carries on government litigation in the Supreme Court; the Office of the Assistant to the Attorney General, which has administrative supervision of the principal sections of the department and the United States attorneys and marshals; the Office of the Assistant Solicitor General, which is in charge of the legislative work of the department; the Office of the Pardon Attorney; Tax Division; Anti-trust Division; Claims Division; Lands

Division; Criminal Division; Customs Division; Federal Bureau of Investigation; Bureau of Prisons; Immigration and Naturalization Service; Board of Immigration Appeals, and the Parole Board.

Kansas—The "Sunflower State." Sometimes called the "Jayhawker State." State flower, sunflower. Population, 1,801,028. Area, 82,276 square miles. Capital, Topeka. Joined the United States as part of the Louisiana Cession in 1803. It formed part of the Missouri Territory till 1821, and then remained unorganized until 1854, when the Territory of Kansas, which included part of the present state of Colorado, was created by the Kansas-Nebraska Bill. Political dissension over the slavery question was rampant, and civil war raged between 1855 and 1857. At one time the state had two governments and two capitals. It was admitted to the Union in 1861. A state constitutional amendment in 1880 brought prohibition, and in 1912 the suffrage was extended to women. In state politics Kansas is generally found to be Republican. In national politics, however, the state went Democratic in the years 1912, 1916, 1932, and 1936.

It has six representatives in Congress.

Kansas-Nebraska Bill—The Missouri Compromise of 1820 had excluded slavery from the Louisiana Purchase north of 36° 30′ north latitude, except from the state of Missouri, and the Compromise of 1850 was not regarded as having disturbed that arrangement. That part of this region lying west and northwest of Missouri, and stretching to the Rocky Mountains, was known as the Platte Country. In 1851–52 petitions for a territorial organization of this region were presented to Congress, and in 1853 a bill organizing it as the Territory of Nebraska was reported in the House. This bill failed in the Senate.

In the next Congress substantially the same bill was reported to the Senate from the Committee on Territories by Stephen A. Douglas. In the meantime, A. Dixon of Kentucky had given notice that he would move an amendment exempting this territory from the operations of the Missouri Compromise. Douglas, not to be outdone in the service of slavery, had the bill recommitted and reported the following measure:

194

Two territories were to be organized, Kansas to include all of this region in the latitude of Missouri and west of that state, and Nebraska the remainder. The southern boundary of Kansas was moved to 37° north latitude, the strip between 36° 37' and 37° being left to the Indians. Moreover, in order to carry into effect the principle of the Compromise of 1850 (so said the bill), it was provided that: 1. The question of slavery was to be left to the people. 2. Questions involving the title to slaves were to be left to local courts with the right to appeal to the United States Supreme Court. 3. The fugitive slave laws were to apply to the territories. Further, so far as this region was concerned, the Missouri Compromise was declared repealed. In this shape the bill, known as the Kansas-Nebraska Bill, was passed and signed by President Pierce. This measure divided the Whig party, most of the Southern Whigs joining the Democrats. All Northerners opposed to the measure were known as "Anti-Nebraskas," and these joined the party known soon after as Republican.

Kentucky—"Blue Grass State." State flower, goldenrod. Population, 2,845,627. Area, 40,395 square miles. Capital, Frankfort. It became a separate territory in 1790 and was admitted to the Union in 1792. Kentucky did not secede during the Civil War, though it was represented in the Confederate Congress by members chosen by Kentuckians who were fighting on the Southern side. The state has generally been Democratic in politics, although the Whigs held sway from 1836 to 1850 under the leadership of its outstanding citizen, Henry Clay. Other prominent statesmen from Kentucky were John Cabell Breckinridge, Vice-President of the United States from 1857 to 1861; John Jordan Crittenden, United States senator for many years and United States Attorney General in 1841 and 1850. Abraham Lincoln was born in a log cabin in Hardin County in 1809. Daniel Boone explored the state in 1767. It has nine representatives.

Keynote Speech—The keynote speech at a political convention is the party theme song, in which the issues it is deemed desirable to call to the attention of the voters are emphasized. It strikes an ex-

195

alted note and stresses ideals. Sometimes a keynote speech contains a telling phrase that is later used as a party rallying cry.

The keynoter is usually a leading party orator, a citizen of credit and renown, a person who inspires confidence. Since keynote speeches are now broadcast they are carefully timed to reach the greatest number of listeners, and it has lately become the custom to have a woman as well as man keynoter.

Kitchen Cabinet—In addition to his official Cabinet, President Andrew Jackson surrounded himself with a circle of informal and unofficial advisers who were called the Kitchen Cabinet. The name was also applied to a group of intimate friends and advisers of President John Tyler and President Andrew Johnson. (See *Brain Trust; Tennis Cabinet.*)

Knifing—A form of political treachery practiced by political organizations which, through motives of revenge or hatred, seek to defeat one of their own party candidates. While ostensibly supporting the candidate, the organization works secretly against him, sometimes trading with the opposition to support an opposition candidate in exchange for opposition support of one of the organization's candidates, each side thus abandoning one of its own men. This kind of cloak-and-dagger work can often be detected by comparing the votes from the various political subdivisions for any particular candidate with that for the other party candidates and with the returns of previous elections, though sometimes a candidate will be so strong or his opponent so unpopular that party lines will be completely forgotten.

Know-Nothings was the name given to the members of the American party. About 1852, when the Whig party was disintegrating, a secret organization said to have been called "The Sons of '76" or "The Order of the Star-Spangled Banner" was formed. The rank and file of its members knew little about the organization, and their constant answer of "I don't know" to questions about the organization caused them to be called "Know-Nothings." All meetings of the party were secret. It avoided the subject of slavery but was vigorously opposed to Catholics and aliens. Its slogan was "Americans must rule America." At its first national convention in 1856, Millard Fillmore of New York was nominated for President and Andrew J. Donelson for Vice-President. They were endorsed by the Whigs. Fillmore received a popular vote of 850,000 but only succeeded in carrying Maryland. In 1860 other candidates were nominated, but under another party name. (See *Constitutional Union Party.*)

Ku-Klux Klan was an organization that sprang up in the South during the period of reconstruction. Its objects were the suppression of the Negro as a factor in politics; its means, terrorization, ending in many cases in murder. It was a secret organization; its origin is unknown, but it is supposed to have sprung up about 1867 from numerous local associations all having the same end in view.

In its constitution or prescript the name of the association is never mentioned, two asterisks (**) being inserted instead; their local lodges were called *dens;* the masters, *cyclops;* the members, *ghouls.* A county was a *province,* governed by a *grand giant* and four *goblins.* A congressional district was a *dominion,* governed by a *grand Titan* and six *furies.* A state was a *realm,* governed by a *grand dragon* and eight *hydras.* The whole country was the *empire,* governed by a *grand wizard* and ten *genii.*

Their banner was triangular, a black dragon on a yellow field with a red border; their mysteries were never to be written but only orally communicated; the distinctive feature of their dress was a covering for the head descending to the breast, holes being cut for the eyes and mouth, the covering being decorated in any startling or fantastic manner.

The order succeeded in its purpose; the midnight raids of men thus clad, who administered whippings or other punishment, had the effect intended, and the Ku-Klux became a terror to all Negroes, keeping them either from exercising their political rights or else causing them to act with their persecutors. The order, however, outran its original purpose, and where mere whippings did not accomplish the desired end, as with Northern whites who had come South and with the bolder Negroes, murder was resorted to. The disorders grew, and in March 1871 a congressional investigating committee was appointed; in the same month President Grant, in a message to

Congress, asked for legislation to enable the restoration of order in the South, as neither life nor property were there secure, and as the transportation of the mails and the collection of the revenue were interfered with. The Ku-Klux Act or Force Bill was promptly passed. This bill provided for the punishment by fine or imprisonment, or both, of attempts to interfere with the privilege of any citizen to vote, giving the Federal courts cognizance of suits arising thereunder and giving Federal judges power to exclude from juries persons whom they judged to be in sympathy with the accused. In cases where state authorities were unable or unwilling to give adequate protection the President was authorized to employ the military and naval power of the United States to secure the same and suspend the writ of habeas corpus.

The second section of the bill, declaring the punishment for any conspiracy to prevent a person from enjoying his legal rights, was declared unconstitutional by the Supreme Court in 1883. The habeas corpus provision was to remain in force only to the end of the next session of Congress. An attempt to renew it failed in 1872.

In October 1871, President Grant issued two proclamations, the first ordering certain associations in South Carolina to surrender their arms and disguises within five days; the second, at the expiration of the five days, suspending the writ of habeas corpus. Many arrests and convictions followed, and the association was crushed within four months.

The Ku-Klux Klan was known by various other names, as White League and Invisible Empire. The name Ku-Klux has since been applied in a general way to troubles between the Negroes and whites in the South.

The clan was revived by Colonel William J. Simmons of Georgia in 1915, but nothing much was heard of it until after World War I, when it suddenly began to grow and spread like a plague all over the United States. By 1924 it had an active membership of several million and was a potent political force, cowing politicians everywhere and holding the balance of power in Oregon, California, Texas, Oklahoma, Arkansas, Ohio, and Indiana.

The new Klan, like the old, used terroristic methods. It stood for white supremacy and was anti-Semitic and anti-Catholic. But as the prejudices and emotions which marked the postwar period diminished, the strength of the Klan ebbed.

Labor, Department of—This was originally a part of the Department of Commerce and Labor, which was created by act of Congress on February 14, 1903. It was made into a separate department in 1913, with its own Secretary, who is a member of the Cabinet. The welfare of the wage earners of the United States and the betterment of working conditions are matters over which the Secretary of Labor has jurisdiction. Child welfare is another of the department's responsibilities. The Fair Labor Standards Act is administered by this branch of the government. In labor disputes the Secretary of Labor has the power to act as mediator and may appoint conciliation commissioners. Much data on labor conditions—cost of living, employment, and pay rolls—are published by the department. Alien immigration and the naturalization laws are under its supervision.

The principal bureaus and divisions of the Department of Labor are the Bureau of Labor Statistics, the Children's Bureau, Division of Labor Standards, United States Conciliation Service, Wage and Hour and Public Contracts divisions, which enforce the provisions of the Fair Labor Standards Act in the matter of wages and hours, and the Women's Bureau.

Lame Duck Session—See *House of Representatives.*

League of Women Voters—This is a non-partisan organization which neither endorses nor supports parties but aims to promote intelligent participation in government by letting people know not only how a democratic government functions, but also what the average citizen's relationship is to his government. It helps people overcome their feeling of frustration by showing that pressure in the general interest can outweigh pressure in any special interest; that strong public opinion has power. In short, the League seems to be dedicated to arousing in women an appreciation and acceptance of the responsibilities of good citizenship.

Founded in 1920, the year of adoption of the Nineteenth Amendment granting equal suffrage to women, and with a membership consisting of persons of every party and background, the League of Women Voters is organized in fifteen hundred communities throughout the country.

Liberal Republican Party—Many Republicans were dissatisfied with Grant's first term as President. They believed that the national government had exceeded the proper limits of its power in its treatment of reconstruction problems. These Republicans met in convention in Cincinnati in 1872. Carl Schurz was elected chairman. A platform was adopted demanding civil-service reform, local self-government, and universal amnesty, recognizing the equality of all men, recommending the resumption of specie payments, but remitting the questions of protection and free trade to Congress because of the existence in the convention of "honest but irreconcilable differences of opinion" on that subject. Horace Greeley and B. Gratz Brown were named for President and Vice-President. This platform and these nominations were adopted by the regular Democratic convention of that year. Nevertheless, about thirty thousand members of that party voted for Charles O'Conor of New York and John Quincy Adams of Massachusetts, the nominees of a purely Democratic convention, notwithstanding that these candidates had declined the nomination. Some of the members of the Cincinnati convention, deeming the nominations made there to be a mistake, met in New York in June and named William S. Groesbeck of Ohio and Frederick L. Olmstead of New York. The Republican nominee, Grant, was elected by an enormous majority, and the Liberal Republican party was thereafter practically dead, although a few congressmen still clung to the name.

Liberator, The—Uncompromising anti-slavery journal launched by William Lloyd Garrison in Boston in 1831 and continued until 1865.

Liberty Bell—This famous bell hangs in Independence Hall, Philadelphia, where the Declaration of Independence was signed. It was rung to hail the adoption of that document in 1776. Later recast in this country, the bell was inscribed, "Proclaim liberty throughout all the land, to all the inhabitants thereof." It was cracked in 1835 while tolling for the death of Chief Justice John Marshall.

Liberty Party—A meeting of Abolitionists held in Warsaw, New York, in 1839, had incidentally nominated James G. Birney for President and Francis J. Lemoyne for Vice-President. The nominations were confirmed by a convention, ostensibly national, that met in Albany on April 1, 1840, and here the name Liberty party was adopted. Its platform was the abolition of slavery. These candidates received 7,059 votes in spite of their having declined the nominations. Thereafter candidates for various local offices were put in nomination.

On August 30, 1844, the national convention of the party met. The topic of greatest interest at that time was the annexation of Texas and the consequent increase in our slave territory. On August 16 a letter of Clay's had been published in which he declared "that, far from having any *personal* objection to the annexation of Texas, *I should be glad to see it,* without dishonor, without war, with the common consent of the Union and upon just and fair terms."

This caused the convention to name its own candidates, and Birney and Thomas Morris of Ohio were nominated. The total vote for Birney was 62,263. Had the electoral vote of New York gone to Clay, it would have elected him. In that state the popular vote stood: Polk 237,488, Clay 232,482, Birney 15,812. Had Birney not been nominated, it is probable that enough of his vote to elect Clay would have been so cast—certainly none of it would have gone to Polk. The same was true in Michigan. Thus Polk, the candidate representing annexation, was elected by the votes of those opposed to the project. This lesson was not forgotten, and the party did not again name its own candidates. In 1848 and 1852 it supported the Free Soil party, and thereafter the Republicans.

Lincoln, Abraham, the sixteenth President of the United States, was born in Hardin County, Kentucky, on February 12, 1809. In 1830 he moved with his family to Macon County, Illinois. From there he made several trips to New Orleans as a flatboatman, and on his return superintended a flour mill near Springfield. In 1832 he enlisted in the Black Hawk War and served as a captain.

When he returned to civil life he entered politics and ran for the State Legislature but was defeated, his first and only defeat in a popular election. He then returned to business pursuits, in which he was unsuccessful. His schooling had been inconsiderable, but he had taken advantage of every opportunity for improvement, and after his want of success in business he was for a while a surveyor, but financial troubles compelled him to drop that employment in 1837. During that time he was studying law in his leisure hours, and in 1836 he was admitted to the bar.

In 1834 he was elected to the Illinois Legislature, in which he served four successive terms; he twice received the vote of his party, the Whig, for the speakership, but was neither time elected. After retiring from the Legislature he practiced law and in 1846 was elected to Congress, being the only Whig Congressman from Illinois. He declined a renomination and was defeated as a candidate for the Senate, and then returned to his law practice.

Lincoln and Douglas had been opposed to each other in so many debates that people naturally turned to the former to answer any of Douglas's speeches. In 1858 Douglas stumped the state to aid his canvass for the United States Senate; Lincoln was nominated to oppose him, and the two held seven joint debates at different points in the state. These debates attracted universal attention and largely increased Lincoln's reputation. The Republican popular vote was larger than the Democratic, but the election was by the Legislature, which chose Douglas.

In 1859 the Ohio Democrats summoned Douglas to aid them in their canvass for governor, and the Republicans naturally appealed to Lincoln, who responded. In 1860, at the request of the Young Men's Republican Club of New York, he delivered an address in that city on the political situation, closing with the words: "Let us have faith that right makes might, and in the faith let us to the end dare to do our duty as we understand it." On May 18, 1860, the Republican National Convention met in Chicago and nominated Lincoln for the presidency. He was elected, and on March 4, 1861, he was inaugurated.

His administration was marked by the Civil War. In 1864 he was re-elected. On the evening of April 14, 1865, he was shot while attending a performance at Ford's Theater, Washington, by John Wilkes Booth, a Southern sympathizer. He lingered until the next morning, when he died.

As stated before, Lincoln was self-educated, and the simplicity and generosity that characterized his early life were maintained by him throughout his career. Even during the darkest hours of the war, with the weight of the whole struggle resting upon him, while numberless matters engrossed his attention, no one was refused an audience, and in every case of appeal to executive clemency relief was granted if there were any mitigating circumstances. Though abhorring slavery and opposing its extension, he was not an Abolitionist, as has frequently been charged; he was of the people and always kept in touch with them. His humor was irrepressible, and even the gravest subject was enlivened by a story; but in his disposition there was a streak of profound melancholy most strongly manifest while the responsibility of the war lay heaviest upon him.

"Little Group of Willful Men"—In March 1917, a few days before Congress adjourned, eleven members of the Senate filibustered against the armed merchant ship bill and succeeded in preventing the passage of the measure. President Wilson had asked Congress for authorization to arm merchant vessels to protect themselves from German submarines. The bill passed the House by a vote of 403 to 13, and most of the Senate membership favored it, but a small minority group managed to hold the floor until adjournment. President Wilson, in a sharp note, said, "A little group of willful men, representing no opinion but their own, have rendered the great government of the United States helpless and contemptible." He asked the Senate to change its rules, and this resulted in the adoption of the Closure Rule of 1917. (See *Cloture*.)

Lobby—The term is applied collectively to the persons who make a business of frequenting the lobbies of legislative assemblies to solicit or influence the members regarding pending legislation. The individual lobbyist may seek to accomplish his purpose corruptly by the payment of money or by other tempting means, or he may legitimately confine himself to persuading members to take a certain line of action toward particular bills. Lobbying has become a lucrative profession which has attracted women as well as men. Much of it is done nowadays in hotels and cocktail bars. It is through the lobby that business and other groups with special interests put pressure on legislators. The lobby is sometimes referred to as the Third House. (See *Pressure Group*.)

Locke's Carolina Constitution—In 1669 Lord Shaftesbury, one of the proprietaries of the Carolina Colony, had a constitution prepared by the philosopher, John Locke, for the government of that colony, by means of which an endeavor was made to establish in America what can only be called a feudal empire.

The constitution contained one hundred and twenty articles. The eight proprietaries who held the grant of the Carolina colonies were to combine the dignity and power of a governor and an upper house of the legislature. Their position and rule were to be hereditary, and their number was never to be increased or diminished, for in case of death of a member without heirs his survivors elected a successor. The territory contained in the grant was divided into counties, each containing 480,000 acres, and this was again divided into five parts, of which one remained the inalienable property of the proprietaries, and another formed the inalienable and indivisible estate of the nobility, of which, according to the constitution, there were two orders—one earl and two barons for each county. The remaining three fifths were reserved for the people and might be held by lords of the manor who were not hereditary legislators.

The members of the nobility might neither be increased nor diminished, election supplying all places left vacant for want of heirs. All political rights were dependent upon hereditary wealth. The cultivators of the soil were each allowed the use of ten acres at a fixed rent but could not purchase land or exercise the right of suffrage. They were adscripts to the soil, were under jurisdiction of their lord without right of appeal to the courts. The supervision of everything in the colonies was vested in a Court of Appeals and seven inferior courts, but no lawyers were allowed to plead for money or reward. The religion was to be that of the Church of

England. Of course all attempts to foist such a scheme of government on the few scattered Huguenots who formed the population met with deserved failure and after twenty years was abandoned.

Locofocos—Previous to 1846 the system of incorporating banks in the state of New York had been by means of special legislation. The removal, in 1833, of United States deposits from the Bank of the United States to state banks and the prospects of failure of the attempts to have that bank's charter renewed led to the formation of many new banks. The practice of former days of purchasing these charters from the legislature was revived, and the scandal assumed such proportions that in 1835 a number of Democrats in New York City, chiefly members of Tammany Hall, organized for the purpose of opposing the banks. They called themselves the Equal Rights party.

A meeting of this faction, held in Tammany Hall on October 29, 1835, was also attended by the regular or Tammany Democrats, who attempted to control the proceedings. Failing in this, they turned off the gas. The Equal Rights men lit locofoco matches and proceeded to hold their meeting. Their opponents, Democrats and Whigs, seized on this circumstance to give them a nickname, and the term clung first to them and subsequently to the whole Democratic party for some years, for the Whigs delighted to brand their opponents as opposed to the "moneyed interests of the country" and would not relinquish a nickname so well suited to their purpose.

The administration of Van Buren, committed as it was to the sub-treasury system, drew the locofocos back into the party, but their influence, while it lasted, was potent, especially in New York.

Louisiana—"Creole State" or, as it is sometimes called, the "Pelican State." State flower, magnolia. Population, 2,363,880. Area, 48,523 square miles. Capital, Baton Rouge. Entered the Union in 1812. Union forces took control of the lower half of the state during the Civil War, and many political problems brought chaos until about 1876. The state has been quite consistently Democratic and has remained on the Democratic side of the fence in national elections since the Civil War.

Huey Long, known as the "Kingfish," was elected governor of

205

the state in 1928 and became a virtual dictator in Louisiana politics. He later went to the United States Senate. In September 1935 he was assassinated and his widow was appointed to the Senate vacancy.

The state has eight representatives in Congress.

Logrolling—A form of political bargaining by which a member of a legislature secures support for a bill in which he is interested by promising in return to support the measure of another member. The term is said to have originated in the practice of American lumbermen helping each other roll large logs down to the water.

Machine—Aaron Burr was apparently the first person to attach the word "machine" to the organization of a political party. It was formerly used to indicate an organization dominated by self-seeking politicians and is still used in a more or less derogatory sense.

Madison, James, was born in Port Conway, Virginia, on March 16, 1751, and died in Montpelier, in the same state, on June 28, 1836. He was graduated from Princeton College and was admitted to the bar. In 1776 he was a member of the Virginia Legislature. From 1780 to 1783, and from 1786 to 1788 he served in the Continental Congress. He was also a member of the convention of 1787; in fact, a resolution offered by him in the Virginia Legislature led to that convention. Between 1789 and 1797 he served in Congress. He was Secretary of State under Jefferson and was elected to succeed him as President in 1809. His administration was forced into the War of 1812 with England, and that struggle was the principal event of his administration. He served two terms. He was in close sympathy with Jefferson, whose views he shared and by whom he was implicitly trusted. He was an able writer and one of the founders of the Democratic-Republican party, now known simply as the Democratic party.

Maine—The "Pine Tree State" or, as it is sometimes called, the "Lumber State." State flower, pine cone. Population, 847,226. Area, 33,215 square miles. Capital, Augusta. Admitted to the Union in 1820. It had been a part of Massachusetts. Prior to the Civil War,

Maine was Democratic for the most part but has since been found mostly in the Republican column. Hannibal Hamlin, prior to being elected Vice-President of the United States (1861–65), was a United States representative, a United States senator, and governor of Maine. Another renowned statesman from Maine was James Gillespie Blaine, twice unsuccessful Republican nominee for the presidency of the United States. It was during the Blaine-Grover Cleveland campaign for the presidency in 1884 that the Reverend S. D. Burchard referred to the Democratic party as "the party whose antecedents are rum, Romanism, and rebellion." Still another was Thomas Brackett Reed, member of the United States House of Representatives, who in 1889 became Speaker of the House. The state has three representatives.

Manifest Destiny—This phrase came into circulation in 1844, when the question of the annexation of Texas was a leading issue of the presidential campaign. It referred to the political doctrine that it was our manifest destiny to spread all over the continent. It was employed afterward on various occasions, President McKinley even using it in speaking of our annexation of the Hawaiian Islands.

Maryland—Known as the "Free State." State flower, black-eyed Susan. Population, 1,821,244. Area, 10,577 square miles. Capital, Annapolis. An original state of the Union. In 1767 a boundary was formed that became known as the Mason and Dixon Line; it was the dividing line between the states of the South where slavery was practiced and the free states of the North. Fort McHenry is located in this state, and the attack upon that fort in 1814 inspired Francis Scott Key to write "The Star-Spangled Banner." One of the state's prominent men was Charles Carroll of Carrollton, a signer of the Declaration of Independence. With few exceptions Maryland has been, in state politics, Democratic. In national politics it has generally gone Democratic since 1868, with brief switches to the Republican side. It was Republican in 1920 and 1928. The state has six representatives.

Mason and Dixon's Line—During the discussion in Congress over the Missouri Compromise, John Randolph of Virginia made

207

frequent use of this phrase to indicate the dividing line between free and slave territory. Originally the line was the parallel of latitude 39° 43′ 26.3″, separating Pennsylvania from Maryland. It took its name from two English mathematicians and astronomers, Charles Mason and Jeremiah Dixon, who between 1763 and 1767 traced the greater part of the line. By popular usage the line was extended along the course of the Ohio River to the Mississippi, and thence westward along the parallel of 36° 30′, the southern boundary of Missouri, though that state itself was slave territory.

Massachusetts—"Bay State." State flower, mayflower. Population, 4,316,721. Area, 8,257 square miles. Capital, Boston. The Pilgrim Fathers landed at Plymouth Rock from Plymouth, England, on the *Mayflower* in 1620. The Massachusetts Bay Company governed the colony from 1629 to 1684, and only those who were admitted to the company or were connected with the Congregational Church were permitted to vote and participate in the government. The Boston Tea Party episode occurred in December 1773, when some patriots dumped British tea into the harbor in protest against taxation without representation.

In modern national politics Massachusetts has been Republican, though the state went Democratic for Woodrow Wilson in 1912 and has been Democratic in the last five presidential elections. The state has furnished such outstanding men as John Adams, second President of the United States; John Quincy Adams, sixth President of the United States, and Daniel Webster, who was a member of the United States House of Representatives as well as Senate, and later became Secretary of State. Calvin Coolidge, who succeeded to the presidency upon the death of President Harding, was governor of Massachusetts in 1919 and 1920.

The state has fourteen representatives.

Mayflower Compact—This celebrated document by which the Pilgrim Fathers combined themselves into "a civill body politick" was signed on the lid of Elder Brewster's chest in the cabin of the *Mayflower* as that vessel lay at anchor in Plymouth Harbor before either passengers or cargo had been discharged. There had been "discontented and mutinous speeches" and threats by some that they "would use their own liberty" when they got ashore. Nevertheless, forty-one of the men signed the document, each putting against his name the number of his family.

The names of the signers who are known as the Pilgrim Fathers were John Carver, William Bradford, Edward Winslow, William Brewster, Isaac Allerton, Myles Standish, John Alden, Samuel Fuller, Christopher Martin, William Mullins, William White, Richard Warren, John Howland, Stephen Hopkins, Edward Tilly, John Tilly, Francis Cooke, Thomas Rogers, Thomas Tinker, John Ridgdale, Edward Fuller, John Turner, Francis Eaton, James Chilton, John Crackston, John Billington, Moses Fletcher, John Goodman, Degory Prist, Thomas Williams, Gilbert Winslow, Edward Margeson, Peter Brown, Richard Britteridge, George Soule, Richard Clarke, Richard Gardiner, John Allerton, Thomas English, Edward Doty, Edward Leister.

The agreement which these men signed reads as follows:

> In the name of God, Amen. We whose names are underwritten, the loyall subjects of our dread soveraigne Lord, King James, by the grace of God, of Great Britaine, Franc, & Ireland king, defender of the faith, &c., haveing undertaken, for the glorie of God, and advancement of the Christian faith, and honour of our king & countrie, a voyage to plant the first colonie in the Northerne parts of Virginia, doe by these presents solemnly & mutualy in the presence of God, and one of another, covenant & combine our selves togeather into a civill body politick, for our better ordering & preservation & furtherance of the ends aforesaid; and by vertue hearof to enacte, constitute, and frame such just & equall lawes, ordinances, acts, constitutions, & offices, from time to time, as shall be thought most meete & convenient for the generall good of the Colonie, unto which we promise all due submission and obedience. In witnes wherof we have hereunder subscribed our names at Cap-Codd the 11. of November, in the year of the raigne of our soveraigne lord, King James, of England, France, & Ireland the eighteenth, and of Scotland the fiftie fourth. Anno: Dom. 1620.

McKinley, William—William McKinley, like his predecessor, Grover Cleveland, came from a large family of modest means. He was born on January 29, 1843, in Niles, Ohio. He attended schools in his native state and was for a short time a student at Allegheny College, but financial reasons forced him to discontinue his education. For a brief period McKinley taught school to make a living. At the opening of the Civil War he enlisted as a private and distinguished himself as a soldier, holding the rank of major at the close of his career in the Army.

After his release from the service he studied law and returned to Ohio to practice in Canton. In 1869 he became prosecuting attorney of Stark County. In 1876 the people elected McKinley to the House of Representatives in Washington, and except for a few months in 1884, he served as a congressman from Ohio until 1891.

McKinley's amiable manner and active participation in politics accounted for a steady increase in his popularity, and in 1891 the people of Ohio chose to elect him governor and to re-elect him in 1893.

In 1896 McKinley defeated William Jennings Bryan, his Democratic opponent, to become President in one of the most exciting campaigns in political history. Bryan was championing free silver in his party platform, and the Republicans' coming out squarely for the gold standard helped to draw a large number of votes. McKinley's close adviser, Marcus A. Hanna, a multimillionaire and a shrewd political promoter, also contributed heavily to the success of the contest.

McKinley was a firm believer in high protective duties and was considered an authority on industrial welfare and tariff issues. During his first term many bills were passed to aid the prosperity of the small independent manufacturer.

Domestic issues, however, were of lesser importance than international problems in the first four years of the McKinley administration. On April 21, 1898, the United States declared war on Spain and supported Cuba in her struggle for independence. In 1898 the formal annexing of the Hawaiian Islands was effected. About this same time the United States was also taking active part with other European powers in the defeat of the Boxer Rebellion in China. It was after the Boxers had been subdued that John Hays, then Secretary of State, made his earnest plea for the "Open Door" policy in the Far East.

210

General prosperity in the country and the easy success and victories on foreign questions put the McKinley administration in good favor, and in 1900, with Theodore Roosevelt as his running mate, McKinley was re-elected President. Not long afterward he was making a tour of the country and stopped off at the Pan-American Exposition in Buffalo, where he was shot on September 6, 1901, by an anarchist, Leon Czolgosz, who was quickly apprehended and afterward electrocuted. The President, who had been fatally wounded, died on September 14 in Buffalo. It was the third assassination of a President within a period of thirty-six years.

It has often been said that William McKinley was not a great man but that he made an excellent President. He rarely quarreled and was tactful and conciliatory by nature. Naturally timid and cautious, he was more inclined to feel out public opinion before making decisions than to be aggressive and independent in his actions. His opponents called him a "statesman with his ear to the ground." Although he did not possess great qualities of leadership, his faults were offset by his dignified, honest manner and character and his popular appeal and ability to preserve harmony among the people with whom he worked and served.

Mecklenburg Declaration—At a midnight meeting of the militia of Mecklenburg County, North Carolina, in May 1775, a declaration was adopted which declared that the people of that county were free and independent of the British Crown. The general tenor of the document and much of its phraseology were word for word those of the Declaration of Independence. A fire in 1800 is said to have destroyed the original record of the meeting. It is a disputed question whether the Declaration of Independence followed the words of the Mecklenburg Declaration or whether the latter, having possibly been rewritten from memory, was colored by the former.

Mending Fences—A politician is said to be engaged in mending his fences when he is busy among his constituents, quietly looking after and strengthening his own political interests. The term had its origin just before the Republican National Convention in 1880, when John Sherman, a prominent candidate for the Republican nomination, was at his farm in Mansfield, Ohio. A reporter in quest of political news found Sherman and his brother-in-law, Colonel Moulton, in a field replacing some fence rails. In reply to the reporter's question as to what Sherman was doing, Colonel Moulton avoided talking politics by saying, "Why, you can see for yourself. He's mending his fences."

Michigan—"Wolverine State." State flower, appleblossom. Population, 5,256,106. Area, 58,216 square miles. Capital, Lansing. Michigan was once part of the Northwest Territory and then of Indiana Territory, from which it was set off under its own name in 1805. It was enlarged several times, but in 1836 Wisconsin was cut off from it, leaving its limits much as they are today. (See *Toledo War*.) It was admitted as a state in 1837. The state has usually been Republican in both state and national elections, although in 1912 it went on the Progressive band wagon and also supported Franklin D. Roosevelt in 1932, 1936, and 1944. Lewis Cass, an outstanding political figure, was governor of Michigan Territory from 1813 to 1831. He was Secretary of War under Jackson, Secretary of State under Buchanan, and United States senator from Michigan from 1845 to 1857. He was an unsuccessful candidate for the presidency in 1848. Michigan has seventeen representatives in Congress.

Midnight Judges—To gain every possible advantage for their party, the Federalists, who were defeated in the presidential election of 1800, created twenty-three new judgeships, all of them quite unnecessary, and on the last day of his term President John Adams was kept busy until late at night signing the commissions of the new judges. Early the next morning he slipped out of Washington without waiting to participate in the inauguration of his successor, Thomas Jefferson. The judges whose commissions Adams signed at the last minute of the twelfth hour became known as Midnight Judges.

Minnesota—Generally known as the "Gopher State." State flower, lady slipper or moccasin flower. Population, 2,792,300. Area, 84,068 square miles. Capital, St. Paul. The portion of Minnesota

212

east of the Mississippi formed part of the Northwest Territory, and the portion west of the river was part of the Louisiana Purchase. It was organized as a territory, together with the Dakotas, in 1849 and was admitted to the Union in 1858. The state has been Republican, but with pronounced independent tendencies. Occasionally the Democrats have managed to elect a governor, but in national elections the state has, on the whole, been Republican from the time it was admitted to the Union. It has nine representatives.

Mississippi—The "Magnolia State." State flower, magnolia. Population, 2,183,276. Area, 47,716. Capital, Jackson. The organization of Mississippi Territory, which included what is now Alabama, began in 1798 and was completed two years later. The state was admitted to the Union in 1817. Its constitution is aimed at maintaining the supremacy of the whites. Mississippi, with few exceptions, has been Democratic politically. Jefferson Davis, though born in Kentucky, spent most of his boyhood and later years in Mississippi. He was chosen president of the Confederacy in 1861 and elected president by popular vote for a term of six years, his inauguration taking place on February 22, 1862. The state has seven representatives.

Missouri—The "Show Me State." State flower, hawthorn. Population, 3,784,664. Area, 69,674 square miles. Capital, Jefferson City. Originally part of the Louisiana Purchase, Missouri was admitted to the Union in 1821. Prior to the state's admission to the Union there was considerable bitterness over the question of slavery. This was settled by the Missouri Compromise, whereby it was admitted to the Union as a slave state, but slavery was prohibited in most of the territory. Missouri has been strongly Democratic, though the Republicans carried the state in 1908, 1920, 1924, and 1928. Champ Clark, a prominent though unsuccessful candidate for the presidential nomination in 1912, was an outstanding Missourian. President Harry S. Truman is from Missouri. The state has thirteen representatives.

Missouri Compromise—On the admission of Louisiana as a state, the remainder of the Louisiana Purchase was organized as the

Territory of Missouri. In 1818 the portion now comprising the state of Missouri applied for admission to the Union. In 1819 a bill for this purpose, containing a clause prohibiting slavery, was passed by the House, but it was defeated by the Senate. In 1820 a bill was sent by the Senate to the House providing for the admission of Maine and containing a rider authorizing Missouri to organize. There was no objection to the admission of Maine, the House having already passed a bill for that purpose, but it refused to allow the Senate to force its views on the Missouri question upon it. The Senate bill was accordingly disagreed to.

A compromise was now patched up on the basis of a resolution of Senator Thomas of Illinois. The Missouri and Maine bills were to be separated. Missouri was to be admitted as a slave state, but slavery was to be prohibited in the remainder of the Louisiana Purchase north of 36° 30′ north latitude. There was also a clause providing for the return of fugitive slaves. A provision in the constitution adopted by Missouri, forbidding its legislature to emancipate slaves and ordering it to prevent the immigration of free Negroes, led to further opposition, and at the next session of Congress, in February 1821, Missouri was required to bind herself that the citizens of other states should enjoy all privileges "to which they are entitled under the Constitution of the United States."

Henry Clay was largely instrumental in bringing about this compromise; he was chairman of the last committee. Yet so little did he foresee its consequences that he is reported to have said to a Missouri delegate after its passage, "Now, go home and prepare your state for gradual emancipation." Maine was admitted in 1820, Missouri in 1821.

Moderator—The presiding officer at a town meeting (*q.v.*).

Monroe, James, fifth President of the United States, was born in Westmoreland County, Virginia, on April 29, 1758, and died on July 4, 1831. After attending William and Mary College he read law under Thomas Jefferson. In 1782 he became a member of the Virginia Legislature, and the following year he was a member of the Continental Congress, in which body he served until 1786. He

214

was United States senator from 1790 to 1794. He served as Minister to France from 1794 to 1796 and was governor of Virginia from 1799 to 1802. He was again appointed Minister to France to negotiate the purchase of Louisiana, and later became Minister to Great Britain and to Spain. In 1811 he was once more governor of Virginia. During Madison's administration he became Secretary of State, retaining that position until the end of Madison's second term. He succeeded Madison to the presidency in 1817, defeating Rufus King, the Federalist candidate, by 183 electoral votes to 34. Party strife died away during his terms in office, which became known as the "Era of Good Feeling." Monroe, who belonged to the Republican party of his day, would have been unanimously elected to a second term but for the action of a single elector from New Hampshire who voted against him because he thought Washington alone should have that honor. Monroe's most important act was the announcement of the doctrine which bears his name (see *Monroe Doctrine*), and the most important measure of his administration was the Missouri Compromise (*q.v.*).

Monroe Doctrine—In his annual message to Congress in 1823, President Monroe announced the doctrine which bears his name. He said: "We owe it, therefore, to candor, and to the amicable relations existing between the United States and those powers, to declare that we should consider any attempt on their part to extend their system to any portion of this hemisphere as dangerous to our peace and safety. With the existing colonies or dependencies of any European power we have not interfered and shall not interfere. But with the governments who have declared their independence and maintained it, and whose independence we have on great consideration and on just principles acknowledged, we could not view any interposition for the purpose of oppressing them or controlling in any other manner their destiny by any European power in any other light than as the manifestation of an unfriendly disposition toward the United States."

President Monroe also said in this same historic message: ". . . the occasion has been judged proper for asserting, as a principle in which the rights and interests of the United States are involved, that

215

the American continents, by the free and independent condition which they have assumed and maintain, are henceforth not to be considered as subjects for future colonization by any European powers."

This momentous declaration of American foreign policy was called forth by the fear that the Holy Alliance, which had lately been formed in Europe, would assist Spain in regaining control of her lost South American colonies, and apprehension over a claim which Russia had advanced to a part of the Pacific coast. England backed this country in the stand taken on the question of interference with the independence of the former Spanish colonies in South America, and the European allies dropped any design which they may have had on the new governments in this hemisphere.

Montana—Known as the "Treasure State." State flower, bitter-root. Population, 559,456. Area, 147,138 square miles. Capital, Helena. Under the Louisiana Purchase Treaty, Montana was ceded to the United States in 1803. The territory became organized in 1864 and in 1889 was admitted to the Union. In the last ten presidential elections it has gone Democratic six times. The terrific battle in the summer of 1876 between the Sioux Indians, led by Sitting Bull, and General Custer is of historical interest. The state has two seats in the House of Representatives.

Muckrake—In a speech delivered on April 14, 1906, at the laying of the cornerstone of the House of Representatives office building in Washington, President Theodore Roosevelt put the word "muckrake" into circulation, when he scored a then popular and sensational brand of journalism in which public men and private corporations were exposed and unmercifully assailed. He said:

"In Bunyan's *Pilgrim's Progress* you may recall the description of the Man with the Muckrake, the man who could look no way but downward with the muckrake in his hand; who was offered a celestial crown for his muckrake but who could neither look up nor regard the crown he was offered but continued to rake to himself the filth of the floor. Muckraking leads to slander that may attack an honest man or even assail a bad man with untruth. An epidemic of

216

indiscriminate assault upon character does no good but very great harm. Mudslinging is as bad as whitewashing. . . . Men with the muckrake are often indispensable to the well-being of society, but only if they know when to stop raking the muck."

Mugwumps—The nomination of James G. Blaine for President in 1884 caused a revolt in the Republican party, many Republicans, especially in New York and New England, throwing their support to Cleveland. These disgruntled Republicans were reproachfully called mugwumps. They had bolted Blaine's nomination because of the scandals with which his name had been associated and because they objected to his handling of foreign affairs while Secretary of State. The election was a close one, and the mugwumps undoubtedly contributed materially to the Cleveland victory, particularly in New York. The name "mugwump" was soon given to all independent voters. (See *Pivotal State; Crédit Mobilier; Tattooed Man.*)

Municipal Government—There are three major types of municipal government in use in American cities today. They are: (1) the mayor-council form; (2) the commission form, and (3) the council-manager form.

The first of these, the mayor-council form, varies in structure, the mayor sometimes being placed in a strong position, with the power to appoint and remove department heads, veto acts of the council, and the right to prepare the city budget for the consideration of the council. In its weaker form the mayor is largely without these powers and is little more than a figurehead.

The commission form, which originated in Galveston, Texas, when that city was visited by a tidal wave at the turn of the century, is usually made up of five commissioners, elected at large, who constitute the legislative body of the municipality, with each commissioner also serving as head of an administrative department. Constitutional provisions which divide government into legislative, executive, and judicial departments are held by the courts to apply to state and not to local governments.

The council-manager form was first used in Sumter, South Carolina, in 1912, and is now in operation in upward of six hundred communities. The main feature of this governmental method is a small council generally elected at large in which is centered the legislative power and control over finances. A professionally trained city manager is employed by the council, and he is charged with the administration of city affairs. He possesses the power to appoint and remove department heads and other administrative personnel. He also draws up the budget for council consideration. The council-manager form of municipal government has proved the most efficient form and is making steady progress.

"My Hat's in the Ring"—In announcing his candidacy for the Republican nomination for the presidency in 1912, Theodore Roosevelt said: "My hat's in the ring. The fight is on and I am stripped to the buff."

National Committees—The national committees of the Democratic and Republican parties are composed of a man and a woman from each state and the possessions of the United States. The members, who serve for four years, are chosen by the states in a variety of ways, in some cases by direct party primary, in others by state conventions, but more generally by the delegates to the national convention.

The chief functions and powers of these national committees involve the calling and organizing of the national nominating conventions (*q.v.*), selecting the time and place where they are to be held, and fixing the voting strength of the various state delegations. The committees also play a leading part in national campaigns, raising and dispensing funds, assigning speakers and organizers to places where they are needed, and acting as general boards of strategy in the conduct of the campaign. (See *Nominating Conventions*.)

National Republican Party—During the administration of John Quincy Adams the unity that had so long prevailed in the Democratic-Republican party showed signs of coming to an end. The differences between the Adams and Clay Republicans and the Jackson Republicans were not merely on the surface; they had roots deep down. Each acknowledged the other to be members of the same

218

party, it is true, but they nevertheless contained the elements of distinct parties. The Adams section was devoted to principles much resembling those of the old Federalists, but they brought to politics many of the popular elements of Jefferson's methods. They favored a national bank, internal improvements, and a protective tariff. In the election of 1828, though defeated, they made an excellent showing, polling 509,000 popular votes to 647,000 for Jackson.

Through lack of tact Adams forfeited the support of many followers, and the leadership naturally fell to Clay, and by common consent the name of National Republican was adopted about 1830. In 1831 the party nominated Clay but adopted no platform. An address to the voters was issued, declaring its principles to be as above stated, but the party was defeated. In practice its main aim now was opposition to President Jackson, and it welcomed as allies men of all shades of opinions on other topics—the Nullifiers of South Carolina, the State's-Right factions of other states. To all these heterogeneous elements the name of Whigs was applied in 1834, and a large proportion of them formed the Whig party, whose existence dated from that year.

National Union of Social Justice—See *Coughlinites; Townsend Plan*.

Navy Department—Originally a part of the War Department, the Navy Department was made a separate branch of the government on April 30, 1798, and Benjamin Stoddert of Massachusetts was the first to fill the office of Secretary of the Navy and sit in the Cabinet. The supervision and maintenance of a naval establishment is in the Secretary's hands, and through him the President, as Commander in Chief of the Navy, exercises his authority. The Secretary, who is a civil rather than naval officer, has under his control the construction of war vessels, as well as the manning, arming, and equipping of them, and of the functioning of naval bases, shipyards, and training stations. The Marine Corps is also under his command. Hydrographic maps of foreign water and the high seas are prepared by the Navy Department. Likewise within his jurisdiction is the Naval Observatory and the Bureau of Aeronautics. The latter is charged with the design, construction, testing, and repairs of naval and Marine Corps aircraft.

The Secretary of the Navy is assisted by the Undersecretary of the Navy, the Assistant Secretary of the Navy, and the Assistant Secretary of the Navy for Air. Bureaus of the department include the Bureau of Naval Personnel, Bureau of Ordnance, Bureau of Ships, Bureau of Yards and Docks, Bureau of Supplies and Accounts, Bureau of Medicine and Surgery, Bureau of Aeronautics.

Nebraska—"Cornhusker State" is the nickname sometimes given to Nebraska. Also called "Tree Planter's State." State flower, goldenrod. Population, 1,315,834. Area, 77,237 square miles. Capital, Lincoln. Ceded to the United States by the Louisiana Purchase Treaty, it was admitted to the Union in 1867. Until the turn of the century state politics were, as a rule, Republican. Its national complexion, however, because of the influence of the Great Commoner, William Jennings Bryan, fluctuated, and the state went Democratic in 1896, as well as from 1908 to 1916 and again in 1932 and 1936.

Bryan was a power in the Democratic party for well over a quarter of a century and was the leader of the free silver movement. His well-known "crown of thorns" speech won him the presidential nomination in 1896, but he was defeated in the ensuing campaign by McKinley. He also lost the presidential campaign in 1900 and 1908. The state has four representatives in Congress.

Nevada—Known as the "Silver State" or "Sagebrush State." State flower, sagebrush. Population, 110,247. Area, 110,540 square miles. Capital, Carson City. Nevada was originally part of Mexico and was ceded to us by the Treaty of Guadalupe Hidalgo in 1848. Organized as a separate territory in 1861, it was admitted to the Union in 1864. In the last ten presidential elections it has been Democratic seven times. It went Republican in 1920, 1924, and 1928. It has one representative in Congress.

New Deal—When Franklin D. Roosevelt came into power in 1932 a nation-wide depression was at the strangling point. He forthwith proclaimed that the "forgotten man" must be given a "new deal." His administration became known as the New Deal Government, and that label remained, though Roosevelt later tried to change it to a "win the war" slogan.

When Roosevelt took office there were 12,000,000 persons out of work and prices were depressed to a very low level; foreign trade was severely shrunken, and the country's financial system was extremely shaky and bank failures were widespread.

Following are some of the acts of the administration:

Proclaimed a ten-day banking holiday throughout the nation which called for the closing of all depositories.

Congress was called into special session to pass a precedent-shattering national-recovery program.

National Industry Recovery Administration (NRA) was set up by Congress in order to obtain wider re-employment, pay decent wages, shorten working hours, and prevent unfair competition.

Agricultural Adjustment Administration (AAA) came into being to aid the farmers.

Laws were passed to insure bank deposits and render government aid for homeowners who faced mortgage foreclosure.

National prohibition was repealed.

Legislation provided for social security payments.

Wage-hour law was enacted for labor.

Later such "alphabet agencies" as RFC, CCC, TVA, WPA, PWA, HOLC, and FHA were established.

Bigger government budgets, larger deficits, heavier taxes were part of the New Deal, and the gold standard was abandoned.

Many of the New Deal policies were formulated by a "brain trust," composed of college professors.

The Supreme Court ruled that some of the measures in the New Deal were unconstitutional, such as the NRA and the AAA, and an attempt was made by the administration to "pump new blood" into the tribunal. (See *Nine Old Men.*)

New Hampshire—The "Granite State." State flower, purple lilac. Population, 491,524. Area, 9,304 square miles. Capital, Concord. An original state of the Union. The national political complexion of the state was Democratic from 1804 to 1852, but it was Republican thereafter until 1912, when it went Democratic. It again decided for the Democratic ticket in 1916 and also in 1936, 1940, and 1944. Franklin Pierce, fourteenth President of the United States (1853–57) was a native of New Hampshire. Daniel Webster, lawyer, statesman, and famed orator, was born in Salisbury. The state has two representatives in Congress.

New Jersey—An original state of the Union. Known as the "Garden State." State flower, violet. Population, 4,160,165. Area, 7,836 square miles. Capital, Trenton. New Jersey's political history has been quite varied. From 1860 to 1896, with one exception, the state was Democratic. It then went Republican until 1932, with the exception of 1912, when it joined the Progressives. Franklin D. Roosevelt carried the state four times. Grover Cleveland, who was born in Caldwell, was twice President of the United States. Woodrow Wilson, who was governor of New Jersey (1911–13), was President from 1913 to 1921. The state has fourteen seats in the House of Representatives.

New Mexico—Known as the "Sunshine State." State flower, yucca. Population, 531,818. Area, 121,666 square miles. Capital, Santa Fe. New Mexico was organized as a territory in 1850 from land ceded by Mexico. In 1854 the region acquired by the Gadsden Purchase was added to New Mexico, which then included Arizona and parts of Nevada and Colorado as these now exist. Later the northeastern and northwestern corners were given to Colorado and Nevada respectively, and in 1863 the western half was formed into the Territory of Arizona. New Mexico entered the Union in 1912. It would probably have acquired statehood much earlier but for the fear that the Mexican element in the population would practically establish a state church. In the nine presidential elections since New Mexico became a state it has been in the Democratic column six times, in the Republican three. It sends two congressmen to Washington.

New York—The "Empire State." State flower, rose. Population, 13,479,142. Area, 49,576 square miles. Capital, Albany. An original state of the Union. From 1795 to 1800 the Federalist party held sway in the state, but under the leadership of De Witt Clinton it went Democratic for a good spell. Since 1861, however, its political tendencies in both national and state affairs have been of an uncertain nature.

The governorship of the state might be said to have been the steppingstone to the presidency of the United States for Martin Van Buren, Grover Cleveland, Theodore Roosevelt, and Franklin Delano Roosevelt. Millard Fillmore, who was born in New York in 1800, succeeded to the presidency upon the death of Zachary Taylor in 1850.

Other notable men of the state were Horace Greeley, George Clinton, Charles E. Hughes, and Alfred E. Smith. Alexander Hamilton was New York's representative at the Annapolis Convention in 1786.

New York has forty-five representatives in Congress.

Nine Old Men—During the fight over President Franklin D. Roosevelt's proposal to appoint a new justice to the Supreme Court for each justice who failed to retire at seventy, the justices were frequently referred to as the Nine Old Men.

In his special message to Congress on February 5, 1937, which followed a series of Supreme Court decisions adverse to the New Deal, President Roosevelt said, "New facts become blurred through old glasses fitted, as it were, for the needs of another generation; older men, assuming that the scene is the same as it was in the past, cease to explore or inquire into the present or future." (See *Supreme Court*.)

Nominating Conventions, National—The presidential campaign of 1832 was the first one in which the candidates were named at national party conventions. Prior to that time candidates were nominated for President and Vice-President by congressional party caucuses. The practice originated with the Federalists following the retirement of Washington, who had been elected unanimously. The Jacksonians were opposed to this method of naming candidates as undemocratic and unconstitutional and by 1828 had succeeded in killing it. National nominating conventions finally became a fully established feature of American politics in the 1840s.

The national committees of the two major parties call and organize the national nominating conventions, selecting the time and place for holding the conventions and determining the method by which the number of delegates will be apportioned among the states. At the 1944 conventions the Democratic and Republican state delegations stood as follows in point of numerical strength:

	Delegates, Democratic Convention	Delegates, Republican Convention
Alabama	24	14
Arizona.	10	8
Arkansas	20	12
California	52	50
Colorado	12	15
Connecticut	18	16
Delaware	8	9
Florida	18	15
Georgia	26	13
Idaho	10	11
Illinois	58	59
Indiana.	26	29
Iowa	20	23
Kansas	16	19
Kentucky	24	22
Louisiana	22	13
Maine	10	13
Maryland	18	16
Massachusetts	34	35
Michigan	38	41
Minnesota	24	25
Mississippi	20	6
Missouri	32	30
Montana	10	8
Nebraska	12	15
Nevada	8	6
New Hampshire	10	11
New Jersey	34	35
New Mexico	10	8
New York	96	93
North Carolina	30	25
North Dakota	8	11
Ohio	52	50
Oklahoma	22	23
Oregon	14	15

	Delegates, Democratic Convention	Delegates, Republican Convention
Pennsylvania	72	70
Rhode Island	10	8
South Carolina	18	4
South Dakota	8	11
Tennessee	26	19
Texas	48	33
Utah	10	8
Vermont	6	9
Virginia	24	19
Washington	18	16
West Virginia	18	19
Wisconsin	26	24
Wyoming	8	9
Alaska	6	3
District of Columbia	6	3
Hawaii	6	5
Philippine Islands	6	2
Puerto Rico	6	2
Canal Zone	6	....
Virgin Islands	2	....
Total	1,176	1,058

Normalcy—Warren G. Harding campaigned successfully for the presidency in 1920 under the watchword "normalcy." He pleaded for a "return to normalcy," meaning conditions as they existed before the war.

North Carolina—Popular nickname is "Old North State," but at times is referred to as the "Tarheel State." State flower, dogwood. Population, 3,571,623. Area, 52,712 square miles. Capital, Raleigh. An original state of the Union. It seceded from the Union in 1861 and was readmitted in 1868. The state has been Democratic in politics with the exception of an eight-year period beginning in 1840, and it went Republican in 1928. Educational qualifications limit the voting privilege. Under this practice the Negro vote may be said to be entirely excluded.

James Knox Polk, who was eleventh President of the United States, was born in Mecklenburg County, and Andrew Johnson, seventeenth President, was born near Raleigh.

The state has twelve representatives in Congress.

North Dakota—Known as the "Flickertail State" or "Sioux State." State flower, wild prairie rose. Population, 641,935. Area, 70,665 square miles. Capital, Bismarck. Admitted to the Union in 1889. The state was part of the Louisiana Purchase and was ceded in 1803. The state is normally Republican, but the Democrats have gained control at various times, particularly in 1912, 1916, and 1932. Franklin D. Roosevelt carried the state four times. The Nonpartisan League, organized in 1915, gained control of the state government in 1918. The state has two representatives in Congress.

Northeast Boundary—The Treaty of 1783 between Great Britain and the United States defined the northern boundary of the latter between the St. Lawrence and the Atlantic. For nearly sixty years, however, the meaning of the language used was in dispute, especially as to the "highlands" and the true source of the Connecticut River. Commissioners appointed under Jay's Treaty of 1794 helped to settle some of the boundary marks, but the question remained unsettled, as a whole, despite efforts made in 1803, in 1814 by the Treaty of Ghent, in 1827, and in other years.

By the convention of 1827, the matter was referred for arbitration to the King of the Netherlands, but his award, rendered in 1831, was accepted by neither nation. In 1838 and 1839 there were some hostilities on the border (called the Aroostook disturbance); Maine sent armed men thither and erected forts, and Congress authorized the President to resist encroachments of British subjects. General Scott, however, arranged for a truce and a joint occupation.

Great Britain finally appointed Lord Ashburton to settle the matter with our government, and he concluded a treaty (see *Ashburton Treaty*) with Daniel Webster, then Secretary of State, on August 9, 1842. This treaty fixed the boundary line favorably to British claims on the whole, though New York and New Hampshire gained some territory. Maine and Massachusetts were to be compensated by the United States for territory given up; grants of land in the disputed region were confirmed, and the navigation of the St. Johns River was made free for people of both nations. Much popular indignation was felt in this country at the yielding of any portion of our claims.

Northwest Boundary—Russia, Spain, Great Britain, and the United States have each at one time or another laid claim to part or all of the territory lying west of the Rocky Mountains and between latitude 42° north, the present northern boundary of California, and 54° 40' north. This whole region was known as Oregon.

Russia withdrew her claims to the territory south of 54° 40' (the present southern limit of Alaska) by a treaty with the United States in 1824 (ratified by our government on January 11, 1825) and by a treaty with Great Britain in February 1825.

The claim of Spain passed to France by treaty, along with the region known as Louisiana, in 1800, and was transferred to the United States in 1803 by the purchase of Louisiana. Spain still held what is now a part of our Pacific coast, but by the treaty of 1819 (ratified by Spain in 1821) she named the latitude of 42° as the northern limits of her territory.

Great Britain and the United States were now the only claimants to Oregon. Both based their claims on discovery, exploration, and occupation. Great Britain, however, showed a willingness to compromise on the Columbia River as the boundary, while the United States would not entertain the thought of compromise short of the forty-ninth degree. At the same time our government claimed as far north as the headwaters of the Columbia, in about latitude 52°, and a strong popular opinion prevailed that the territory up to 54° 40' belonged to us. This was probably caused by the terms of the treaty with Russia, which of course had no force as between this country and Great Britain.

The Peace Treaty of 1783, which closed the Revolution, settled our northern boundary as far west as the Mississippi, which was at that time the western limit of our territory. After the purchase of Louisiana the convention of 1818 between England and the United States carried the boundary as far west as the Rocky Mountains, along the forty-ninth parallel of latitude, leaving the region west of those mountains open to joint occupation for ten years. A convention, ratified by the United States in April 1828, continued this joint occupation indefinitely, providing, however, that either nation might terminate the arrangement by a year's notice.

The yielding to British claims as to the northeast boundary by the

227

Treaty of 1842 led to a popular desire, especially marked in the Democratic party, to enforce our extreme claims in the Northwest and gave rise to the political cry of "Fifty-four Forty or Fight." In the latter part of Tyler's administration (1844–45) Calhoun, then Secretary of State, had made an offer to accept the forty-ninth degree as the boundary, which a calm view of the facts seems to show was the utmost the United States could rightfully claim. England, however, insisted on the Columbia River from the forty-ninth parallel to the Pacific. On Calhoun's refusal an arbitration was proposed, which was also declined.

A strong war feeling was now aroused in Great Britain, to avoid the consequences of which Polk's Secretary of State, Buchanan, in July 1845, again offered to accept the forty-ninth parallel. This was refused by England and also withdrawn by Buchanan because of the indignation aroused in this country at the thought of yielding. Congress debated the matter and advised the notice necessary to terminate the joint occupancy, which was done. Great Britain was avowedly making war preparations.

Finally, however, in June 1846, the British Ambassador made an offer to accept as the boundary the forty-ninth parallel, as far as the channel between Vancouver's Island and the mainland, and from that point a line through the middle of that channel and the Strait of Fuca to the Pacific. Both nations were to have free navigation of the channel and the Columbia River. By the advice of the Senate ratifications were exchanged to a convention on this basis on July 17, 1846. The Treaty of Washington, 1871, provided for the decision by the Emperor of Germany of a dispute which had arisen under the settlement of 1846. The United States claimed the Canal de Haro as the channel through which the boundary was to run, while Great Britain claimed the Rosario Strait; San Juan and other islands were thus in dispute; Emperor William in 1872 decided in favor of the United States, and the boundary was thus at last and completely defined.

Notification of Election—The President of the United States is not officially notified that the people have chosen him for the highest office in the land. He learns of his election in the same way that any American learns who is the successful candidate. He reaches Washington a day or two before inauguration day and, calling at the White House, pays his respects to the retiring President, with whom he rides to the Capitol for the inaugural ceremonies. (See *Inauguration Day.*)

Nullification is the act of nullifying or declaring void a law. In our history the term is applied to the nullification by a state of a national law. The Cherokee Case is the first successful instance of it, but the word usually has relation to the case of South Carolina, where the result was different. The nullification doctrine of Hayne differed slightly from that of Calhoun, Hayne declaring that the right to nullify resided in the state legislature, while Calhoun maintained that it must be exercised by the people in a state convention. These doctrines were called into being under the following circumstances.

The tariffs of 1824 and of 1828 had gradually introduced a system of protection of home manufactures. The South, employing unskilled and untaught slave labor, had no manufactures and therefore objected to a system protecting Northern manufactures at its expense. A tariff bill, slightly reducing some duties, became a law on July 14, 1832, but the South, and pre-eminently South Carolina, was not satisfied.

This state now took steps to carry into execution threats previously made. A state convention was called to meet on November 19, 1832, and on November 24 an ordinance of nullification was passed. This ordinance declared the tariff acts of 1828 and 1832 void; forbade the payment of duty under these acts after February 1, 1833; declared an appeal to the Supreme Court of the United States regarding the validity of the ordinance to be contempt of the state court; caused every juror and every state officer to swear to support the ordinance; and declared that if force were used against her she would consider herself no longer a member of the Union.

President Jackson acted with energy. He issued a proclamation pointing out that nullification was inconsistent with the Constitution, and "disunion by armed force" treason. General Scott was ordered to Charleston. The collector of that city was instructed to take precautions to insure the payment of duties, and a naval force entered its harbor. In January 1833 a private meeting of the Nullifiers had decided to postpone the operations of the ordinance until after the adjournment of Congress, and duties were paid after the first of February as they had been before. Nullification had been crushed by the energy of Andrew Jackson. Toward the end of February 1833 a new tariff bill was passed, though by no means one entirely satisfactory to the South, and on March 16 a state convention repealed the ordinance of nullification.

O.P.F. stands for Old Public Functionary, a term which James Buchanan used to describe himself in his annual message to Congress in 1857. Thereafter he was referred to by his contemporaries as O.P.F.

Oaths—Most government officials are sworn into office. Here are the executive, the judiciary, and the legislative oaths.

President: "I do solemnly swear [or affirm] that I will faithfully execute the office of President of the United States, and will, to the best of my ability, preserve, protect, and defend the Constitution of the United States."

Supreme Court Justices: "I do solemnly swear that I will administer justice without respect to persons, and do equal right to the poor and to the rich; and that I will faithfully discharge all the duties incumbent on me as Judge, according to the best of my abilities and understanding, agreeably to the Constitution and laws of the United States."

Senators and Representatives: "I do solemnly swear [or affirm] that I will support and defend the Constitution of the United States against all enemies, foreign and domestic; that I will bear true faith and allegiance to the same; that I take this obligation freely, without any mental reservation or purpose of evasion, and that I will well and faithfully discharge the duties of the office on which I am about to enter. So help me God."

Ohio—"Buckeye State." State flower, scarlet carnation. Population, 6,907,612. Area, 41,222 square miles. Capital, Columbus. Admitted to the Union in 1803. Ohio has had a pronounced bearing on, and was a decisive force in, national affairs. It gave to the nation as presidents: Benjamin Harrison, Ulysses S. Grant, Rutherford B. Hayes, James A. Garfield, William McKinley, William Howard Taft, and Warren G. Harding. Nicholas Longworth, who practiced law in Cincinnati, was Speaker of the House of Representatives from 1925 to 1931. He married the daughter of President Theodore Roosevelt at the White House in 1906.

Until the Jackson era, Ohio was true Jeffersonian in national politics. The state then swerved back and forth until 1856, when the Republicans took over, and it remained in the Republican column until 1912. Ohio went Democratic again in 1916, 1932, 1936, and 1940. The state has twenty-three representatives in Congress.

Oklahoma—Known as the "Sooner State." State flower, mistletoe. Population, 2,336,434. Area, 69,919. Capital, Oklahoma City. In 1834 Oklahoma, most of which was part of the Louisiana Purchase of 1803, was set aside as an Indian reservation. Opened to white settlers in 1889, it was admitted to the Union in 1907. The state, which has eight representatives in Congress, is usually Democratic in national politics.

Old Potato—In 1932, Al Smith, who had been at odds with Franklin D. Roosevelt, met the latter after Roosevelt had won the presidential nomination and greeted him with "Hello, old potato!"

Old Tip or **Old Tippecanoe** was the familiar name bestowed by his supporters on General William Henry Harrison, the "Log Cabin and Hard Cider Candidate," when he ran against Martin Van Buren for the presidency in 1840. General Harrison had defeated some Indians at the Battle of Tippecanoe in the War of 1812. (See *Hard Cider Campaign; Tippecanoe and Tyler Too.*)

On the Fence—A person is said to be on the fence in a political sense when he is undecided whether or not to support a particular measure or man, or when he stands uncertainly between two parties.

231

Political opportunists are sometimes contemptuously said to be "on the fence, ready to drop on either side."

Ordinance of 1784—At the close of the Revolution it was regarded as unjust that the states having unsettled Western possessions should hold the same solely for their own benefit, and it was agreed that these should be ceded to the general government. In 1784 Jefferson presented to the Continental Congress, in Philadelphia, Virginia's deed of cession of all her territory northwest of the Ohio, and, as chairman of a committee appointed for the purpose, he submitted a plan for the government of that tract and of any other that might be ceded within certain geographical limits.

This is known as the Ordinance of 1784. As reported, it provided, among other regulations, for the division of the territory into embryo states and ordained that it should forever remain a part of and subject to the government of the United States, and finally it abolished slavery in the territory after the year 1800. Its concluding section declared it to be a compact between the thirteen original states and "those newly described," and to be unalterable except by the consent of Congress and of the state concerned. The vote on the section prohibiting slavery showed six states in favor of the section and three against it, but as it could not be adopted by less than a majority of all the states, it failed. In this shape the ordinance was carried.

Oregon—"Beaver State," or, as sometimes known, "Webfoot State." State flower, Oregon grape. Population, 1,089,684. Area, 96,981 square miles. Capital, Salem. Organized as a territory in 1848, Oregon was admitted to the Union in 1859. In national politics the state is normally Republican, but in state elections it is independent. An equal suffrage law was proclaimed by the state in 1912. It has four representatives in Congress.

"Our Country, Right or Wrong"—Commodore Stephen Decatur at a dinner in Norfolk, Virginia, in 1816, gave this toast: "Our country! In her intercourse with foreign nations may she always be in the right; but our country, right or wrong."

232

Over the main gate of Buchenwald, the German horror camp of World War II, was the inscription: *Recht oder unrecht Mein Vaterland* [My country, right or wrong].

"Our Lives, Our Fortunes, and Our Sacred Honor." The last words of the Declaration of Independence. The closing sentence reads: "And, for the support of this Declaration, with a firm reliance on the protection of divine Providence, we mutually pledge to each other, our Lives, our Fortunes, and our sacred Honor."

Pair—When two legislators who would have voted on opposite sides of a question agree that the vote of one cancels the other, it is called a pair. Under such an agreement, which leaves the result unaffected, neither member votes, but each may indicate the position he would have taken. It enables one or both to be absent and is often resorted to during the enforced absence of a legislator.

Palace Guard—The trusted favorites and cronies of a person holding high office; a term often applied to the circle of close political friends and informal advisers of the President in Washington. The implication is that these persons are like the zealously loyal household guard of royalty. (See *Brain Trust; Kitchen Cabinet.*)

Parlor Pink—An intellectual holding extreme political and social views who cries up some foreign country or political or social system at the expense of our own. In his transferred nationalism, the parlor pink is usually a theoretical rather than a practical politician.

Party—Edmund Burke defined a political party as "a body of men united, for promoting by their joint endeavors the national interest, upon some particular principle in which they are all agreed." But in the United States party interest has sometimes outweighed the national interest.

Patronage—Procedure whereby officials who have been elected or appointed to public office may reward their supporters or adherents

233

by appointing them to positions in the government employ. It also takes in the awarding of contracts or favors to individuals or committees. (See *Civil Service; To the Victors Belong the Spoils.*)

"Peace at Any Price; Peace and Union"—Campaign slogan of the Know Nothing (National American) party when it ran Millard Fillmore for President in 1856.

Peanut Politics is an expression signifying the use of mean and petty tactics to gain some peculiarly trifling political advantage. Small-minded men who employ such tactics are called peanut politicians.

Pennsylvania—"Keystone State." State flower, mountain laurel. Population, 9,900,180. Area, 45,333 square miles. Capital, Harrisburg. An original state of the Union. Pennsylvania has an envious record in American history. The Continental Congresses of 1775 and 1776 were held in Philadelphia, and also the Constitutional Convention of 1787. It was the seat of the Federal Government for a decade, beginning in 1790. It furnished such early public leaders as Benjamin Franklin, who, though born in Boston, settled in Pennsylvania; John Dickinson, who wrote the Declaration of Rights; Robert Morris, signer of the Declaration of Independence; Thomas Mifflin, who was aide-de-camp to George Washington and later governor of Pennsylvania; and Albert Gallatin, who served twice as Secretary of the Treasury. James Buchanan, fifteenth President of the United States, was a Pennsylvanian. From 1797 to 1860 the state's electoral votes went to the Jeffersonian and Democratic parties almost every time. But since then, aside from 1912, when it supported Theodore Roosevelt and the Progressive party, the state has been Republican, though Franklin D. Roosevelt carried Pennsylvania in 1936, 1940, and 1944. It has thirty-three representatives in Congress.

Pernicious Activity—President Cleveland on July 14, 1886, directed a circular "to the heads of departments in the service of the general government," warning them and their subordinates against using "their official positions in attempts to control political activities in their localities." He said, "Officeholders are neither disfranchised nor forbidden the exercise of political privileges; but their privileges are not enlarged, nor is their duty to party increased to pernicious activity by officeholding." (See *Political Activity Act.*)

Petition, Right of—The right of petition is a right antedating the Constitution. It is embodied in the Magna Charta and again in the English Bill of Rights. It was a part of the common law in this country at the time of the adoption of the Constitution. The First Amendment to that instrument created no new right by providing that "Congress shall make no law . . . abridging . . . the right of the people peaceably to assemble and to petition the government for a redress of grievances." It simply declared an old right and guarded it from interference on the part of Congress. The power to protect the right was not taken from the states. That power had resided in them, and it was left in their hands. Citizens must look to the state governments for its enforcement. But the right is implied in the idea of a republican government and is therefore guaranteed by the national government (Constitution, Article IV, Section 4).

A petitioner is not guilty of libel on account of the facts recited in his petition, even if these are false, unless malice is proven. Before December 12, 1853, all petitions to the House of Representatives were presented in the House, and the introduction of petitions relating to the abolition of slavery led to heated debates, and between 1836 and 1844 to rules that practically nullified the right. On the above date the rules were modified so that petitions were endorsed with the name of the member presenting them and the committee to which they were to be referred. After the clerk had entered them in full on the journal and they had been transmitted to the proper committee they were printed in the *Congressional Record*.

Pewter Muggers was a name given to a faction of the Democratic party in New York City about 1828, in which year, with the help of the Adams men (the administration party) and the Anti-Masons, they defeated the Tammany candidates for several important offices. The name originated from the resort in Frankfort Street which the leaders of the faction patronized.

235

Pierce, Franklin, the fourteenth President of the United States, was born in Hillsborough, New Hampshire, on November 23, 1804, and died in Concord, New Hampshire, on October 8, 1869. He was a graduate of Bowdoin College and a lawyer. He served in the State Legislature from 1829 to 1833, and in Congress from 1833 to 1837. He was a Senator from 1837 to 1842. In politics he was a Democrat. On the outbreak of the Mexican War he enlisted as a private but came out a brigadier general. He was injured at Contreras when his horse was shot from under him. Pierce was the dark-horse candidate of the Democratic convention in 1852, winning the presidential nomination over a strong field, which included Douglas and Buchanan. In the ensuing election he defeated the Whig candidate, General Winfield Scott, the popular vote being 1,601,474 for Pierce and 1,386,578 for Scott.

In 1853 and 1854 an expedition under Commodore Perry was sent to Japan and a treaty made which opened the ports of that country to the commerce of the civilized world. In January 1854, Senator Stephen A. Douglas introduced into Congress the Kansas-Nebraska Bill (*q.v.*), the effect of which was to invalidate the Missouri Compromise, as it permitted the introduction of slavery into those territories. A desperate struggle between the pro-slavery and anti-slavery parties followed, and civil war raged in Kansas for several years. Pierce's administration was also marked by the Gadsden Purchase (see *Annexations*), which settled the Mexican boundary. Pierce was the only President to serve without a change in his Cabinet. His Secretary of War was Jefferson Davis.

Although Pierce was a brilliant and able man and succeeded in averting war between the North and South over the slavery question, he failed to please either side, and his party refused to renominate him. A handsome man and a splendid orator, Franklin Pierce was born on Friday, inaugurated on Friday, and died on Friday.

Pigeonholing—Laying aside for consideration at a later time any bill by any committee of the legislature. It is often done for the express purpose of killing a bill through inaction. (See *Tabling.*)

Pivotal State—When the votes of the states are so equally divided that the result of an election depends upon the vote of one particu-

236

lar state, the state swinging the election is called a pivotal state. In the presidential election of 1884 a different result in New York would have meant a different result in the election. Cleveland carried the state over Blaine by a plurality of only 1,047 votes in a total of 1,150,000 votes. A shift of 524 votes to Blaine would have won him the state and the presidency. (See *Rum, Romanism, and Rebellion.*)

Platform, Political—A public declaration of principles and policies for which a political party or an individual stands and seeks the support of the electorate. Political platforms began to make their appearance in American politics when the national nominating conventions became fully established in the 1840s. Despite their often equivocal character, these platforms have served a useful purpose in drawing attention to some of the principal points at issue in political campaigns and in furnishing the grounds of contention for politicians, orators, editors, commentators, and people generally. Candidates do not always stand squarely upon the platforms adopted by the conventions which nominate them, but this does not usually prove a serious handicap.

Plumed Knight—Nickname of James G. Blaine. In nominating Blaine for President at the Republican National Convention in Cincinnati in 1876, Robert G. Ingersoll said: "Like an armed warrior, like a plumed knight, James G. Blaine marched down the halls of the American Congress and threw his shining lance full and fair against the brazen foreheads of the defamers of his country, and the maligners of his honor."

Pocket Veto—When a bill passes both houses of Congress it is sent to the President, who may either sign it or veto it, or do neither, in which case the bill after ten days becomes a law without his signature, unless Congress has previously adjourned and the President cannot return it.

If Congress adjourns before the ten days (not counting Sundays) elapse and the President fails to sign the bill, it automatically dies. This is the so-called pocket veto, a term apparently first applied by

237

the Whigs to the disposition in this way of two internal-improvement bills by Jackson. (See *Veto.*)

Political Action Committee—The C.I.O. executive committee on July 7, 1943, set up the Political Action Committee which was intended to support the interests of labor in the two-party political system. Fur began to fly in the political field when the P.A.C., led by Sidney Hillman, sought to choose a vice-presidential candidate for the Democratic convention in July 1944. The P.A.C. amassed many votes for its endorsed candidates in the state primaries.

Hillman was later summoned before a special House committee which was then investigating campaign expenditures. Republican National Chairman Herbert Brownell assailed the "arrogance" of P.A.C., which he said was "dominated by the Communist element."

In an interview Hillman was asked why, if the P.A.C. was nonpartisan, it was supporting the Democratic ticket (Roosevelt and Truman). He replied that he felt there would have been no endorsement of the national ticket if Wendell Willkie had been nominated. He added that he thought Wendell Willkie and Roosevelt had a broad approach to present-day problems and that "we didn't take any position until Willkie was eliminated."

Political Activity Act—Senator Carl A. Hatch, Democrat of New Mexico, fought for almost two years to put through a bill which would prohibit all Federal job holders except policy-making officials from participating in politics in any way except to vote, on threat of removal from office. The Hatch Bill applies particularly to United States attorneys, marshals, customs and revenue collectors who in the past were delegates to presidential nominating conventions.

Among other things, the sweeping measure forbids solicitation of campaign contributions from persons on relief and prohibits use of relief funds to influence persons in voting. Violators are to be fined one thousand dollars and imprisoned for a year. Cabinet officers and other policy-making officials, as well as members and employees of Congress, are exempted from the measure.

It was signed by President F. D. Roosevelt on August 2, 1939, with this comment: "It is because for so many years I have striven in public life and in private life for decency in political campaigns, both on the part of government servants, of candidates, of newspapers, of corporations, and of individuals, that I regard this new legislation as at least a step in the right direction."

The President said further that he was confident "the purpose of the proponents of this legislation" was that the new law be administered so that "the right of free speech will remain, even to those who serve their government, and that the government itself shall have full right to place all facts in its possession before the public." (See *Campaign Expenditures.*)

Polk, James Knox, eleventh President of the United States, was born in Mecklenburg County, North Carolina, November 2, 1795, and died in Nashville, Tennessee, June 15, 1849. He was graduated from the University of North Carolina in 1818, and two years later was admitted to the bar. In 1823 he was elected to the Tennessee Legislature and in 1825 was sent to Congress, where he served until 1839, the last four years as Speaker of the House. He was governor of Tennessee from 1839 to 1843. He was a dark-horse candidate for the presidential nomination at the Democratic convention of 1844, the delegates swinging to him when Martin Van Buren failed to get the necessary two-thirds vote. The party platform advocated the admission of Texas as a state and took a firm stand on the Oregon boundary dispute with Great Britain. Polk, who was known as "The Napoleon of the Stump," beat Henry Clay, the Whig nominee, in a close election, the popular vote being 1,337,243 for Polk and 1,299,-068 for Clay. The electoral vote was 170 for Polk, 105 for Clay.

The outstanding events of his administration were the Mexican War and the settlement of Northeast boundary dispute. At the close of the war we acquired California and a vast territory in the Southwest. In addition to Texas, Iowa and Wisconsin were admitted to the Union. The Department of the Interior was established, and the first tariff-for-revenue-only measure was enacted.

Polk served only one term, dying only three months after his retirement from office.

Poll Tax—A poll tax is a direct tax levied at so much per head or *poll* of the population. It is usually about one dollar and a qualification for voting. Congress has power by Article I, Section 9, of the Constitution to levy a poll tax in proportion to the census, but it has never exercised this power. Many of the states, however, have levied poll taxes, though far fewer do so now than formerly.

For a number of years past Congress has taken up the question of the poll tax, with a view to passing a law to abolish it in seven states of the South—Alabama, Arkansas, Mississippi, South Carolina, Tennessee, Texas, and Virginia. In 1945 the House of Representatives passed a bill to eliminate the tax in those states, but the measure died in the Senate. President Truman, at a recent news conference for high school journalists in Chicago, held that the repeal of the poll tax must be left to the states.

Populist Party—This was the popular name of the People's party organized in 1890. The platform adopted at the party convention in Omaha, July 4, 1892, contained this statement:

"We have witnessed for more than a quarter of a century the struggles of the two great political parties for power and plunder, while grievous wrongs have been inflicted upon the suffering poor. We charge that the controlling influences dominating both these parties have permitted the existing dreadful conditions to develop without serious effort to prevent or restrain them. Neither do they now promise any substantial reform. They have agreed together to ignore, in the coming campaign, every issue but one. They propose to drown the outcries of a plundered people with the uproar of a sham battle over the tariff, so that capitalists, corporations, national banks, rings, trusts, watered stock, the demonitization of silver, and the oppressions of the usurers may be all lost sight of."

The platform demanded a national currency, safe, sound, and flexible; the free and unlimited coinage of silver and gold at the ratio of 16 to 1; the amount of the circulating medium to be increased to not less than $50 per capita; a graduated income tax; postal savings banks; government ownership of railroads, telegraphs, telephones, and the reclaiming by the government of all lands held by railroads and other corporations in excess of their actual needs and all lands owned by aliens, to be held for actual settlers only.

At this convention General James B. Weaver of Iowa was nominated for President and James G. Field of Virginia for Vice-President. The party polled more than a million votes, carrying North Dakota, Colorado, Idaho, Kansas, and Nevada with 22 electoral votes. In 1896 the Populists joined the Democrats in backing Bryan but nominated Thomas E. Watson for Vice-President. They backed Bryan again in 1900 and Adlai E. Stevenson for Vice-President. In 1904 the party nominated Thomas E. Watson for President and Thomas H. Tibbles of Nebraska for Vice-President. The Populist movement, which had been originally organized with the Farmer's Alliance as its core, faded gradually as the Democratic party appropriated many of its liberal doctrines.

Pork Barrel—Term applied to an appropriations bill providing funds to be spent for various Federal projects in different localities. Such a bill enables congressmen to bring home the "bacon"—hence the name.

Post Office Department—This department of government was established February 20, 1792, but the Postmaster General did not become a member of the Cabinet until 1829. As head of the Federal Postal Service, the Postmaster General superintends the business of the department and has charge of making the mail-carrying contracts with railroads, steamship companies, airplane concerns, and other kinds of carriers. Subject to the approval of the President, the Postmaster General negotiates postal treaties with foreign governments. A detective agency is maintained by the Post Office Department to safeguard property entrusted to its care and to see that the mails are not used for purposes of fraud.

Four assistant postmasters general are appointed by the President to help the Postmaster General carry on the work of the department. There are numerous offices and divisions of the Post Office Department, among them the Office of Budget and Administrative Planning; the Bureau of the First Assistant Postmaster General, which contains the first four divisions of the Post Office Service, where the Special Administrative Aide acts as adviser to the First Assistant; the Bureau of the Second Assistant Postmaster General, comprising the Division of Air Mail Service, Division of International Postal

241

Service, Division of Railway Adjustments, Division of Railway Mail Service; the Bureau of the Third Assistant Postmaster General, composed of the Division of Letter and Miscellaneous Mail, Division of Newspaper and Periodical Mail, Division of Finance and Disbursing Office, Division of Money Orders, Division of Parcel Post, Division of Postal Savings, Division of Registered Mail, Division of Stamps; the Bureau of the Fourth Assistant Postmaster General, composed of the Division of Motor Vehicle Service, Division of Post Office Quarters, Division of Topography, Division of Engineering and Research, Division of Traffic, Division of Equipment and Supplies, Division of Federal Building Operations, and Mail Equipment Shops; the Bureau of the Chief Inspector; Office of the Solicitor; Office of the Purchasing Agent.

President by Three Votes—When upon the retirement of Washington John Adams was elected President in 1796 by a vote of 71 electoral votes to 68 for Jefferson, he was called President by Three Votes.

President's Message—The Constitution provides (Article II, Section 3) that the President "shall from time to time give the Congress information of the state of the Union, and recommend to their consideration such measures as he shall judge necessary and expedient." In consequence of this provision, it has become customary for the President to deliver his annual message to Congress as soon as it assembles. Washington and Adams read theirs in person to Congress, but Jefferson sent his to the House to be read for him, and later Presidents down to the time of Woodrow Wilson followed Jefferson's example. As often as not, nowadays messages are read in person, and always so in the case of special messages on extraordinary occasions. President Roosevelt's message asking that war be declared on the Axis powers was broadcast to the world.

The longest message ever sent by a President to Congress is said to have been that of President Truman reporting on the state of the Union, January 21, 1946. It contained twenty-five thousand words. But many presidential messages, notably those of Franklin D. Roosevelt, have been brief, pungent, and forceful.

242

Presidential Succession—The Constitution, Article II, Section 1, provides that "in case of the removal of the President from office, or of his death, resignation, or inability to discharge . . . the duties of the said office, the same shall devolve on the Vice-President," the power to provide for further contingencies being left to Congress. This Congress did by means of the act of March 1, 1792.

In cases of death, of removal by impeachment, or of resignation, no difficulties are met with, but the power to declare the "inability" of the President in cases where the same is not on the surface, as in insanity, is lodged nowhere. In such a case the Vice-President would probably take it upon himself to act as President, and the Supreme Court would be the final judge of the validity of his acts. The law of 1792 declared that in case of inability of the Vice-President the office devolves on the president pro tempore of the Senate, and after him on the Speaker of the House, until a new election can be ordered. It also provided that the Secretary of State should notify the executives of the states of any vacancy in the Executive office by reason of failure on the part of the Vice-President, and if at that date there be still two months intervening before the first Wednesday in December (the day on which the electors vote), then an election for President shall be ordered to be held within thirty-four days preceding the latter day. If the intervening time be less than two months, and the current presidential term expire on the fourth of March following, then no election for the unexpired term takes place; but if the time be less than two months, and the term does not so expire, then a new election shall be ordered for the following year.

The Twelfth Amendment provides that in cases in which the House has not exercised its right of choosing a President (when the choice falls to it) by the following March 4, the Vice-President shall act as President; but it fails to provide for a contingency where neither President nor Vice-President is selected, and where no president pro tempore of the Senate has been chosen.

The assassination of Garfield at a time when the House was not organized and while there was no president pro tempore of the Senate led to agitation of the subject, and in 1883 a bill was introduced into the Senate to regulate this matter, but it was not con-

243

sidered by the House. In December 1885, substantially the same bill was again introduced and this time passed. It was approved on January 19, 1886.

Its provisions are as follows: In case of inability on the part of both President and Vice-President, the Executive office falls to the Cabinet officers in the following order, provided the officer on whom it devolves has been confirmed by the Senate and is by birth and otherwise qualified to hold the office: the secretaries of State, Treasury, and War, the Attorney General, the Postmaster General, the secretaries of the Navy and of the Interior. No mention was made of the secretaries of Agriculture, Commerce, and Labor, as those departments had not then been organized. The officer thus selected serves out the unexpired term.

Presidential Timber—A man is said to be of presidential timber if he has a stainless record and the background, character, and ability to make a creditable run for the presidency. Viscount Bryce in his classic work, *The American Commonwealth,* explaining why great men are not chosen President, says:

> Eminent men make more enemies, and give those enemies more assailable points, than obscure men do. They are therefore in so far less desirable candidates. It is true that the eminent man has also made more friends, that his name is more widely known, and may be greeted with louder cheers. Other things being equal, the famous man is preferable. But other things never are equal. The famous man has probably attacked some leaders in his own party, has supplanted others, has expressed his dislike to the crotchet of some active section, has perhaps committed errors which are capable of being magnified into offences. No man stands long before the public and bears a part in great affairs without giving openings to censorious criticism. Fiercer far than the light which beats upon a throne is the light which beats upon a presidential candidate, searching out all the recesses of his past life. Hence, when the choice lies between a brilliant man and a safe man, the safe man is preferred. Party feeling, strong enough to carry in on its back a man without conspicuous positive merits, is not always strong enough to procure forgiveness for a man with positive faults.

Presidential Vote—The state-by-state popular vote for President in the 1944 election was as follows:

State	Total Vote	Democrat	Pct.	Republican	Pct.	Other	Pct.	Plurality
Alabama	244,743	198,918	81.3	44,540	18.2	1,285	0.5	154,378
Arizona	137,213	80,926	58.9	56,287	41.1	.....	..	24,639
Arkansas	214,954	148,965	69.3	65,551	30.5	438	0.5	83,414
California	3,518,814	1,988,564	56.5	1,512,965	43.0	17,285	0.5	475,599
Colorado	505,039	234,331	46.4	268,731	53.2	1,977	0.4	34,400
Connecticut	831,993	435,146	52.3	390,527	46.9	6,320	0.8	44,619
Delaware	125,361	68,166	54.4	56,747	45.3	448	0.4	11,419
Florida	482,803	339,377	70.3	143,215	29.7	211	0.0	196,162
Georgia	328,111	268,187	81.7	56,506	17.2	3,418	1.5	211,681
Idaho	208,321	107,399	51.5	109,137	48.1	785	0.4	7,262
Illinois	4,036,061	2,079,479	51.6	1,939,314	48.0	17,268	0.4	149,165
Indiana	1,672,091	781,403	46.7	875,891	52.4	14,797	0.9	94,480
Iowa	1,052,601	499,876	47.5	547,267	51.0	5,458	0.5	47,391
Kansas	733,776	287,458	39.2	442,096	60.2	4,222	0.6	154,638
Kentucky	867,921	472,589	54.5	392,448	45.2	2,884	0.3	80,141
Louisiana	358,506	288,000	80.3	70,382	19.7	124	0.0	217,618
Maine	296,400	149,631	47.5	155,434	52.4	335	0.1	14,803
Maryland	609,419	316,138	51.9	293,281	48.1	.....	..	22,857
Massachusetts	1,960,625	1,035,296	52.8	921,350	47.0	4,019	0.2	113,946
Michigan	2,205,217	1,106,899	50.2	1,084,423	49.2	13,895	0.6	22,476
Minnesota	1,126,159	589,864	52.4	527,416	46.8	8,879	0.8	62,448
Mississippi	172,379	160,792	93.3	11,587	6.7	.....	..	149,205
Missouri	1,571,678	807,357	51.4	761,175	48.4	3,146	0.2	46,182
Montana	207,355	112,556	54.3	93,163	44.9	1,636	0.8	19,393

Presidential Vote—The state-by-state popular vote for President in the 1944 election was as follows:

State	Total Vote	Democrat	Pct.	Republican	Pct.	Other	Pct.	Plurality
Nebraska	563,126	233,246	41.4	329,880	58.6	.....	..	96,634
Nevada	54,234	29,623	54.6	24,611	45.4	.....	..	5,012
New Hampshire	229,630	119,668	52.1	109,916	47.9	46	0.0	9,752
New Jersey	1,963,761	987,874	50.3	961,335	49.0	14,552	0.7	26,539
New Mexico	152,221	81,389	53.5	70,688	46.4	144	0.1	10,701
New York	6,311,630	3,304,238	52.4	2,987,647	47.3	20,045	0.3	316,591
North Carolina	789,554	527,399	66.6	262,155	33.2	.....	..	265,244
North Dakota	220,171	100,144	45.5	118,535	53.8	1,492	0.7	18,391
Ohio	3,153,056	1,570,763	49.8	1,582,293	50.2	.....	..	11,530
Oklahoma	720,973	401,549	55.7	319,424	44.3	.....	..	82,125
Oregon	480,147	248,635	51.8	225,365	46.9	6,147	1.3	23,270
Pennsylvania	3,794,787	1,940,479	51.1	1,835,048	48.4	19,260	0.5	105,431
Rhode Island	297,948	174,431	58.5	123,517	41.5	.....	..	50,914
South Carolina	103,375	90,601	87.6	4,610	4.5	8,164	7.9	85,991
South Dakota	232,073	96,711	41.7	135,362	58.3	.....	..	38,651
Tennessee	510,692	308,707	60.5	200,311	39.2	1,674	0.3	108,396
Texas	1,150,343	821,605	71.4	191,425	16.6	137,313	12.0	630,180
Utah	247,979	150,088	60.5	97,891	39.5	.....	..	52,197
Vermont	125,347	53,820	42.9	71,527	57.1	.....	..	17,707
Virginia	388,485	242,276	62.4	145,243	37.4	966	0.2	97,033
Washington	856,328	486,774	56.8	361,689	42.2	7,865	1.0	124,885
West Virginia	715,596	392,777	54.9	322,819	45.1	.....	..	69,958
Wisconsin	1,339,152	650,412	48.6	674,532	50.4	14,207	1.0	24,119
Wyoming	101,340	49,419	48.8	51,921	51.2	.....	..	2,502
Totals	47,969,828	25,610,946	53.4	22,018,177	45.9	340,705	.7	3,592,769

Presidents de Facto and de Jure—When a person has actual possession of a public office and exercises its functions, he is said to be an officer *de facto,* or in fact; while a person who is rightfully entitled to an office, but does not actually fill it, is said to be an officer *de jure,* or of right. In the presidential contest of 1876, it was claimed by many supporters of Samuel J. Tilden, the losing nominee, that he had been defrauded of the election, and they spoke of him as President de Jure, and his successful opponent, Rutherford B. Hayes, as President de Facto; that is, the rightful President as distinguished from the actual one.

Presidents of the United States—A list of the presidents of the United States, with information concerning their party affiliations, years of service, etc., follows. For the powers of the President, see *Executive.* Biographical sketches of the presidents will also be found elsewhere in this book.

Name	Born	Party	Elected from	Years of Service	Died
1. George Washington	Va., 1732	Fed.	Va.	1789–1797	1799
2. John Adams	Mass., 1735	Fed.	Mass.	1797–1801	1826
3. Thomas Jefferson	Va., 1743	Rep.-Dem.	Va.	1801–1809	1826
4. James Madison	Va., 1751	Rep.-Dem.	Va.	1809–1817	1836
5. James Monroe	Va., 1758	Rep.-Dem.	Va.	1817–1825	1831
6. John Quincy Adams	Mass., 1767	Rep.-Dem.	Mass.	1825–1829	1848
7. Andrew Jackson	S. C., 1767	Dem.	Tenn.	1829–1837	1845
8. Martin Van Buren	N. Y., 1782	Dem.	N. Y.	1837–1841	1862
9. William Henry Harrison	Va., 1773	Whig	O.	1841 (one month)	1841
10. John Tyler	Va., 1790	Dem.	Va.	1841–1845	1862
11. James K. Polk	N. C., 1795	Dem.	Tenn.	1845–1849	1849
12. Zachary Taylor	Va., 1784	Whig	La.	1849–1850	1850
13. Millard Fillmore	N. Y., 1800	Whig	N. Y.	1850–1853	1874
14. Franklin Pierce	N. H., 1804	Dem.	N. H.	1853–1857	1869
15. James Buchanan	Pa., 1791	Dem.	Pa.	1857–1861	1868
16. Abraham Lincoln	Ky., 1809	Rep.	Ill.	1861–1865	1865
17. Andrew Johnson	N. C., 1808	Dem.	Tenn.	1865–1869	1875
18. Ulysses S. Grant	O., 1822	Rep.	Ill.	1869–1877	1885
19. Rutherford B. Hayes	O., 1822	Rep.	O.	1877–1881	1893
20. James A. Garfield	O., 1831	Rep.	O.	1881 (6 mos.)	1881
21. Chester A. Arthur	Vt., 1830	Rep.	N. Y.	1881–1885	1886
22. Grover Cleveland	N. J., 1837	Dem.	N. Y.	1885–1889	1908
23. Benjamin Harrison	O., 1833	Rep.	Ind.	1889–1893	1901

Name	Born	Party	Elected from	Years of Service	Died
24. Grover Cleveland		Dem.	.... N. Y.	1893–1897	
25. William McKinley	O., 1843	.... Rep.	.... O.	.. 1897–1901	1901
26. Theodore Roosevelt ...	N. Y., 1858	.. Rep.	.... N. Y.	1901–1909	1919
27. William H. Taft	O., 1857	.... Rep.	.... O.	.. 1909–1913	1930
28. Woodrow Wilson	Va., 1856	... Dem.	.... N. J.	1913–1921	1924
29. Warren G. Harding ...	O., 1865	.... Rep.	.... O.	.. 1921–1923	1923
30. Calvin Coolidge	Vt., 1872	... Rep.	.... Mass.	1923–1929	1933
31. Herbert Hoover	Ia., 1874	.... Rep.	.... Calif.	1929–1933	
32. Franklin D. Roosevelt .	N. Y., 1882	.Dem.	.... N. Y.	1933–1945	1945
33. Harry S. Truman	Mo., 1884	.. Dem.	.... Mo.	. 1945–	

Press Conferences—Franklin D. Roosevelt, during his terms as President, held frank and informal conferences with the press. Through these conferences and his reports to the nation by radio, he took the public into his confidence to a much greater degree than any other President. He held nearly a thousand news conferences with reporters during his tenure of office. (See *Fireside Chats*.)

Pressure Group—Any group of persons, large or small, which openly or secretly endeavors to influence the government for its own advantage. Because some groups have worked under cover from motives of purely personal gain, the term has come to have a sinister meaning, but there is nothing wrong with a pressure group which works openly for legitimate ends. By the counteraction of different group pressures upon one another a balance is maintained among the various conflicting economic, social, and political forces at work in the country. Our government is designed to function under pressure from all sides. (See *Lobby*.)

Primary—The balloting of the voters of a party for the purpose of nominating candidates for office, or for choosing delegates to a nominating convention. The former is called the direct primary, the latter the indirect primary.

The direct primary has a long history. It had its beginning in Crawford County, Pennsylvania, shortly after the Civil War. It gained headway in the West and South, but it was not until the turn of the century, when such leaders as La Follette, Bryan, Theodore Roosevelt, and Wilson advocated the system, that it spread throughout the country and largely superseded the old convention system.

The reasons for the primary were set forth by Robert M. La Follette, one of the leading liberal United States senators of the first quarter of this century, in a speech delivered at Milwaukee in 1902.

"The question of primary elections," said Senator La Follette, "is one of government for the people and by the people. Under our system of government by political parties, two elements, equal in importance, are involved in the exercise of suffrage; one, the making of the ballot; the other, the casting of the ballot. The right to cast the ballot is considered sacred. No man would be willing to delegate his power to cast the ballot at general elections. No man shall be compelled to delegate his power to make his ballot. Boss Tweed said: 'You may elect whichever candidate you please to office, if you will allow me to select the candidates.' The boss can always afford to say, 'You may vote any ticket you please so long as I make all the tickets.' The character of the men nominated and the influences to which they owe their nominations determine the character of the government.

"The result and the only result sought by a primary election is to give every man an equal voice in the selection of all candidates; to lodge in the people the absolute right to say who their candidates shall be; to root out forever the power of the political boss to control the selection of officials through the manipulation of caucuses and conventions."

It was but a step from the direct primary for local and state candidates to the presidential primary, and Senator La Follette's state, Wisconsin, was the first to have such a law. This was in 1905. A decade later some twenty-five states had presidential primary laws, most of them providing that party voters should not only choose delegates to the national convention but should also indicate their choice of a presidential nominee. The delegates then vote for the candidate who wins the state primary. About twenty states, electing approximately half the delegates to the national conventions, now hold presidential primaries.

There is a wide divergence in the primary laws of the states, not only as to the method by which candidates secure a place on the official ballot but also as to the method used in voting for the candidates. In many states candidates are "designated" for the

249

ballot by petition, the aspirant for office being required to secure a specified number of signatures to his petition in order to qualify. In other states a simple declaration of intention to run for office and the payment of a fee is sufficient.

In voting for the candidates some states use the so-called "open" primary, a voter being given the ballots of all parties. After marking the ballot of his choice he discards the rest. In the so-called "closed" primary the voter is given only the ballot of the party to which he has declared his adherence. In a few states in the South, where the winning of the Democratic primary is equivalent to election, it often happens that with a number of candidates in the field none receives a majority of the votes cast. When this occurs the two highest candidates are pitted against each other in a second or run-off primary.

On May 26, 1941, the Supreme Court of the United States, in a 4 to 3 decision, held that "the authority of Congress includes the authority to regulate primary elections when they are a step in the exercise of the people of their choice of representatives in Congress." The court remarked that it was the first time the question had been specifically passed on by the Supreme Court.

Prohibition—Legislative method used in the control of the liquor traffic. It forbids the manufacture and sale of alcoholic beverages of an intoxicating nature. Among the earliest states in America to put prohibition into effect were Maine, in 1846 (and reinforced in 1851), and later came Vermont, Rhode Island, and Massachusetts. The laws in the two latter states, however, were later repealed. The Middle Western states launched a forceful campaign for prohibition after 1880, and some of them passed dry laws. The movement later spread to the Southern states. By 1916 half of the states in the country had adopted some form of prohibition.

When the United States entered World War I, the prohibition forces saw an opportunity to extend the movement and try to make it nation-wide. In November 1917 a law was passed by Congress which prohibited the manufacture of liquors, but beer and wine were not affected. Shortly afterward President Woodrow Wilson proclaimed a reduction in the alcoholic content of beer.

Congress later in the same year passed a resolution providing for national prohibition. This was to be submitted to the states, and it became the Eighteenth Amendment to the Constitution. The necessary three fourths of the states had ratified it by January 1919.

Then the National Prohibition Act (Volstead Act) was passed by Congress on October 28, 1919. Wilson vetoed the measure, but Congress passed it over his veto. The Supreme Court later sustained the validity of both the Eighteenth Amendment and the National Prohibition Act. The law remained in effect until repealed by virtue of ratification of the Twenty-first Amendment to the Constitution.

Federal agencies found it exceedingly difficult to enforce the law inasmuch as a large proportion of the populace was strongly opposed to prohibition. There was a great deal of bootlegging, smuggling, many "speak-easies," gang warfare, and an increase in crime. The anti-prohibition movement made marked progress each year until the law was repealed in 1933.

Prohibition Party—William Kennedy Brown, a clergyman and educator who was born in Pennsylvania in 1834 and after entering the ministry devoted much thought to the question of temperance and the political status of women, may well be considered a pioneer in the temperance movement in the United States. In conjunction with Julius A. Spencer he formed a political movement calling for temperance reform. From this movement sprang the Prohibition party, in the platform of which was a plank calling for woman suffrage. This party was the first of the major national political organizations to advocate woman suffrage.

The Prohibition party has had a presidential ticket in the field each election since its inception in 1872. The most votes a Prohibition presidential candidate ever received was about 270,000, polled by John Bidwell, a soldier, agriculturist, and politician, in 1892.

Puerto Rico—An island washed by the Atlantic Ocean on the north and the Caribbean Sea on the south. A dependency of the United States. Population, 1,869,255. Area, 3,435 square miles. Capital, San Juan. During the Spanish-American War in 1898 the island was taken under control by the American forces and later ceded to the United States by Spain. The island has a large measure of self-government, and its citizens are granted American citizenship. The governor of the island is appointed by the President of the United States. The dependency has a resident commissioner in Washington.

Qualifications of Voters—See *Voters, Qualifications of.*

Quorum—In all select bodies made up of a definite number of persons, such as legislative assemblies, boards, and commissions, the common-law rule is that a majority (one more than half) constitutes a quorum, but where the number is indefinite, as in the case of a town meeting or general body of electors, the majority rule does not prevail, and any number legally met may transact business. The weight of authority is to the effect that less than a quorum of a select body, if met at the time and place set for a duly called meeting, may keep the meeting alive by adjournment.

Radical Democracy—In 1864 the Union men opposed to Lincoln's renomination issued a call for a convention which met accordingly on May 31. The circular had attacked the administration vigorously. Their platform called for the suppression of the Rebellion, the preservation of the habeas corpus, of the right of asylum, and the Monroe Doctrine. It recommended a popular vote and only a single term for presidents, an amendment to the Constitution prohibiting slavery, and called for the confiscation of the land of rebels and its distribution among actual settlers. The name Radical Democracy was adopted; they were also known as Radical Men. General John C. Frémont was nominated; he accepted the nomination but withdrew in Lincoln's favor on September 21.

Recess Appointments—Under Article II, Section 2, of the Constitution the President has the power to fill up all vacancies during the recess of the Senate by granting commissions which expire at the end of the next session.

Referendum—Submitting a matter to the electorate for decision by direct popular vote. Provision is made in the Constitution for

252

referring amendments to that document to the states for ratification. (See *Amendments.*)

"Remember Pearl Harbor"—This phrase became a byword and rallying cry throughout America during World War II. Millions of people were saying it, and it made its appearance on thousands of posters shortly after the Japanese attack on the United States Hawaiian naval base at Pearl Harbor on December 7, 1941. President Roosevelt said it was "a day that will live in infamy."

Removal from Office—Although the Constitution is silent on the question of the power of removal from office, the Supreme Court has held that it is incidental to the power to appoint. Chief Justice Taft said in the case of Myers *vs.* United States (272 U.S. 52), decided in 1926, "The power to remove inferior executive officers, like that to remove superior executive officers, is an incident of the power to appoint them, and is in its nature an executive power. The power of Congress . . . to vest the appointment of such inferior officers in the heads of departments carries with it authority incidentally to invest the heads of departments with power to remove."

Repeating—Fraudulent casting by a voter of more than one ballot at the same election. A person who does this is called a repeater.

Republican Party—This was the original name of the Democratic party. It is also the name of the principal opponent of that party from 1854 to the present time. The dissolution of the Whig party in 1852 left a number of factions agreeing in nothing but in their opposition to the Democratic party and having none of the elements necessary to the formation of a united party. But from these there sprang the most powerful party the Democratic party has yet had to encounter—a consistent advocate of broad construction and internal improvements, more popular than the Federal party and more homogeneous and courageous than the Whigs.

The name was adopted partly because its associations were thought well suited to draw together many of the discordant ele-

253

ments. It was suggested at a meeting of a number of members of Congress and was first formally adopted at a Michigan convention in July 1854. The old Whigs, the Free-Soilers, many Know-Nothings, and some few Democrats were the elements that went to make up the party; the Abolitionists were a species of allies. Its success in the states was at first marked, eleven senators and a plurality of the House belonging to the party.

In 1856 a national convention was called and Frémont was nominated. The platform declared against the repeal of the Missouri Compromise and the extension of slavery and in favor of the Pacific railroads, of the admission of Kansas as a free state, and of the improvement of "rivers and harbors of national character." Frémont was defeated by a small majority.

Between 1856 and 1860 the party gained largely in compactness, the uncompromising attitude of the slave power uniting Northerners more closely and drawing away from the party those not in sympathy with it. The platform of 1860 was, with slight exceptions, the same as in 1856, except that a protective tariff was demanded and that threats of secession were condemned. In the convention only a few of the Southern states were represented.

Abraham Lincoln was nominated and elected. His election was declared by the Southern states to be sufficient cause for their secession, and thus was the country plunged into Civil War. During the war the history of the government is the history of the party. The war policy of the President was supported by the party, as were also the measures intended to cripple slavery.

In 1864 Lincoln was renominated and re-elected by a large majority. His assassination followed hard upon his inauguration, and the Vice-President, Johnson, became President. Between him and Congress there sprang up, almost at once, a conflict on the subject of the reconstruction of the seceded states, Congress demanding "substantial guarantees" of the preservation of the rights of the Negroes as a condition precedent to admission. Johnson's impeachment and acquittal followed.

The measures of Congress on the subject of reconstruction were approved by the party. That the party was carried somewhat too far on this subject was shown by the declaration of the unconstitu-

254

tionality of parts of the Civil Rights Bill by a Supreme Court, the members of which were appointed by Republican presidents.

In 1868 Grant was nominated and elected. The party placed itself on record as opposed to the intimidation of Negro voters by Southern whites, and the Fifteenth Amendment to the Constitution is due to its efforts, as were also the Thirteenth and Fourteenth. In 1872 Grant was renominated, but a portion of the party, disapproving of its coercive measures toward the South, held a separate convention under the name of Liberal Republican party. Grant was neverthe-less elected, but his second term was marred by scandals arising from the corruption of subordinates selected by him.

The state elections just previous to 1876 had been unfavorable to the party, and the Democrats, with Tilden as their candidate, waged a vigorous campaign against Hayes, the Republican nominee. The result was long in doubt and was settled only by the Electoral Commission. Hayes was declared elected. During his administra-tion specie payments were resumed. In the convention of 1880 a determined stand was made by Grant's friends to secure his nomina-tion on the ground that, having been out of office for one term, his renomination could not be considered as for a "third term," but although his supporters clung to him throughout, Garfield was nominated and elected. The assassination of Garfield soon after his election brought Vice-President Arthur to the presidency.

In 1884 Blaine was chosen to represent the party. He was per-sonally obnoxious to a considerable number of Republicans, there-after called mugwumps, and in New York, always a doubtful and in this case the deciding state, the defection was sufficient to give the electoral vote of the state to the Democratic candidate, Cleveland, by the small plurality of 1,047, in a total vote of more than 1,100,000. Thus, after an uninterrupted sway of twenty-four years, the party's candidate for the presidency was defeated.

With the exception of Cleveland's two unconsecutive terms, the Republican party was dominant until 1912, when the splitting of the party by the Bull Moose or Progressive faction let Woodrow Wil-son in for an eight-year stretch. But the country went Republican again in 1920 and so remained until 1932, when Franklin D. Roose-velt became President.

255

Revolutionary—An instigator of political revolution, an advocate of the forcible substitution of a new government for the old. "Radical" or "red" is the term generally applied to such an extremist in the United States, the word "revolution" having acquired hallowed historical associations.

"Reward Your Friends and Punish Your Enemies"—These words of Samuel Gompers were the political slogan of the American Federation of Labor when he was head of that organization.

Rhode Island—"Little Rhody." State flower, violet. Population, 713,346. Area, 1,214 square miles. Capital, Providence. An original state of the Union. In both national and state politics the state is usually found in the Republican ranks, but in the last five presidential elections it has given its electoral votes to the Democratic party. It has two representatives in Congress.

Riders—When a legislative bill is saddled with a provision which has nothing to do with the main purpose of the measure to which it is attached, it is called a rider. It is a method by which provisions which would fail of passage if contained in a separate measure are passed as part of some necessary and important piece of legislation. By tacking a rider onto a bill a minority can sometimes make the passage of the bill in any form dependent on its carrying the rider. It is also resorted to as a means of circumventing the executive veto, as the Executive may feel obliged to sign a good bill despite a bad amendment. Riders are generally attached to appropriation bills.

Rogue's Island—When the state of Rhode Island stood out against ratification of the Constitution it was nicknamed Rogue's Island.

Roll-Call Vote—If one fifth of the members present of either of the houses of Congress desire a record of the yeas and nays on any question, the vote must be taken by roll call and published in the *Congressional Record*. In this way the people know just how each representative votes on particular measures. (Constitution, Article I, Section 5.)

Roorback—A forgery or fictitious story of a detrimental or defamatory nature published for the purpose of political intrigue. It
originated in the presidential election of 1844, when a story was
published reflecting on James K. Polk, the Democratic candidate,
which purported to be an excerpt from *Roorback's Tour through
the Western and Southern States in 1836.*

Roosevelt, Franklin Delano, thirty-second President of the
United States, was perhaps the most unique Executive in the history
of the nation. Of aristocratic Dutch lineage and member of a family
of wealth, he became President on March 4, 1933, and served three
full terms, shattering the third-term tradition, and died on April
12, 1945, at Warm Springs, Georgia, after serving a little over a
year of his fourth term.

His childhood was spent in luxury. He attended Groton private
school in Massachusetts and in June 1904 was graduated from Harvard University and later took up law. While at college this six-
foot broad-shouldered boy was active in sports and liked tennis,
swimming, and sailing.

In 1910 he was elected state senator from Dutchess County, New
York, and his oratory and capabilities won him quick recognition.
When Woodrow Wilson, in 1912, defeated William H. Taft and
"Bull Moose" Theodore Roosevelt, he was rewarded with appoint-
ment as Assistant Secretary of the Navy. At that time he disclaimed
being anti-Tammany but said he was opposed to the control of the
New York State democracy by Charles F. Murphy, the leader of
the Tammany organization.

With Europe aflame with conflict during the 1916 presidential
campaign he became very active in expanding the naval establishment.

When Wilson declined to run for a third term in 1920, Roosevelt
was nominated vice-presidential candidate on the ticket headed by
James M. Cox, but was defeated. The Democrats, at this time, were
committed to Wilson's policies respecting the entry of the United
States into the League of Nations and ratification of the Versailles
Treaty, and they were overwhelmingly defeated by the Warren G.
Harding-Calvin Coolidge ticket.

While swimming at his summer home in Campobello, New Brunswick, in August 1921, Roosevelt was stricken with infantile paralysis. He was carried away on a stretcher and for months his life hung in the balance. He had an indomitable spirit and fought the disease, but his legs were useless, though he could still swim. Each year he spent much time in the pool at Warm Springs, Georgia, and later established the Warm Springs Foundation so that others with the same affliction might be benefited.

The cultured and wealthy young lawyer returned to his law practice and later he and Alfred E. Smith, many times governor of New York State and defeated Democratic presidential candidate, were brought into close political relationship, an alliance which was destined to have a marked bearing on national affairs.

When Al Smith sought the presidential candidacy at San Francisco in 1920 it was Roosevelt who seconded the nomination, but Smith lost out to Cox. Four years afterward, wearing crutches, Roosevelt went to Madison Square Garden and made a notable nominating speech in behalf of Al Smith, labeling him the "Happy Warrior." Smith again lost the nomination—this time to John W. Davis, who was defeated by Calvin Coolidge.

Again in 1928, at Houston, Texas, Roosevelt was the nominator of Al Smith, whom he referred to as "Friend Al," and on this occasion Smith was successful in getting the nomination. Much against his will, Roosevelt ran for governor of New York State on the Smith ticket, and while he was elected Smith went down to defeat.

Within the next three or four years a split came in the Roosevelt-Smith alliance, and Roosevelt was pushed to the fore in the 1932 pre-convention campaign for the presidential nomination. Smith came out openly against Roosevelt for the nomination and applied the term "demagoguery" to Roosevelt's New Deal and forgotten-man philosophy and announced himself as a candidate. However, Roosevelt and John Nance Garner of Texas were selected to head the ticket, and Roosevelt flew from Albany to Chicago to accept the nomination.

Smith kept out of the limelight for months but finally relented and gave his support to Roosevelt. Their personal relationship was resurrected and their greetings were "Hello, old potato," and "How are you, Al?" Roosevelt was elected and received more than 22,000,-000 popular votes.

When Roosevelt assumed the presidency on March 4, 1933, having defeated Herbert Hoover, more than 12,000,000 persons were unemployed, prices were at a low ebb, foreign trade was in a bad way, and the banking system was tottering. One of his first acts was to declare a national banking holiday, and all financial depositories in the country were closed for ten days.

Roosevelt was extended exceptionally wide powers for a peacetime Executive, and for the next three months he put through an extensive recovery program of an unprecedented character. He created such "alphabet agencies" as the NRA, AAA, CCC, WPA, PWA, HOLC, and FHA. He later attempted to "pack," as his critics charged, the United States Supreme Court, because the court had ruled some of his pet legislation unconstitutional.

He was unanimously renominated in 1936 and overwhelmingly defeated Alf M. Landon, who was then governor of Kansas.

When he sought a third term his critics cried "indispensable man," "dictatorship," and "one-man government." However, he went on to defeat Wendell L. Willkie, Republican, by 449 to 82 electoral votes, and four years later was elected to a fourth term by defeating Thomas E. Dewey, governor of New York.

Roosevelt played a dominant role in charting a victory for the Allies. When the Nazi armies went roughshod through Belgium and Holland he declared that Britain and the British Navy must be preserved if America was to be safe, and he traded fifty old destroyers to Britain for air bases in the Atlantic.

Then came the sneak attack by the Japs on Pearl Harbor on Sunday, December 7, 1941—a day, Roosevelt said, "which will live in infamy."

He crossed the Atlantic again and again to hold conferences with Prime Minister Winston Churchill of Great Britain and other world leaders—at Tehran, Cairo, Iran, etc. He proclaimed to Congress his Four Freedoms—freedom of speech, freedom of religion, freedom from want, and freedom from fear.

Roosevelt outlined a huge wartime program; production goals were expanded; hundreds of billions of dollars in war costs continued to mount until the Allies had a vast superiority of arms over their enemies.

In the fall of 1942 Roosevelt received congressional authorization for rigid control of prices, wages, and profits, and rationing and price ceilings came into effect. The military situation began to improve; the Axis powers surrendered unconditionally, and then the Japs called an end to the great World War II.

Roosevelt was conceded a master politician even by his opponents. He was an able conversationalist, a good storyteller, and enjoyed a good joke, even though it was on himself. He smoked almost incessantly, holding his cigarette in an ivory cigarette holder.

Two attempts were made on his life—in April 1929, when a bomb addressed to him was found in a post office, and in February 1933, when Giuseppe Zangara fired five shots at him in Miami. The shots killed Mayor Anton J. Cermak of Chicago.

Roosevelt was born in Hyde Park on January 30, 1882, and died unexpectedly at Warm Springs, Georgia, on April 12, 1945. His legal residence was at Hyde Park, New York, where his grave is located.

Roosevelt, Theodore, twenty-sixth President of the United States, was born in New York City on October 27, 1858. His ancestors were, for the most part, Dutch and English. Though not of strong physique in boyhood, he liked sports and outdoor life. In 1880 he was graduated from Harvard University, shortly afterward joining the Republican party. He was elected to the New York Assembly, serving from 1881 to 1883. Some of his colleagues considered him a "dandy" because of his fastidiousness in dress. In 1886 he made an unsuccessful campaign for the New York mayoralty.

In 1897 he became Assistant Secretary of the Navy. At the outbreak of the Spanish-American War he organized a volunteer cavalry outfit which became known as the Roughriders. Later, as colonel of the regiment, he rendered distinguished service, and the famous charge up San Juan Hill, near Santiago, was led by him. When the war terminated he was tendered the New York State gubernatorial nomination by the Republicans and was elected by a plurality of over 18,000.

He was a vigorous executive, and Republican leaders offered him the vice-presidential candidacy on the McKinley ticket in 1900, though he was reluctant to accept. When McKinley died before serving out his term Roosevelt was raised to the presidency and took the oath of office on September 14, 1901. He continued the policies of McKinley, supporting the legislation against trusts and lending his assistance to treaties calling for reciprocal trade. He urged that the country's financial system be revised and that the Navy be increased, and gained the rights and territory for the construction of the Panama Canal. He was also instrumental in the establishment of a Census Bureau on a permanent basis as well as a Department of Commerce and Labor.

Political cartoonists of the day often caricatured him with his "big stick," because he had once said: "Speak softly and carry a big stick."

He was elected in 1904 by 2,000,000 votes, which was one of the largest pluralities ever accorded a candidate. His opponent was Alton B. Parker. For his efforts in bringing about a termination of the Russo-Japanese War in 1905 he was awarded the Nobel Prize for Peace. The second Peace Conference at The Hague was brought about largely through his efforts.

When his term expired he declined to run for re-election for a third term and threw his support to William Howard Taft. After Taft was elected Roosevelt went to Africa to hunt big game.

Upon his return he aligned himself with the progressive element of the Republican party and was prevailed upon to become a candidate for the presidential nomination. When Taft, however, won the nomination Roosevelt formed a third party, the Progressive party, which became known as the Bull Moose party, and he became that party's presidential candidate. The Republican vote was thus split between Taft and Roosevelt in practically all the states. In about twenty-eight states Roosevelt had a majority over Taft. He received 4,000,000 votes to Taft's 3,000,000 and 88 electoral votes as against 8 for Taft. Though Woodrow Wilson, Democrat, was the successful candidate, he received only a minority of the total popular vote.

Roosevelt thereafter took to writing magazine articles and was contributing editor of the *Outlook* up to 1914. In this year he went on an expedition to Brazil and discovered a new river.

During World War I he was a strong advocate of preparedness and urged intervention by the United States. He was a frequent critic of President Wilson and in the presidential campaign of 1916 supported Charles E. Hughes, the unsuccessful candidate of the Republican party.

He died on January 6, 1919, and is buried in Oyster Bay, New York.

Rugged Individualism—An expression used by Herbert Hoover during the 1928 presidential campaign in a speech delivered in New York on October 22. "We were challenged," he said, "with a peacetime choice between the American system of rugged individualism and a European philosophy of diametrically opposed doctrines —doctrines of paternalism and state socialism."

"Rum, Romanism, and Rebellion"—Reverend Samuel D. Burchard, speaking for a deputation of clergymen calling upon James G. Blaine, the Republican presidential candidate, at the Fifth Avenue Hotel, New York City, October 29, 1884, said:

"We are Republicans, and don't propose to leave our party and identify ourselves with the party whose antecedents have been Rum, Romanism, and Rebellion."

This slighting allusion to Catholics which Blaine allowed to go unrebuked may have cost him the election. Cleveland carried New York State by only 1,047. With 524 of these votes Blaine would have carried the state and won the presidency.

Run Like Sam Hill—This familiar phrase originated in New England, where everybody knows not only what it means to run like Sam Hill but understands when someone says, "Where in Sam Hill are you going?" The person whose name is suggestive of speed was Colonel Samuel Hill of Guilford, Connecticut, who had a remarkable political career. He represented his town at eighteen sessions of the legislature, twice serving as Speaker, and at the same time held the offices of town clerk, clerk of the proprietors, and probate judge in Guilford. It is said that the moderator of the town meeting would announce, "We are here to elect Sam Hill and someone to go with him to the next General Court." A born politician,

Sam Hill established a political dynasty which enabled his son and his grandson to hold public office for life.

Scalawag—A scamp. The name was applied in the South after the Civil War to native white Southerners who joined the Republican party and helped in the work of reconstruction.

Scrub Race for President—In the presidential campaign of 1824 all the candidates—John Quincy Adams, Andrew Jackson, William H. Crawford, and Henry Clay—were of the same political party, and consequently the contest was purely a personal one. Adams received 84 electoral votes, Jackson 99, Crawford 41, and Clay 37, a total of 261 votes. Since none had a majority, the election was thrown into the House of Representatives, which had to choose from the three highest candidates. This eliminated Clay, whose supporters then voted for Adams, who carried thirteen states and was elected President. Clay, whose views were largely in accord with those of Adams, was made Secretary of State, which, it was alleged, was the price Clay asked for throwing his strength to Adams, but this was always denied.

Seat of Government—Previous to the final removal to Washington in 1800 the seats of government were: Philadelphia, May 10, 1775; Baltimore, December 20, 1776; Philadelphia, March 4, 1777; Lancaster, Pennsylvania, September 27, 1777; York, Pennsylvania, September 30, 1777; Philadelphia, July 2, 1778; Princeton, New Jersey, June 30, 1783; Annapolis, Maryland, November 26, 1783; Trenton, New Jersey, November 1, 1784; New York, January 11, 1785, where the Constitutional Government was organized in 1789.

Sectional President—Southerners applied this term to Lincoln, who, they claimed, represented only the Northern, not the Southern, section of the country.

Senate, The, is the upper and smaller branch of the legislative division of the Federal Government. The name is also applied to the corresponding divisions of the state legislatures, but when the term is used without qualification the United States Senate is

263

meant. This division of Congress is composed of two senators from each state, regardless of the size or population of the state, and the Constitution provides that "no state without its consent shall be deprived of its equal suffrage in the Senate." The ninety-six senators are elected for terms of six years each, but the terms are so arranged that one third of them terminate every two years. The Senate, therefore, is a legislative body having continuous existence and organization.

To qualify as a senator one must be at least thirty years old, a citizen for not less than nine years, and when elected an inhabitant of the state he is chosen to represent. The Senate is the judge of the elections and qualifications of its own members.

The Vice-President of the United States is the president of the Senate, but he has no vote except in case of a tie. The senators choose their other officers, and also a president pro tempore in the absence of the Vice-President or when he exercises the office of President. Like the House of Representatives, the Senate determines the rules of its own proceedings and may punish its members for disorderly behavior and by a two-thirds vote expel a member.

The Senate has the sole power to try impeachments. It must confirm the appointments made by the President and must ratify all treaties by a two-thirds vote. It may, of course, reject both appointments and treaties made by the President.

The Seventeenth Amendment to the Constitution, proclaimed May 31, 1913, provides for the direct election of United States senators by the people. Prior to the amendment senators were elected by the legislatures of the states, as they were originally considered the spokesmen of the states in the Federal Government, while the members of the House were considered the mouthpieces of the people. By the same amendment, vacancies in the representation of any state may be filled by the state executive making temporary appointment until the people fill the vacancies by election. (See *Congress; House of Representatives.*)

Separation of Powers—The government of the United States is divided into three great departments—the executive, the legislative, and the judicial—each with separate powers and functions which cannot be encroached on by the others. When the Constitution was before the people for ratification it was nicknamed the Triple-Headed Monster, in allusion to this division of the Federal Government. (See *Checks and Balances*.)

Sergeant at Arms—The sergeant at arms of a legislative body is the officer who, under the direction of the presiding head, preserves order, serves processes, and makes arrests when they are ordered by the assembly. He is usually elected by the legislative body.

Share-the-Wealth—See *Townsend Plan; Coughlinites*.

Sic Semper Tyrannis—This Latin phrase meaning "thus always to tyrants" is the motto of the state of Virginia. They were the words which John Wilkes Booth shouted when he leaped to the stage of Ford's Theater after shooting Abraham Lincoln.

Sidewalks of New York—Campaign song of Alfred E. Smith when he ran for President in 1928. It was played on any and all occasions when Smith made public appearances. In 1933, when newspapers reported that the author of the song was destitute, Smith is said to have taken action to assure that the man who wrote this famous campaign song would never be in want.

Slander and Libel—The Constitution (Article I, Section 6) gives senators and representatives full freedom of speech while engaged in their legislative duties, and they cannot be sued for what they say on the floor of either house, in committee meetings, or in official publications. Members of legislative bodies throughout the country enjoy a similar immunity under local law.

Solid South—Not long after the termination of the Civil War the Southern states banded together and became unswerving in their devotion to the Democratic party, so much so that around 1880 the characterization Solid South was applied to those states. This solidarity was the outgrowth of attempts by the Republican party to organize the vast Negro vote in the hope of keeping the Negro rule in effect in the South. This was strongly resented by the white people, who, when called upon, threw aside their convictions on po-

265

litical issues and had as their main aim the maintenance of white supremacy. For more than thirty years after the close of the Civil War the South never broke its political solidarity in national elections.

Sons of the Wild Jackass—Senator George H. Moses, former United States Senator from New Hampshire, who died in Concord on December 20, 1944, enjoyed a distinct reputation as one of the most pungent phrasemakers in the United States. His most nationally publicized phrase was his designation of some Senate members of a farm bloc as "sons of the wild jackass." Later, when queried as to the origin of the phrase, he said he had adopted it from the Old Testament.

South Carolina—The "Palmetto State." State flower, yellow jessamine. Population, 1,899,804. Area, 31,055 square miles. Capital, Columbia. Original state of the Union. It was the first state to secede in 1860. The state has, with few exceptions, always been Democratic in its politics. White supremacy is assured by its constitution, which prescribes a literacy test or ability to pay taxes on a few hundred dollars' worth of property. In this way the Democratic party is kept in the ascendancy.

Andrew Jackson, seventh President of the United States, was born in South Carolina. John C. Calhoun, who was Vice-President of the United States from 1825 to 1832 and a strong advocate of states' rights, was also a South Carolinian.

The state has six representatives in Congress.

South Dakota—"Coyote State." State flower, the pasque. Population, 642,961. Area, 77,047 square miles. Capital, Pierre. Ceded to the United States by the Louisiana Purchase Treaty. Admitted to the Union in 1889. Politically the state almost invariably shows a Republican majority, although it went Progressive in 1912 (Taft was not even on the ticket), and Democratic in 1932 and 1936. It has two representatives in Congress.

"Speak Softly and Carry a Big Stick"—Theodore Roosevelt used this phrase in a speech at the Minnesota State Fair, September 2,

1901. "There is a homely old adage," he said, "which runs: 'Speak softly and carry a big stick; you will go far.' If the American nation will speak softly and yet build and keep at the pitch of highest training a thoroughly efficient navy, the Monroe Doctrine will go far."

He was often caricatured showing his teeth and carrying a big stick.

Speaker of the House of Representatives, The, is elected by that body from its own membership, and as a member of the House he may speak and vote on all questions arising before it. All official documents, such as acts and warrants, issued under the authority of the House, are signed by the Speaker, on whom also devolves the duty of presiding over sessions of the House, recognizing members who desire to speak, ruling on questions of order, and referring bills to the proper committees.

The Speaker is, of course, invariably a leading member of the dominant party in the House. He was formerly a more powerful figure than he is today; he was, in fact, practically a dictator, appointing the committees at the beginning of each Congress and deciding with the heads of certain committees which bills should be debated and also which should be allowed to pass.

Joseph G. Cannon, popularly known as the "Hayseed Member from Illinois" and later as "Uncle Joe," was the most notorious Speaker in the annals of Congress. He was elected Speaker of the Fifty-first Congress (1901–03) and immediately began his arbitrary and partisan control of procedure known as "Canonnism." In 1907 the members who were barred from desirable committee places became extremely restless under his domination. Champ Clark of Missouri made an unsuccessful attempt to break his power in 1909, but it was not until the following year that the Democrats, with the help of insurgent Republicans, succeeded in passing a resolution enlarging the Committee on Rules and excluding the Speaker from membership on the committee. Since 1911 Congress has elected its committees.

Speaker Cannon was a political character, a typical old-school politician. In 1916 the House commemorated Uncle Joe's eightieth

267

birthday, which, considering his extreme reactionism, his misconduct as Speaker, and his failure during "near fifty years" of service in the House to connect his name with any constructive piece of legislation, was a remarkable tribute to the man himself.

Spoils System—The doctrine that places in the public service are the proper spoils of a victorious political party made an early appearance in American politics. It was not, however, until Jackson's administration in 1830 that the system came into full flower. Jackson maintained that every citizen had an equal right to public office. He advocated "rotation in office," which involved frequent changes, and his removals for political reasons alone far outnumbered those of all the presidents before him together. Although the civil service has to some extent cut into the spoils system, politicians still have many offices at their command with which to reward their followers. (See *Civil Service; Few Die and None Resign; To the Victors Belong the Spoils.*)

Square Deal—On July 4, 1903, President Theodore Roosevelt said in a speech at Springfield, Illinois: "A man who is good enough to shed his blood for his country is good enough to be given a square deal afterward. More than that no man is entitled to, and less than that no man shall have."

Stabilization Act—The economic issues which harassed the country during World War II centered around inflation and its many facets. On September 7, 1942, President Roosevelt asked Congress to authorize rigid control of prices, salaries, wages, and profits. A Stabilization Act resulted. And from the Supreme Court the President drafted Justice James F. Byrnes to be Economic Stabilizer Director. Rationing, starting with gasoline and sugar, was expanded; price ceilings were clamped on more and more commodities. But the threat of inflation remained. Novel restrictions were placed upon the people. They were not permitted to jump to new jobs at higher wages unless the change would aid the war effort. Salary raises were denied them unless the Treasury Department or War Labor Board gave approval. All prices were virtually frozen by the President on

April 8, 1943. The barriers were drastically tightened against wage boosts in what was termed a "hold-the-line" order against inflation.

Stalwarts—This is a name by which a faction of the Republican party was known. The name arose about the time of the national convention of 1880 and was applied to the wing of the party that supported the claims of General Grant to a nomination for a third term; the name was due to the tenacity with which these supporters clung to him. They were led by Senator Roscoe Conkling of New York. Opposed to them were the Half-Breeds, as they were called, under the leadership of James G. Blaine.

The contest between these factions was very warm during Garfield's short administration, the quarrel being on the division of the offices. Blaine was Secretary of State, and the administration was regarded as identified with the Half-Breeds. The outcome of the quarrel was the resignation of Senator Conkling and his colleague, in the expectation of an immediate re-election, which would have served as a rebuke to the President. In this Conkling was disappointed. He failed of re-election.

Meanwhile Garfield's death and the accession of Arthur, a Stalwart, together with the latter's judicious conduct, healed the party split, at least on the surface. Nevertheless, the enormous Democratic majority in the New York State election for governor in 1882, caused as it was by the abstention of Republican voters, showed that the gulf had not yet been bridged. The withdrawal of Conkling from political life, however, aided in uniting the party, and these lines of division soon disappeared.

State, Department of—This, the oldest of the executive departments of the government, was created by act of Congress on July 27, 1789, as the Department of Foreign Affairs, with John Jay as the Secretary for Foreign Affairs. On September 15, 1789, the name was changed to the Department of State. The head of the department is the Secretary of State, and Thomas Jefferson was the first to fill that office. The Secretary of State is the highest-ranking officer of the Cabinet, and in the event of the death of the President and the death or absence of the Vice-President he assumes the position of acting President. The Secretary has charge of all business between our government and foreign governments. He conducts all correspondence with United States ambassadors, ministers, and consuls abroad and with foreign representatives in the United States. Under his direction are the negotiations of treaties, and his department is the liaison office between the state executives and the President. Granting of passports and issuing of visas come under his jurisdiction. He has charge of the foreign commerce service abroad, and commercial attachés gather information for submission to his department. Certain functions relating to presidential elections come under him, and the appointment of electors by the various states is certified through his department. Laws and resolutions of Congress, as well as constitutional amendments, are published by this department. The Secretary of State has charge of the great seal of the United States.

The organization of the Department of State includes the following offices: the Office of Controls, handling passports and visas; Office of Transportation and Communications; Office of Wartime Economic Affairs; Office of Economic Affairs; Office of American Republic Affairs; Offices of European, Near Eastern, and African Affairs; Office of Far Eastern Affairs; Office of Special Political Affairs; Office of Public Information; Office of Departmental Administration; Office of Foreign Service Administration.

State of the Union—See *President's Message.*

Steam Roller—Theodore Roosevelt, seeking the presidential nomination at the Republican convention in 1912, became very indignant at the "steam roller" tactics of those supporters of President Taft which forced the latter's nomination.

Steering Committee—The order in which business is dealt with in the Senate and the House of Representatives in Washington is determined by an informal group of members in each house called a steering committee, which in both houses is controlled by the leaders of the majority party.

Straw Vote—As a straw will show the way the wind blows, so may an unofficial or straw vote indicate the trend of political sentiment before an election. Modern scientific sampling methods of taking polls have resulted in amazingly accurate forecasts of elections. The Gallup Poll's forecast for the division of civilian votes in the 1944 presidential election (Roosevelt *vs.* Dewey) compared as follows with the election results:

	Forecast	Election	Deviation
Roosevelt	51.5%	53.3%	1.8%

Not only was the Gallup Poll right within 2 per cent, but so was every other national poll making use of the sampling technique. These polls included the Fortune Survey conducted by Elmo Roper, the Office of Public Research conducted by Hadley Cantril, the Crossley Poll conducted by Archibald Crossley, and the National Opinion Research Center, conducted by Harry Field.

Stump—Political orators formerly harangued the people largely out of doors, using the best vantage point they could find, which in pioneering days was often the stump of a tree. Hence such terms as "stump speech," "stump speaker," "stumping the state."

Submission Men—See *Anti-War Democrats.*

Supreme Court of the United States—This court, which is the highest in the land, consists of a Chief Justice and eight Associate Justices, who are appointed by the President, with the consent of the Senate, for life. Originally, under the Judiciary Act of 1789, there were a Chief Justice and five Associate Justices. The number has been changed from time to time, but for many years now the court has consisted of a full bench of nine judges, with six constituting a quorum. The last attempt to change the number of justices was made by President Franklin D. Roosevelt, but his effort proved unsuccessful. (See *Nine Old Men.*)

The Supreme Court has original jurisdiction only of "cases affecting ambassadors, other public ministers and consuls, and those in which a state shall be a party"; that is to say, only such cases can be commenced in the Supreme Court, but cases decided in other Federal courts can, under certain conditions, be reviewed by the highest court by virtue of its appellate jurisdiction. Its jurisdiction

JUSTICES OF THE UNITED STATES SUPREME COURT

Name	Service Term	Yrs.	Born	Died
John Jay, N. Y.	1789–1795	6	1745	1829
John Rutledge, S. C.	1789–1791	2	1739	1800
William Cushing, Mass.	1789–1810	21	1733	1810
James Wilson, Pa.	1789–1798	9	1742	1798
John Blair, Va.	1789–1796	7	1732	1800
Robert H. Harrison, Md.	1789–1790	1	1745	1790
James Iredell, N. C.	1790–1799	9	1751	1799
Thomas Johnson, Md.	1791–1793	2	1732	1819
William Paterson, N. J.	1793–1806	13	1745	1806
John Rutledge, S. C.	1795–1796	..	1739	1800
Samuel Chase, Md.	1796–1811	15	1741	1811
Oliver Ellsworth, Conn.	1796–1799	4	1745	1807
Bushrod Washington, Va.	1798–1829	31	1762	1829
Alfred Moore, N. C.	1799–1804	5	1755	1810
John Marshall, Va.	1801–1835	34	1755	1835
William Johnson, S. C.	1804–1834	30	1771	1834
Brockholst Livingston, N. Y.....	1806–1823	17	1757	1823
Thomas Todd, Ky.	1807–1826	19	1765	1826
Joseph Story, Mass.	1811–1845	34	1779	1845
Gabriel Duval, Md.	1811–1836	25	1752	1844
Smith Thompson, N. Y.	1823–1843	20	1767	1843
Robert Trimble, Ky.	1826–1828	2	1777	1828
John McLean, Ohio	1829–1861	32	1785	1861
Henry Baldwin, Pa.	1830–1846	14	1779	1844
James M. Wayne, Ga.	1835–1867	32	1790	1867
Roger B. Taney, Md.	1836–1864	28	1777	1864
Philip P. Barbour, Va.	1836–1841	5	1783	1841
John Catron, Tenn.	1837–1865	28	1786	1865
John McKinley, Ala.	1837–1852	15	1780	1852
Peter V. Daniel, Va.	1841–1860	19	1785	1860
Samuel Nelson, N. Y.	1845–1872	27	1792	1873
Levi Woodbury, N. H.	1845–1851	6	1789	1851
Robert C. Grier, Pa.	1846–1870	24	1794	1870
Benj. R. Curtis, Mass.	1851–1857	6	1809	1874
John A. Campbell, Ala.	1853–1861	8	1811	1889
Nathan Clifford, Me.	1858–1881	23	1803	1881
Noah H. Swayne, Ohio	1862–1881	20	1804	1884
Samuel F. Miller, Iowa	1862–1890	28	1816	1890
David Davis, Ill.	1862–1877	15	1815	1886
Stephen J. Field, Cal.	1863–1897	34	1816	1899
Salmon P. Chase, Ohio	1864–1873	9	1808	1873
William Strong, Pa.	1870–1880	10	1808	1895
Joseph P. Bradley, N. J.	1870–1892	22	1813	1892
Ward Hunt, N. Y.	1873–1882	10	1811	1886
Morrison R. Waite, Ohio	1874–1888	14	1816	1888

Name	Service Term	Yrs.	Born	Died
John M. Harlan, Ky.	1877–1911	34	1833	1911
William B. Woods, Ga.	1880–1887	7	1824	1887
Stanley Matthews, Ohio	1881–1889	8	1824	1889
Horace Gray, Mass.	1881–1902	21	1828	1902
Samuel Blatchford, N. Y.	1882–1893	11	1820	1893
Lucius Q. C. Lamar, Miss.	1888–1893	5	1825	1893
Melville W. Fuller, Ill.	1888–1910	22	1833	1910
David J. Brewer, Kan.	1889–1910	21	1837	1910
Henry B. Brown, Mich.	1890–1906	16	1836	1913
George Shiras, Jr., Pa.	1892–1903	11	1832	1924
Howell E. Jackson, Tenn.	1893–1895	2	1832	1895
Edward D. White, La.	1894–1910	16	1845	1921
Rufus W. Peckham, N. Y.	1895–1910	14	1838	1909
Joseph McKenna, Cal.	1898–1925	27	1843	1926
Oliver W. Holmes, Mass.	1902–1932	29	1841	1935
William R. Day, Ohio	1903–1922	19	1849	1923
William H. Moody, Mass.	1906–1910	4	1853	1917
Horace H. Lurton, Tenn.	1910–1914	5	1844	1914
Charles E. Hughes, N. Y.	1910–1916	6	1862	....
Willis Van Devanter, Wy.	1911–1937	26	1859	1941
Joseph R. Lamar, Ga.	1910–1916	6	1857	1916
Edward D. White, La.	1910–1921	11	1845	1921
Mahlon Pitney, N. J.	1912–1922	12	1858	1924
Jas. C. McReynolds, Tenn.	1914–1941	26	1862	1946
Louis D. Brandeis, Mass.	1916–1939	23	1856	1941
John H. Clarke, Ohio	1916–1922	6	1857	....
William H. Taft, Conn.	1921–1930	9	1857	1930
George Sutherland, Utah	1922–1938	16	1862	1942
Pierce Butler, Minn.	1922–1939	27	1866	1939
Edward T. Sanford, Tenn.	1923–1930	7	1865	1930
Harlan F. Stone, N. Y.	1925–1941	16	1872	....
Charles E. Hughes, N. Y.	1930–1941	11	1862	....
Owen J. Roberts, Penn.	1930–1945	15	1875	....
Benjamin N. Cardozo, N. Y.	1932–1938	6	1870	1938
Hugo L. Black, Ala.	1937–....	..	1886	....
Stanley F. Reed, Ky.	1938–....	..	1884	....
Felix Frankfurter, Mass.	1939–....	..	1882	....
William O. Douglas, Conn.	1939–....	..	1898	....
Frank Murphy, Michigan	1940–....	..	1893	....
Harlan F. Stone, N. Y.	1941–1946	5	1872	1946
James F. Byrnes, S. C.	1941–1942	1	1879	....
Robert H. Jackson, N. Y.	1941–....	..	1892	....
Wiley B. Rutledge, Iowa	1943–....	..	1894	....
Harold H. Burton, Ohio	1945–....	..	1888	....
Fred M. Vinson, Ky.	1946–....	..	1890	....

Names in bold-face type are Chief Justices.

is in general distinct from the state courts, but it is sometimes concurrent with them. Cases decided in the highest courts of any state may be reviewed by the Supreme Court, but only when Federal questions are involved; that is, when the controversy deals with the Constitution, laws, or treaties of the United States. (See *Judiciary*.)

Swapping Horses in Midstream—In a speech delivered on June 9, 1864, Abraham Lincoln said: "I have not permitted myself, gentlemen, to conclude that I am the best man in the country; but I am reminded in this connection of a story of an old Dutch farmer, who remarked to a companion once that it was not best to swap horses when crossing a stream." Another version used in the Hoover-Roosevelt campaign of 1932 was "Don't change barrels going over Niagara Falls."

Swinging Round the Circle—When President Andrew Johnson went to Chicago in 1866 to lay the cornerstone of a monument to Stephen A. Douglas he took occasion to make a number of political speeches along the way. He described the trip as "swinging round the circle."

Tabling—To table a measure—that is, to lay it on the Speaker's table for future consideration—has the practical effect under American parliamentary practice of killing it. Like the pigeonholing of a bill by a legislative committee, the tabling of a measure by an assembly is usually done with the express purpose of letting it die through inaction. In Congress, once a bill has been thus put aside, a two-thirds vote is necessary to take it from the table, as this has to be done under a suspension of the rules.

Taft, William H.—Our twenty-seventh President was William H. Taft, a Republican, who was born in Cincinnati, Ohio, on September 15, 1857. His early youth was a distinguished one, with a long list of accomplishments leading eventually to his election as President of the United States in 1908. He was graduated from Yale and Cincinnati Law School. He started his career as a law reporter for his home-town newspapers. Shortly afterward he started practicing law, and from then until 1908 some of his more important titles

274

were: assistant prosecuting attorney, judge of Cincinnati Superior Court, United States Solicitor General, United States circuit judge, governor of the Philippines, and Secretary of War during Theodore Roosevelt's administration.

It is generally conceded that Taft's term of office was a partial failure, not because of the character or intelligence of this dignified and congenial gentleman, both of which were beyond question. It was due rather to a dissension of his advisers and members of the Republican party while he was in office, that he was overshadowed in following such a dominating personality as Theodore Roosevelt as President, and that his temperament was not suited to the practical politics associated with the duties of filling public office. As a trained lawyer he had a judicial mind, and it is believed that the bench was what he always longed for. His greatest wish was granted when during Harding's administration he was chosen to be Chief Justice of the United States Supreme Court, over which he presided from 1921 to 1930.

In 1908, when he defeated William Jennings Bryan for the presidency, he polled the largest electoral and popular vote recorded to that date. When he ran for re-election in 1912 he received only eight electoral votes, which is evidence of his decline in popularity with the people. One of his more important failings was making broad rash statements that could be misinterpreted, such as the time he was questioned by reporters upon alighting from a train in Washington.

"What will become of the labor situation, Mr. President?"

"God only knows," was his reply. He meant the remark as one of sincere sympathy and concern. At this time there was a great deal of unrest among the laboring people, and the phrase was immediately publicized by his opponents as indicative of his general attitude—his disregard and lack of interest on issues vitally affecting the state of the nation.

Actually Mr. Taft was responsible for a number of social reforms and civil improvements. During his term of office the Interstate Commerce Commission was strengthened, the Land Grant and Mann acts were passed, a postal banking system was established, and New Mexico and Arizona were admitted to the Union.

Early in 1930 he became very ill and in March of that year died in Washington, where he was buried.

Take a Walk—Phrase used by Al Smith when he walked out on President Roosevelt when the latter was renominated for the presidency in 1936. By 1940, when Roosevelt decided to run for a third term, Smith was so incensed at "Friend Frank" that he voted for Wendell Willkie, the Republican candidate.

Tammany—In 1789 the Columbian Order was organized in New York City by William Mooney. In 1805 it was incorporated and the name of Tammany Society was assumed, the name being taken from that of an Indian chief. Its organization was supposed in a general way to imitate Indian customs, consisting of sachems or chiefs, a sagamore or master of ceremonies, the members being called braves, its meeting place the wigwam, etc. It was at first a social organization, but about 1800 the majority of its members were in sympathy with Aaron Burr, and the society entered politics under his standard.

From the first the qualities that have always been most prominent in it prevailed, thorough organization and a thorough canvass. Tammany was for a short time allied with De Witt Clinton, but they separated and Tammany came to be recognized as the regular Democratic faction. It had thus gained a position in New York politics.

It has since been a factor to be reckoned with. Its field of greatest activity is in the local politics of New York City, but in the politics of the state its influence is considerable because of the large vote cast in New York City.

About 1830 there was added to its organization the general committee, containing representatives of every election district. This unwieldy body was practically controlled by sub-committees, where the leaders of the organization made their will felt. Tweed was its boss in the days of his success, and his overthrow dealt it a severe blow; but it has always recovered its position. Its organization and traditions both tend to make it subject to the control of a small clique, and its large following in a state always doubtful gives it a strong influence in national politics.

Tarring and Feathering—A form of direct political action expressive of disapproval, often used in connection with riding on a rail. It was very unpopular among British revenue officers in the days immediately preceding the American Revolution.

Tattooed Man—A name applied to James G. Blaine following the publication of a sensational political cartoon in a New York newspaper during the presidential campaign of 1884. Blaine was pictured as Phryne before the Athenian judges. Stripped of his robe, he was shown to be tattooed with the names of the scandals in which his enemies alleged he had a hand.

Taylor, Zachary, was born in Orange County, Virginia, on November 24, 1784, and died while President, in Washington, on July 9, 1850. As a young man he accompanied his father to Kentucky, where he remained until he joined the Army. He served in the Black Hawk and Seminole Indian wars, and as a professional soldier rose until at the outbreak of the Mexican War he was a major general. His distinguished services in that war made him a soldier-hero. While in command of the Southwestern Department he had purchased a plantation in Baton Rouge, Louisiana, and it was from there, as the war was ending, that the Whigs nominated him for the presidency in 1848. Nicknamed "Old Rough and Ready," his enormous personal popularity helped him carry the election. He defeated Lewis Cass of Michigan. The popular vote was 1,360,101 for Taylor and 1,220,544 for Cass.

Zachary Taylor was President only sixteen months when he died in the White House and was succeeded by Millard Fillmore.

Tennessee—"Volunteer State." State flower, iris. Population, 2,915,841. Area, 42,246 square miles. Capital, Nashville. Admitted to the Union in 1796. Tennessee seceded at the outbreak of the Civil War. It was taken back into the Union in 1866, the first of the seceding states to re-establish itself. In both state and national politics it has been consistently Democratic. It has ten representatives in Congress.

Tennis Cabinet—A group of President Theodore Roosevelt's friends who were in the government service during his administra-

277

tion and played tennis with him and with one another on the White House courts.

Territories—At the present time the territories of the United States are Alaska and Hawaii. Alaska became a territory under an act of Congress passed in 1912. Hawaii voluntarily became a territory in 1898. All but three of the thirty-five states which Congress has admitted to the Union were organized as territories before their admission. Texas, California, and West Virginia did not go through this process.

Texas—"Lone-Star State." State flower, bluebonnet. Population, 6,414,824. Area, 267,339 square miles. Capital, Austin. Annexation to the United States was agreed to in 1845, and it was admitted as a state of the Union the same year. Aside from a short period, the state has been uniformly Democratic in politics since its admission.

The city of Galveston in 1901 instituted a commission plan of city government, which system later was adopted by many other cities but is now being gradually abandoned.

General Sam Houston was the state's most outstanding citizen. John Nance Garner, Vice-President of the United States from 1933 to 1941, was Texas's representative in the House of Representatives for more than thirty years. After Governor James E. Ferguson was impeached in 1917, his wife, Miriam, familiarly known as "Ma" Ferguson, entered politics and was made governor from 1925 to 1927.

The state has twenty-one representatives in Congress.

Third Term—President Franklin D. Roosevelt became the first President in our history to be elected to a third term. In the campaign he won a smashing majority and then won the nomination and the election for a fourth term.

"Tippecanoe and Tyler Too" was the campaign slogan of the Whigs in the Hard Cider Campaign of 1840 (*q.v.*), when they ran General William Henry Harrison against Martin Van Buren for the presidency. Harrison was nicknamed Old Tippecanoe because he defeated some Indians in the battle of Tippecanoe during the War of 1812. Bands of minstrels were formed to sing songs in honor of Old Tip and his running mate for Vice-President, John Tyler. They sang:

> "What has caused this great commotion—motion—motion
> The country through?
> It is the ball a rolling on
> For Tippecanoe and Tyler too,
> For Tippecanoe and Tyler too,
> And with them we will beat little Van—Van—Van
> Van is a used-up man—
> And with them we will beat little Van."

Titles of Nobility—The Constitution provides (Article I, Section 9, Clause 8) that no title of nobility shall be granted by the United States, and no person holding any office of profit or trust under them shall, without the consent of Congress, accept any present, emolument, office, or title of any kind whatever from any king, prince, or foreign state.

In May 1810 Congress proposed an amendment to the Constitution barring all citizens of the United States from accepting any title of nobility from a foreign country under penalty of forfeiture of citizenship and incapacity to hold Federal or state office. It was ratified by Maryland, Kentucky, Ohio, Delaware, Pennsylvania, New Jersey, Vermont, Tennessee, Georgia, Massachusetts, and New Hampshire, but these were not enough, and the amendment failed.

To the Victors Belong the Spoils—This familiar political phrase had its origin in 1832, when President Jackson nominated Martin Van Buren, who later became President, for the post of Minister to England. The Senate rejected Van Buren. During the debate it was charged that Van Buren had introduced in Washington the political spoils system practiced in New York. Replying to this charge, Senator William L. Marcy of New York said:

"It may be, sir, that the politicians of New York are not so fastidious as some gentlemen are as to disclose the principles on which they

279

act. . . . They see nothing wrong in the rule that to the victors belong the spoils of the enemy."

Too Proud to Fight—Phrase used by President Woodrow Wilson shortly after the sinking of the steamship *Lusitania* by a German submarine on May 7, 1915. He said, in part:

"The example of America must be a special example. The example of America must be the example not merely of peace because it will not fight, but of peace because it is the healing and elevating influence of the world and strife is not. There is such a thing as a nation being so right that it does not need to convince others by force that it is right. There is such a thing as a man being too proud to fight."

Toledo War—In 1835 a dispute which had smoldered for some years between the state of Ohio and the Michigan Territory came to a head. The controversy arose over a tract of land which included the city of Toledo and was claimed by both the state and the territory: hence the name of the Toledo War. The militia were called out on both sides. Finally the national government interfered. President Jackson removed Governor Mason of the Michigan Territory for his officiousness, and Congress, in 1836, settled the controversy by admitting Michigan as a state on condition of her yielding the claim to the tract in dispute, the Upper Peninsula being given her as compensation. Under this act Michigan became a state in January of the next year.

Toleration Acts—In May 1647, a toleration act was passed in Rhode Island. Following the adoption of various acts and orders relating to government and the punishment of crime, the General Court of Elections decreed: "These are the laws that concern all men, and these are the penalties for the transgression thereof, which by common consent are ratified and established throughout the whole colony; and otherwise than thus, what is herein forbidden, all men may walk as their consciences persuade them, every one in the name of God."

In Maryland, Protestants and Catholics in the General Assembly passed a resolution in 1649 that "whereas the enforcing of conscience in matters of religion hath frequently fallen out to be of dangerous consequence in those commonwealths where it has been practised, and for the more quiet and peaceable government of this province, and the better to preserve mutual love and unity among the inhabitants . . . no person or persons whatsoever within this province . . . professing to believe in Jesus Christ, shall from henceforth be any ways troubled or molested or discountenanced for or in respect of his or her religion, nor in the free exercise thereof, within the province or the islands thereunto belonging, nor any way compelled to the belief or exercise of any other religion against his or her conscience."

This act, since it was limited to Christians, was not so broad as the Rhode Island measure, which established complete and absolute toleration for everybody.

Tories were American colonists who at the time of the Revolution remained loyal to the British king. Many of these loyalists, as they were also called, migrated to Canada. Tories today are extreme conservatives who stand for the old order and are opposed to all change.

Town Meeting—The New England town meeting is about as pure a form of democracy as can be found anywhere. Once a year, customarily in March, the people meet to discuss and settle town affairs, vote taxes, appropriate money, elect or nominate town officers, and enact bylaws. All voters in the town are expected to attend and may address the meeting and vote on any question that arises. The presiding officer is called the moderator. The officials chosen to administer the affairs of the town include the selectmen (usually three in number), a town clerk, a town treasurer, a school committee, assessors of taxes, overseers of the poor, and constables. It was in the colonial town meetings that the people discussed their rights and liberties under the crown and public opinion as to these matters was formed.

Townsend Plan—Dr. Francis Everett Townsend, a retired doctor of Long Beach, California, in 1934 conceived the idea for a pension plan which would give to persons over sixty years of age two hundred dollars a month regardless of sex, color, or income. The

281

movement spread rapidly across the country and developed into a major political issue. In the fall of 1935 a Townsend Plan convention injected the pension scheme into the 1936 presidential campaign, and the author claimed to have a following of more than three million persons. At the time he threatened to put a third-party ticket in the field but decided later to aim toward the election of congressmen who looked kindly on his movement. An alliance was formed with the National Union of Social Justice, led by Reverend Charles E. Coughlin of Detroit, who did his crusading via the radio. A Share-the-Wealth movement, headed by Huey P. Long of Louisiana and later by Gerald L. K. Smith, allied itself with the pension movement. The year 1936 proved a troublesome one for the Townsend project, and much dissension arose in its ranks, and many groups discontinued their support. Townsend settled in California from South Dakota but was born in Illinois in 1867.

Treason is the only crime defined by the Constitution. According to Article III, Section 3, treason against the United States consists only "in levying war against them, or in adhering to their enemies, giving them aid and comfort." Since the charge of treason was formerly often used by kings to compass the death of political opponents and gain possession of their property, the Constitution provides that conviction of treason must be "on the testimony of two witnesses to the same overt act, or on confession in open court," and that forfeiture of property shall last no longer than the criminal's life. An act of Congress in 1790 made death the penalty for treason, but by an act passed in 1862 it was left to the discretion of the court whether the penalty should be death or imprisonment for not less than five years and a fine of not less than $10,000. Every person convicted of treason is debarred from holding Federal office.

Treason is sometimes called high treason to distinguish it from petit treason, which is the killing of a person to whom the offender owes duty or obedience, as a husband or master. It is now treated in England and the United States as murder. Misprision of treason is the concealment of a treasonable act by one who has knowledge of it. Treason can be committed against a single state as well as the United States. (See *Dorr Rebellion*.)

Treasury, Department of—One of the three original executive departments of the government, the Department of the Treasury was organized on September 2, 1789, with Alexander Hamilton as Secretary. Finances of a national nature come under the jurisdiction of the Secretary of the Treasury, who as the head of the department figures ways and means of bettering the revenues of the country and supporting the government's credit. The collection of internal revenue and customs is under his superintendency, as is also the collection of taxes on income, tobacco, and other articles. The engraving and printing of paper currency and the minting of coins are under his jurisdiction, and in peacetime he also has direction of the Coast Guard service. Plans for public buildings as well as their construction and maintenance are handled through this department, which also serves as purchasing agent for the national government. Fighting the unlawful traffic in narcotics is another function of the Department of the Treasury.

Among the chief bureaus, divisions, and offices of the department are the Bureau of the Comptroller of the Currency, Bureau of Customs, Bureau of Engraving and Printing, Bureau of Internal Revenue, Bureau of the Mint, Bureau of Narcotics, Division of Monetary Research, Division of Personnel, Division of Research and Statistics, Division of Tax Research, Foreign Funds Control, Office of the Tax Legislative Counsel, Procurement Division for Federal supplies, Secret Service, Coast Guard, War Finance Division, Office of the Fiscal Assistant Secretary, Bureau of Accounts, Bureau of the Public Debt, Office of the Treasurer of the United States.

Triple-Headed Monster—Nickname given to the Constitution when it was before the people for adoption. It refers to the division of the Federal Government into three branches—the executive, the legislative, and the judicial. (See *Checks and Balances.*)

Truman, Harry S., thirty-third President of the United States, was born on a farm in Lamar, Missouri, May 8, 1884. The first Missourian to become President, he was educated in the public schools of that state, and following World War I, in which he served with distinction, rising to the rank of captain, he studied law in Kansas

City. He was elected a judge of the Jackson County, Missouri, Court in 1922, and in 1934 was elected United States senator from Missouri. Re-elected in 1940, he became head of the so-called Truman Committee, a special senatorial committee charged with investigating the national defense program. This committee saved the country hundreds of millions of dollars. In 1944 Truman was elected Vice-President but served less than three months, when in consequence of the death of Franklin D. Roosevelt on April 12, 1945, he succeeded to the presidency.

"Turn the Rascals Out"—This political slogan, with its suggestion of knavery, is a popular old American campaign cry which all parties have used, depending on whether a party was in power or not. It seems to have originated at the time the spoils system was introduced and expressed as practical a political philosophy as did the slogan, "To the victors belong the spoils." For originally the rallying cry was, "Turn the rascals out and give the jobs to our boys."

Un-American Activities Committee—Martin Dies, while still in his late twenties, was elected to the House of Representatives from Texas in 1931. Shortly afterward he became a member of the important House Rules Committee. When the New Deal got under way he gave many of its measures his full support, but by 1937 he had joined the anti-Roosevelt Democrats in the House of Representatives and he strongly fought against the reorganization of the Supreme Court.

At the beginning of Roosevelt's second term Dies pressed Congress almost continuously to investigate all sorts of matters—the press, the radio, aliens, etc. In 1938 he finally succeeded in getting an appropriation of $25,000 and set up the Committee to Investigate un-American Activities and became its chairman. At this time the Nazi Bund camps, with Fritz Kuhn as leader, were spreading, and the Communists were becoming more active.

When the committee began its hearings a great deal of controversy arose and considerable excitement was created. Dies was characterized by his critics as a "demagogue," a "Fascist," "the Gestapo from

Texas," etc. On the other hand, there were some supporters who felt that the times called for such investigations as he was conducting. President Roosevelt, at one of his press conferences, berated the committee and the methods it was using. Not a few suits for damages were brought against Dies, and in March 1944 he engaged in a debate with Walter Winchell on the radio, in which he came off second best.

When the Dies Committee report was published in January 1940, there was much hue and cry. Many wanted the committee discontinued, while others asked that it be continued for another year, and the House appropriated another $75,000. Further yearly appropriations enabled the committee to continue until the end of 1944. Lack of funds appears to have practically caused its demise early in 1945.

Uncle Sam, with his starry blue swallowtail coat, his striped trousers and his stovepipe hat, has stood for the United States, as John Bull has symbolized Great Britain, for more than a century. His tall, spare figure, long, thin face, and scraggly beard are supposed to be typical of the New England countryman of the last century, and formerly he was always pictured indulging in the old New England pastime of whittling.

The legend connected with the name is that during the War of 1812 there was a government meat inspector in Troy, New York, named Samuel Wilson, and when a new government workman, seeing many cases of provisions marked "U.S.," asked what the letters stood for, he was told that they referred to Uncle Sam Wilson. The story spread until at length Uncle Sam came to personify the United States.

Unicameral System—A legislature consisting of only one chamber.

Unit Rule—A practice observed at nominating conventions which permits the majority of a state delegation to determine how the state shall vote as a unit.

United Nations—The organization of the United Nations under the San Francisco charter was practically completed at the first meeting held in London early in 1946. Here is the setup as given by the New York *Times:*

THE GENERAL ASSEMBLY

President
Paul-Henri Spaak of Belgium.

Vice-Presidents
The heads of the delegations of the United States, the United Kingdom, the U.S.S.R., France, China, South Africa, and Venezuela.

Members

Argentina	Ethiopia	Panama
Australia	France	Paraguay
Belgium	Greece	Peru
Bolivia	Guatemala	Philippines
Brazil	Haiti	Poland
Canada	Honduras	Saudi Arabia
Chile	India	Syria
China	Iran	Turkey
Colombia	Iraq	Ukraine
Costa Rica	Lebanon	Union of S. Africa
Cuba	Liberia	U.S.S.R.
Czechoslovakia	Luxembourg	United Kingdom
Denmark	Mexico	United States
Dominican Republic	Netherlands	Uruguay
Ecuador	New Zealand	Venezuela
Egypt	Nicaragua	White Russia
El Salvador	Norway	Yugoslavia

Committees of the General Assembly

GENERAL
Provisionally composed of fourteen members as follows: the president of the General Assembly, the seven vice-presidents, and the chairmen of the six committees listed hereafter.

POLITICAL AND SECURITY
Dr. D. Z. Manuilsky, the Ukraine.

ECONOMIC AND FINANCIAL
Waclaw Konderski, Poland.

286

SOCIAL, HUMANITARIAN, AND CULTURAL

Peter Fraser, New Zealand.

TRUSTEESHIP

Dr. Roberto MacEachen, Uruguay.

BUDGETARY

Faiz al-Khoury, Syria.

LEGAL

Dr. Roberto Jiminez, Panama.

(All the foregoing committees except the Steering Committee are composed of representatives of all fifty-one members of the UN.)

THE SECURITY COUNCIL

Members

Australia (Until 1948)   Netherlands (Until 1947)
Brazil (Until 1948)   Poland (Until 1948)
China (Permanent)   U.S.S.R. (Permanent)
Egypt (Until 1947)   United Kingdom (Permanent)
France (Permanent)   United States (Permanent)
Mexico (Until 1947)

MILITARY STAFF COMMITTEE

The Chiefs of Staff (or their representatives) of the United States, the United Kingdom, the U.S.S.R., France, and China.

ATOMIC ENERGY COMMITTEE

Composed of the members of the Security Council plus Canada.

THE ECONOMIC AND SOCIAL COUNCIL

President

Sir H. Ramaswami Mudaliar.

Belgium (Until 1949)   India (Until 1948)
Canada (Until 1949)   Lebanon (Until 1947)
Chile (Until 1949)   Norway (Until 1948)
China (Until 1949)   Peru (Until 1949)
Colombia (Until 1947)   Ukraine (Until 1947)
Cuba (Until 1948)   U.S.S.R. (Until 1948)
Czechoslovakia (Until 1948)   United Kingdom (Until 1948)
France (Until 1949)   United States (Until 1947)
Greece (Until 1947)   Yugoslavia (Until 1947)

287

THE INTERNATIONAL COURT OF JUSTICE

Until 1955

Sir A. D. McNair (Great Britain)   Alejandro Alvarez (Chile)
Jules Basdevant (France)   Jose G. Guerrero (El Salvador)
J. Philadelpho de Barros Azevedo (Brazil)

Until 1952

G. H. Hackworth (United States)   Febela Alfaro (Mexico)
Sergei B. Krylov (U.S.S.R.)   Helge Klaestad (Norway)
Charles de Visscher (Belgium)

Until 1949

John M. Read (Canada)   Bohdan Winiarski (Poland)
Milovan Zoricitch (Yugoslavia)   Hsu Mo (China)
Abdel Hamid Badawi (Egypt)

Secretary General
Trygve Lie of Norway.

PERMANENT HEADQUARTERS

Somewhere in Fairfield County, Connecticut, and Westchester County, New York, the exact location to be chosen by the General Assembly.

TEMPORARY HEADQUARTERS

New York, New York.

United Nations Charter—One of the greatest assemblies in history —delegates from fifty nations—meeting in San Francisco, signed on June 26, 1945, the United Nations Charter. It was adopted by the United States Senate on August 8, 1945, by a vote of 89 to 2, and came into force on October 24, 1945, when the Union of Soviet Socialist Republics deposited its instrument of ratification, the twenty-ninth nation to do so. The members of the United Nations, now numbering fifty-one, are:

Argentina	Canada
Australia	Chile
Belgium	China
Bolivia	Colombia
Brazil	Costa Rica

Cuba	New Zealand
Czechoslovakia	Nicaragua
Denmark	Norway
Dominican Rep.	Panama
Ecuador	Paraguay
Egypt	Peru
El Salvador	Philippines
Ethiopia	Poland
France	Saudi Arabia
Greece	Syria
Guatemala	South Africa
Haiti	Turkey
Honduras	Uruguay
India	United Kingdom
Iran	United States
Iraq	U.S.S.R.
Lebanon	Byelorussia S.S.R.
Liberia	Ukraine S.S.R.
Luxembourg	Venezuela
Mexico	Yugoslavia
Netherlands	

THE CHARTER OF THE UNITED NATIONS

We, the peoples of the United Nations

Determined to save succeeding generations from the scourge of war, which twice in our lifetime has brought untold sorrow to mankind, and

To reaffirm faith in fundamental human rights, in the dignity and worth of the human person, in the equal rights of men and women and of nations large and small, and

To establish conditions under which justice and respect for the obligations arising from treaties and other sources of international law can be maintained, and

To promote social progress and better standards of life in larger freedom, and for these ends

To practice tolerance and live together in peace with one another as good neighbors, and

To unite our strength to maintain international peace and security, and

289

To insure, by the acceptance of principles and the institution of methods, that armed force shall not be used, save in the common interest, and

To employ international machinery for the promotion of the economic and social advancement of all peoples, have resolved to combine our efforts to accomplish these aims.

Accordingly, our respective governments, through representatives assembled in the city of San Francisco, who have exhibited their full powers found to be in good and due form, have agreed to the present Charter of the United Nations and do hereby establish an international organization to be known as the United Nations.

CHAPTER I

Purposes

ARTICLE I

The purposes of the United Nations are:

1. To maintain international peace and security, and to that end: to take effective collective measures for the prevention and removal of threats to the peace and for the suppression of acts of aggression or other breaches of the peace, and to bring about by peaceful means, and in conformity with the principles of justice and international law, adjustment or settlement of international disputes or situations which might lead to a breach of the peace;

2. To develop friendly relations among nations based on respect for the principle of equal rights and self-determination of peoples, and to take other appropriate measures to strengthen universal peace;

3. To achieve international cooperation in solving international problems of an economic, social, cultural or humanitarian character, and in promoting and encouraging respect for human rights and for the fundamental freedoms for all without distinction as to race, sex, language or religion; and

4. To be a center for harmonizing the actions of nations in the attainment of these common ends.

Principles

ARTICLE 2

The organization and its members, in pursuit of the purposes stated in Article 1, shall act in accordance with the following principles:

1. The organization is based on the principle of the sovereign equality of all its members.

2. All members, in order to ensure to all of them the rights and benefits resulting from membership, shall fulfill in good faith the obligations assumed by them in accordance with the present charter.

3. All members shall settle their international disputes by peaceful means in such a manner that international peace, and security, and justice, are not endangered.

4. All members shall refrain in their international relations from the threat or use of force against the territorial integrity or political independence of any member or state, or in any other manner inconsistent with the purposes of the United Nations.

5. All members shall give the United Nations every assistance in any action it takes in accordance with the provisions of the present charter, and shall refrain from giving assistance to any state against which the United Nations is taking preventive or enforcement action.

6. The organization shall ensure that states not members act in accordance with these principles so far as may be necessary for the maintenance of international peace and security.

7. Nothing contained in the present charter shall authorize the United Nations to intervene in matters which are essentially within the domestic jurisdiction of any state or shall require the members to submit such matters to settlement under the present charter; but this principle shall not prejudice the application of enforcement measures under Chapter VII.

CHAPTER II

MEMBERSHIP

ARTICLE 3

The original members of the United Nations shall be the states which, having participated in the United Nations Conference on International Organization at San Francisco, or have previously signed the declaration of the United Nations of Jan. 1, 1942, sign the present charter and ratify it in accordance with Article 110.

ARTICLE 4

1. Membership in the United Nations is open to all other peaceloving states which accept the obligations contained in the present charter and which, in the judgment of the organization, are able and willing to carry out these obligations.

2. The admission of any such state to membership in the United

Nations will be effected by a decision of the General Assembly upon the recommendation of the Security Council.

ARTICLE 5

A member of the United Nations against which preventive or enforcement action has been taken by the Security Council may be suspended from the exercise of the rights and privileges of membership by the General Assembly upon the recommendation of the Security Council. The exercise of these rights and privileges may be restored by the Security Council.

ARTICLE 6

A member of the United Nations which has persistently violated the principles contained in the present charter may be expelled from the organization by the General Assembly upon the recommendation of the Security Council.

CHAPTER III

ORGANS

ARTICLE 7

1. There are established as the principal organs of the United Nations: A General Assembly, a Security Council, an Economic and Social Council, an International Court of Justice, a Trusteeship Council and a Secretariat.

2. Such subsidiary organs as may be found necessary may be established in accordance with the present charter.

ARTICLE 8

The United Nations shall place no restrictions on the eligibility of men and women to participate in any capacity and under conditions of equality in the principal and subsidiary organs.

CHAPTER IV

The General Assembly

COMPOSITION

ARTICLE 9

The General Assembly shall consist of all the members of the United Nations.

Each member shall not have more than five representatives in the General Assembly.

292

FUNCTIONS AND POWERS

ARTICLE 10

The General Assembly may discuss any questions or any matters within the scope of the present Charter or relating to the powers and functions of any organs provided in the present Charter, and, except as provided in Article 12, may make recommendations to the members of the United Nations or to the Security Council, or both, on any such questions or matters.

ARTICLE 11

1. The General Assembly may consider the general principles of cooperation in the maintenance of international peace and security, including the principles governing disarmament and the regulations of armaments, and may make recommendations with regard to such principles to the members or to the Security Council or both.

2. The General Assembly may discuss any questions relating to the maintenance of international peace and security brought before it by any member of the United Nations, or by the Security Council, or by a State, which is not a member of the United Nations, in accordance with the provisions of Article 35, Paragraph 2, and, except as provided in Article 12, may make recommendations with regard to any such questions to the State or States concerned or to the Security Council, or both. A question on which action is necessary shall be referred to the Security Council by the General Assembly either before or after discussion.

3. The General Assembly may call the attention of the Security Council to situations which are likely to endanger international peace and security.

4. The powers of the General Assembly set out in this article shall not limit the general scope of Article 10.

ARTICLE 12

1. While the Security Council is exercising in respect of any dispute or situation the functions assigned to it in the present Charter, the General Assembly shall not make any recommendation with regard to that dispute or situation unless the Security Council so requests.

2. The Secretary General, with the consent of the Security Council, shall notify the General Assembly at each session of any matters relative to the maintenance of international peace and security which

are being dealt with by the Security Council and shall similarly notify the General Assembly, or the members of the United Nations if the General Assembly is not in session, immediately the Security Council ceases to deal with such matters.

ARTICLE 13

1. The General Assembly shall initiate studies and make recommendations for the purpose of:

(a) Promoting international cooperation in the political field and encouraging the progressive development of international law and its codification;

(b) Promoting international cooperation in the economic, social, cultural, educational and health fields and assisting in the realization of human rights and basic freedoms for all without distinction as to race, sex, language or religion.

2. The further responsibilities, functions and powers of the General Assembly with respect to matters mentioned in Paragraph (b) above are set forth in Chapters IX and X.

ARTICLE 14

Subject to the provisions of Article 12, the General Assembly may recommend measures for the peaceful adjustment of any situation, regardless of origin, which it deems likely to impair the general welfare or friendly relations among nations, including situations resulting from a violation of the provisions of the present Charter setting forth the purposes and principles of the United Nations.

ARTICLE 15

1. The General Assembly shall receive and consider annual and special reports from the Security Council; these reports shall include an account of the measures that the Security Council has adopted or applied to maintain international peace and security.

2. The General Assembly shall receive and consider reports from the other bodies of the organization.

ARTICLE 16

The General Assembly shall perform such functions with respect to the international trusteeship system as are assigned to it under Chapters XII and XIII, including the approval of the trusteeship agreements for areas not designated as strategic.

294

ARTICLE 17

1. The General Assembly shall consider and approve the budget of the organization.

2. The General Assembly shall consider and approve any financial and budgetary arrangements with specialized agencies referred to in Article 57 and shall examine the administrative budgets of such specialized agencies with a view to making recommendations to the agencies concerned.

3. The expenses of the organization shall be borne by the members as apportioned by the General Assembly.

VOTING

ARTICLE 18

1. Each member of the United Nations shall have one vote in the General Assembly.

2. Decisions of the General Assembly on important questions shall be made by a two-thirds majority of those present and voting. These questions shall include: recommendations with respect to the maintenance of international peace and security, the election of the non-permanent members of the Security Council, the election of the members of the Economic and Social Council, the election of the members of the United Nations which are to designate the members on the Trusteeship Council in accordance with the provisions of Article 86 (c), the admission of new members to the United Nations, the expulsion of members, the suspension of the rights and privileges of members, questions relating to the operations of the trusteeship system, and budgetary questions.

3. Decisions on other questions—including the determination of additional categories of questions to be decided by a two-thirds majority—shall be made by a majority of those present and voting.

ARTICLE 19

A member which is in arrears in the payments of its financial contributions to the organization shall have no vote if the amount of its arrears equals or exceeds the amount of the contributions due from it for the preceding two full years. The General Assembly may, nevertheless, permit such a member to vote if it is satisfied that the failure to pay is due to conditions beyond the control of the member.

PROCEDURE

ARTICLE 20

The General Assembly shall meet in regular annual sessions and in such special sessions as occasion may require. Special sessions shall be convoked by the Secretary General at the request of the Security Council or of a majority of the members of the United Nations.

ARTICLE 21

The General Assembly shall adopt its own rules of procedure. It shall elect its president for each session.

ARTICLE 22

The General Assembly may establish such subsidiary organs as it deems necessary for the performance of its functions.

CHAPTER V
The Security Council

COMPOSITION

ARTICLE 23

1. The Security Council shall consist of eleven members of the United Nations. The United States of America, the United Kingdom of Great Britain and Northern Ireland, the Union of Soviet Socialist Republics, the Republic of China, and France, shall be permanent members of the Security Council. The General Assembly shall elect six other members of the United Nations to be non-permanent members of the Security Council, due regard being specially paid, in the first instance to the contribution of members of the United Nations to the maintenance of international peace and security and to the other purposes of the organization, and also to equitable geographical distribution.

2. The non-permanent members of the Security Council shall be elected for a term of two years. In the first election of the non-permanent members, however, three shall be chosen for a term of one year. A retiring member shall not be eligible for immediate re-election.

3. Each member of the Security Council shall have one representative.

Primary Responsibility

ARTICLE 24

1. In order to insure prompt and effective action by the United Nations, its members confer on the Security Council primary responsibility for the maintenance of international peace and security, and agree that in carrying out its duties under this responsibility the Security Council acts on their behalf.

2. In discharging these duties the Security Council shall act in accordance with the purposes and principles of the United Nations. The specific powers granted to the Security Council for the discharge of these duties are laid down in Chapters VI, VII, VIII and XII.

3. The Security Council shall submit annual and, when necessary, special reports to the General Assembly for its consideration.

ARTICLE 25

The members of the United Nations agree to accept and carry out the decisions of the Security Council in accordance with the provisions of the present charter.

ARTICLE 26

In order to promote the establishment and maintenance of international peace and security with the least diversion for armaments of the world's human and economic resources, the Security Council shall be responsible for formulating, with the assistance of the Military Staff Committee, referred to in Article 47, plans to be submitted to the members of the United Nations for the establishment of a system for the regulation of armaments.

Voting

ARTICLE 27

1. Each member of the Security Council shall have one vote.

2. Decisions of the Security Council on procedural matters shall be made by an affirmative vote of seven members.

3. Decisions of the Security Council on all other matters shall be made by an affirmative vote of seven members including the concurring votes of the permanent members; provided that, in decisions under Chapter VI and under Paragraph 3 of Article 52 a party to a dispute shall abstain from voting.

PROCEDURE

ARTICLE 28

1. The Security Council shall be so organized as to be able to function continuously. Each member of the Security Council shall for this purpose be represented at all times at the seat of the organization.

2. The Security Council shall hold periodic meetings at which each of its members may, if it so desires, be represented by a member of the Government or by some other specially designated representative.

3. The Security Council may hold meetings at such places other than the seat of the organization as in its judgment may best facilitate its work.

ARTICLE 29

The Security Council may establish such subsidiary organs as it deems necessary for the performance of its functions.

ARTICLE 30

The Security Council shall adopt its own rules of procedure, including the method of selecting its president.

ARTICLE 31

Any member of the United Nations which is not a member of the Security Council may participate without a vote in the discussion of any question brought before the Security Council whenever the latter considers that the interests of that member are specially affected.

ARTICLE 32

Any member of the United Nations which is not a member of the Security Council or any State not a member of the United Nations, if it is a party to a dispute under consideration by the Security Council, shall be invited to participate in the discussion relating to the dispute. The Security Council shall lay down such conditions as it may deem just for the participation of a State which is not a member of the United Nations.

CHAPTER VI

PACIFIC SETTLEMENT OF DISPUTES

ARTICLE 33

1. The parties to any dispute, the continuance of which is likely to endanger the maintenance of international peace and security, shall, first of all, seek a solution by negotiation, inquiry, mediation, conciliation, arbitration, judicial settlement, resort to regional agencies or arrangements, or other peaceful means of their own choice.

2. The Security Council shall, when it deems necessary, call upon the parties to settle their dispute by such means.

ARTICLE 34

The Security Council may investigate any dispute, or any situation which might lead to international friction or give rise to a dispute, in order to determine whether its continuance is likely to endanger the maintenance of international peace and security.

ARTICLE 35

1. Any member of the United Nations may bring any dispute or any situation of the nature referred to in Article 34 to the attention of the Security Council, or of the General Assembly.

2. A state which is not a member of the United Nations may bring to the attention of the Security Council or of the General Assembly any dispute to which it is a party, if it accepts in advance, for the purposes of the dispute, the obligations of pacific settlement provided in the present charter.

3. The proceedings of the General Assembly in respect of matters brought to its attention under this article will be subject to the provisions of Articles 11 and 12.

ARTICLE 36

1. The Security Council may, at any stage of a dispute of the nature referred to in Article 33 or of a situation of like nature, recommend appropriate procedures or methods of adjustment.

2. The Security Council should take into consideration any procedures for the settlement of the dispute which have already been adopted by the parties.

3. In making recommendations under this article the Security Council should take into consideration that legal disputes should as

a general rule be referred by the parties to the International Court of Justice in accordance with the provisions of the statute of the court.

ARTICLE 37

1. Should the parties to a dispute of the nature referred to in Article 33 fail to settle it by the means indicated in that article, they shall refer it to the Security Council.

2. If the Security Council deems that the continuance of the dispute is in fact likely to endanger the maintenance of international peace and security, it shall decide whether to take action under Article 36 or to recommend such terms of settlement as it may consider appropriate.

ARTICLE 38

Without prejudice to the provisions of Articles 33–37 of this chapter, the Security Council may, if all the parties to any dispute so request, make recommendations to the parties with a view to a peaceful settlement of the dispute.

CHAPTER VII

ACTION WITH RESPECT TO THREATS TO THE PEACE, BREACHES OF THE PEACE AND ACTS OF AGGRESSION.

ARTICLE 39

The Security Council shall determine the existence of any threat to the peace, breach of the peace, or act of aggression and shall make recommendations, or decide what measures shall be taken in accordance with the provisions of Articles 41 and 42, to maintain or restore international peace and security.

ARTICLE 40

In order to prevent an aggravation of the situation, the Security Council may, before making the recommendations or deciding upon the measures provided for in Article 41, call upon the parties concerned to comply with such provisional measures as it deems necessary or desirable. Such provisional measures shall be without prejudice to the rights, claims, or position of the parties concerned. The Security Council shall duly take account of failure to comply with such provisional measures.

ARTICLE 41

The Security Council may decide what measures not involving the use of armed force are to be employed to give effect to its decisions, and it may call upon members of the United Nations to apply such measures. These may include complete or partial interruptions of economic relations and of rail, sea, air, postal, telegraphic, radio, and other means of communication, and the severance of diplomatic relations.

ARTICLE 42

Should the Security Council consider that measures provided for in Article 41 would be inadequate, or have proved to be inadequate, it may take such action by air, sea or land forces as may be necessary to maintain or restore international peace and security. Such action may include demonstrations, blockade, and other operations by air, sea or land forces of members of the United Nations.

ARTICLE 43

1. All members of the United Nations, in order to contribute to the maintenance of international peace and security, undertake to make available to the Security Council, on its call and in accordance with a special agreement or agreements, armed forces, assistance, and facilities, including rights of passage, necessary for the purpose of maintaining international peace and security.

2. Such agreement or agreements shall govern the numbers and types of forces, their degree of readiness and general location, and the nature of the facilities and assistance to be provided.

3. The agreement or agreements shall be negotiated as soon as possible on the initiative of the Security Council. They shall be concluded between the Security Council and member states or between the Security Council and groups of member states and shall be subject to ratification by the signatory states in accordance with their constitutional processes.

ARTICLE 44

When the Security Council has decided to use force it shall, before calling upon a member not represented on it to provide armed forces in fulfillment of the obligations assumed under Article 43, invite that member, if the member so desires, to participate in the decisions of the Security Council concerning the employment of contingents of that member's armed forces.

ARTICLE 45

In order to enable the United Nations to take urgent military measures, members shall hold immediately available national air force contingents for combined international enforcement action. The strength and degree of readiness of these contingents and plans for their combined action shall be determined, within the limits laid down in the special agreement or agreements referred to in Article 43, by the Security Council with the assistance of the Military Staff Committee.

ARTICLE 46

Plans for the application of armed force shall be made by the Security Council with the assistance of the Military Staff Committee.

ARTICLE 47

1. There shall be established a Military Staff Committee to advise and assist the Security Council on all questions relating to the Security Council's military requirements for the maintenance of international peace and security, the employment and command of forces placed at its disposal, the regulation of armaments, and possible disarmament.

2. The Military Staff Committees shall consist of the Chiefs of Staff of the permanent members of the Security Council or their representatives. Any member of the United Nations not permanently represented on the committee shall be invited by the committee to be associated with it when the efficient discharge of the committee's responsibilities requires the participation of that member in its work.

3. The Military Staff Committee shall be responsible, under the Security Council, for the strategic direction of any armed forces placed at the disposal of the Security Council. Questions relating to the command of such forces shall be worked out subsequently.

4. The Military Staff Committee, with the authorization of the Security Council and after consultation with appropriate regional agencies, may establish regional subcommittees.

ARTICLE 48

1. The action required to carry out the decisions of the Security Council for the maintenance of international peace and security shall be taken by all the members of the United Nations, or by some of them, as the Security Council may determine.

2. Such decisions shall be carried out by the members of the United Nations directly and through their action in the appropriate international agencies of which they are members.

ARTICLE 49

The members of the United Nations shall join in affording mutual assistance in carrying out the measures decided upon by the Security Council.

ARTICLE 50

If preventive or enforcement measures against any state are taken by the Security Council, any other state, whether a member of the United Nations or not, which finds itself confronted with special economic problems arising from the carrying out of those measures shall have the right to consult the Security Council with regard to a solution of those problems.

ARTICLE 51

Nothing in the present charter shall impair the inherent right of individual or collective self-defense, if an armed attack occurs against a member of the organization, until the Security Council has taken the measures necessary to maintain international peace and security. Measures taken by members in the exercise of this right of self-defense shall be immediately reported to the Security Council and shall not in any way affect the authority and responsibility of the Security Council under the present Charter to take at any time such action as it may deem necessary in order to maintain or restore international peace and security.

CHAPTER VIII

Regional Arrangements

ARTICLE 52

1. Nothing in the present Charter precludes the existence of regional arrangements or agencies for dealing with such matters relating to the maintenance of international peace and security as are appropriate for regional action, provided that such arrangements or agencies and their activities are consistent with the purposes and principles of the organization.

2. The members of the United Nations entering into such arrange-

ments or constituting such agencies shall make every effort to achieve peaceful settlement of local disputes through such regional arrangements or by such regional agencies before referring them to the Security Council.

3. The Security Council should encourage the development of peaceful settlement of local disputes through such regional arrangements or by such regional agencies either on the initiative of the states concerned or by reference from the Security Council.

4. This article in no way impairs the application of Articles 34 and 35.

ARTICLE 53

1. The Security Council shall, where appropriate, utilize such arrangements or agencies for enforcement action under its authority. But no enforcement action shall be taken under regional arrangements or by regional agencies without the authorization of the Security Council, with the exception of measures against any enemy state, as described below, provided for pursuant to Article 107, or in regional arrangements directed against renewal of aggressive policy on the part of any such state, until such time as the organization may, on request of the governments concerned, be charged with the responsibility for preventing further aggression by such a state.

2. The term "enemy state" as used in Paragraph 1 of this article applies to any state which during the second World War has been an enemy of any signatory of the present charter.

ARTICLE 54

The Security Council shall at all times be kept fully informed of activities undertaken, or in contemplation, under regional arrangements or by regional agencies for the maintenance of international peace and security.

CHAPTER IX

INTERNATIONAL ECONOMIC AND SOCIAL COOPERATION

ARTICLE 55

With a view to the creation of conditions of stability and well-being which are necessary for peaceful and friendly relations among nations based on respect for the principle of equal rights and self-determination of peoples, the United Nations shall promote:

304

(a) Higher standards of living, full employment, and conditions of economic and social progress and development;

(b) Solutions of international economic, social, health, and related problems and international cultural and educational cooperation and

(c) Universal respect for, and observance of, human rights and fundamental freedoms for all without distinction as to race, sex, language, or religion.

ARTICLE 56

All members pledge themselves to take joint and separate action in cooperation with the organization for the achievement of the purposes set forth in Article 55.

ARTICLE 57

1. The various specialized agencies established by inter-governmental agreement, and having wide international responsibilities as defined in their basic instruments in economic, social, cultural, educational, health and related fields, shall be brought into relationship with the United Nations in accordance with the provisions of Article 63.

2. Specialized agencies thus brought into relationship with the organization are hereinafter referred to as "the specialized agencies."

ARTICLE 58

The organization shall make recommendations for the coordination of the policies and activities of the specialized agencies.

ARTICLE 59

The organization shall, where appropriate, initiate negotiations among the States concerned for the creation of any new specialized agency required for the accomplishment of the purposes set forth in Article 55.

ARTICLE 60

Responsibility for the discharge of the organization's functions set forth in this chapter shall be vested in the General Assembly and, under the authority of the General Assembly, in the Economic and Social Council, which shall have for this purpose the powers set forth in Chapter X.

CHAPTER X
Economic and Social Council

COMPOSITION

ARTICLE 61

1. The Economic and Social Council shall consist of eighteen members of the United Nations elected by the General Assembly.

2. Subject to the provisions of Paragraph 3, six members of the Economic and Social Council shall be elected each year for a term of three years. A retiring member shall be eligible for immediate re-election.

3. At the first election, eighteen members of the Economic and Social Council shall be chosen. The term of office of six members so chosen shall expire at the end of one year, and of six other members at the end of two years, in accordance with arrangements made by the General Assembly.

4. Each member of the Economic and Social Council shall have one representative.

FUNCTIONS AND POWERS

ARTICLE 62

1. The Economic and Social Council may make or initiate studies and reports with respect to international economic, social, cultural, educational, health, and related matters and may make recommendations with respect to any such matters to the General Assembly, to the members of the United Nations, and to the specialized agencies concerned.

2. It may make recommendations for the purpose of promoting respect for, and observance of, human rights and fundamental freedoms for all.

3. It may prepare draft conventions for submission to the General Assembly, with respect to matters falling within its competence.

4. It may call, in accordance with the rules prescribed by the United Nations, international conferences on matters falling within its competence.

ARTICLE 63

1. The Economic and Social Council may enter into an agreement, approved by the General Assembly, with any of the agencies referred to in Article 57, defining the terms on which the agency concerned shall be brought into relationship with the United Nations.

2. It may coordinate the activities of the specialized agencies through consultation with and recommendations to such agencies and through recommendations to the General Assembly and to the members of the United Nations.

ARTICLE 64

1. The Economic and Social Council is authorized to take appropriate steps to obtain regular reports from the specialized agencies. It may make arrangements with the members of the United Nations and with the specialized agencies to obtain reports on the steps taken to give effect to its own recommendations and falling within its competence which are made by the General Assembly.

2. It may communicate its observance on these reports to the General Assembly.

ARTICLE 65

The Economic and Social Council may furnish information to the Security Council and shall assist the Security Council upon its request.

ARTICLE 66

1. The Economic and Social Council shall perform such functions as falls within its competence in connection with the carrying out of the recommendations of the General Assembly.

2. It may, with the approval of the General Assembly, perform services at the request of the members of the United Nations and at the request of the specialized agencies.

3. It may perform such other functions as are specified elsewhere in the present Charter and such functions as may be assigned to it by the General Assembly.

VOTING

ARTICLE 67

1. Each member of the Economic and Social Council shall have one vote.

2. Decisions of the Economic and Social Council shall be taken by a majority of the members present and voting.

PROCEDURE

ARTICLE 68

The Economic and Social Council shall set up commissions in economic and social fields and for the promotion of human rights, and such other commissions as may be required for the performance of its functions.

ARTICLE 69

The Economic and Social Council shall invite any member of the United Nations to participate, without vote, in its deliberations on any matter of particular concern to that member.

ARTICLE 70

The Economic and Social Council may make arrangements for representatives of the specialized agencies to participate, without vote, in its deliberations and in those of the commissions established by it, and for its representatives to participate in the deliberations of the specialized agencies.

ARTICLE 71

The Economic and Social Council may make suitable arrangements for consultation with non-governmental organizations which are concerned with matters within its competence. Such arrangements may be made with international organizations, and, where appropriate, with national organizations after consultation with the member of the United Nations concerned.

ARTICLE 72

1. The Economic and Social Council shall adopt its own rules of procedure, including the method of selecting its president.

2. The Economic and Social Council shall meet as required in accordance with its rules, which shall include provision for the convening of meetings on request of a majority of its members.

CHAPTER XI

DECLARATION REGARDING NON-SELF-GOVERNING TERRITORIES

ARTICLE 73

Members of the United Nations which have or assume responsibilities for the administration of territories whose peoples have not yet attained a full measure of self-government recognize the principle that the interests of the inhabitants of these territories are paramount, and accept as a sacred trust the obligation to promote to the utmost, within the system of international peace and security established by the present charter, the well-being of the inhabitants of these territories, and, to this end:

(a) To insure, with due respect for the culture of the peoples concerned, their political, economic, social, and educational advancement, their just treatment, and their protection against abuses;

(b) To develop self-government, to take due account of the political aspirations of the peoples, and to assist them in the progressive development of their free political institutions, according to the particular circumstances of each territory and its peoples and their varying stages of advancement;

(c) To further international peace and security;

(d) To promote constructive measures of development, to encourage research, and to cooperate with one another and with appropriate international bodies with a view to the practical achievement of the social, economic, and scientific purposes set forth in this paragraph; and

(e) To transmit regularly to the secretary general for information purposes, subject to such limitation as security and constitutional considerations may require, statistical and other information of a technical nature relating to economic, social, and educational conditions in the territories for which they are respectively responsible other than those territories to which Chapters XII and XIII apply.

ARTICLE 74

Members of the United Nations agree that their policy in respect to the territories, to which this chapter applies, no less than in respect of their metropolitan areas, must be based on the general principle of good-neighborliness, due account being taken of the interests and well-being of the rest of the world, in social, economic and commercial matters.

CHAPTER XII

International Trusteeship System

ARTICLE 75

The United Nations shall establish under its authority an international trusteeship system for the administration and supervision of such territories as may be placed thereunder by subsequent individual agreements. These territories are hereafter referred to as trust territories.

ARTICLE 76

The basic objectives of the trusteeship system in accordance with the purposes of the United Nations laid down in Article 1 of the present Charter, shall be:

309

(a) To further international peace and security;

(b) To promote the political, economic, social and educational advancement of the inhabitants of the trust territories, and their progressive development toward self-government or independence as may be appropriate to the particular circumstances of each territory and its peoples and the freely expressed wishes of the peoples concerned, and as may be provided by the terms of each trusteeship agreement;

(c) To encourage respect for human rights and for fundamental freedoms for all without distinction as to race, sex, language or religion, and to encourage recognition of the interdependence of the peoples of the world; and

(d) To insure equal treatment in social, economic and commercial matters for all members of the United Nations and their nationals, and also equal treatment for the latter in the administration of justice, without prejudice to the attainment of the foregoing objectives, and subject to the provisions of Article 80.

ARTICLE 77

1. The trusteeship system shall apply to such territories in the following categories as may be placed thereunder by means of trusteeship agreements:

(a) Territories now held under mandate;

(b) Territories which may be detached from enemy states as a result of the second World War; and

(c) Territories voluntarily placed under the system by states responsible for their administration.

2. It will be a matter for subsequent agreement as to which territories in the foregoing categories will be brought under the trusteeship system and upon what terms.

ARTICLE 78

The trusteeship system shall not apply to territories which have become members of the United Nations, relationship among which should be based on respect for the principle of sovereign equality.

ARTICLE 79

The terms of trusteeship for each territory to be placed under the trusteeship system, including any alteration or amendment, shall be agreed upon by the states directly concerned, including the mandatory power in the case of territories held under mandate by a member of the United Nations, and shall be approved as provided for in Articles 83 and 85.

ARTICLE 80

1. Except as may be agreed upon in individual trusteeship agreements made in accordance with the provisions of this chapter, placing each territory under the trusteeship system, and until such agreements have been concluded, nothing in this chapter shall be construed in or of itself to alter in any manner the rights whatsoever of any states or any peoples or the terms of existing international instruments to which members of the United Nations may respectively be parties.

2. Paragraph 1 of this article shall not be interpreted as giving grounds for delay or postponement of the negotiation and conclusion of such agreements for placing mandated and other territories under the trusteeship system as provided for in Article 77.

ARTICLE 81

The trusteeship agreement shall in each case include the terms under which the trust territory will be administered and designate the authority which shall exercise the administration of the trust territory. Such authority, hereafter called the administering authority, may be one or more states of the United Nations itself.

ARTICLE 82

There may be designated, in any trusteeship agreement, a strategic area or areas which may include part or all of the trust territory to which the agreement applies, without prejudice to any special agreement or agreements made under Article 43.

ARTICLE 83

1. All functions of the United Nations relating to strategic areas, including the approval of the terms of the trusteeship agreements and of their alteration or amendment, shall be exercised by the Security Council.

2. The basic objectives set forth in Article 76 shall be applicable to the people of each strategic area.

3. The Security Council shall, subject to the provisions of the trusteeship agreements and without prejudice to security considerations, avail itself of the assistance of the Trusteeship Council to perform those functions of the United Nations under the trusteeship

system relating to political, economic, social and educational matters in the strategic areas.

ARTICLE 84

It shall be the duty of the administering authority to insure that the trust territory shall play its part in the maintenance of international peace and security. To this end the administering authority may make use of volunteer forces, facilities, and assistance from the trust territory in carrying out the obligations toward the Security Council undertaken in this regard by the administering authority, as well as for local defense and the maintenance of law and order within the trust territory.

ARTICLE 85

1. The functions of the United Nations with regard to trusteeship agreements for all areas not designated as strategic, including the approval of the terms of the trusteeship agreements and of their alteration or amendment, shall be exercised by the General Assembly.

2. The Trusteeship Council, operating under the authority of the General Assembly, shall assist the General Assembly in carrying out these functions.

CHAPTER XIII

The Trusteeship Council

Composition

ARTICLE 86

1. The Trusteeship Council shall consist of the following members of the United Nations:

(a) Those members administering trust territories;

(b) Such of those members mentioned by name in Article 23 as are not administering trust territories; and

(c) As many other members elected for three-year terms by the General Assembly as may be necessary to insure that the total number of members of the Trusteeship Council is equally divided between those members of the United Nations which administer trust territories and those which do not.

2. Each member of the Trusteeship Council shall designate one specially qualified person to represent it therein.

312

FUNCTIONS AND POWERS

ARTICLE 87

The General Assembly and, under its authority, the Trusteeship Council, in carrying out their functions, may:

(a) Consider reports submitted by the administering authority;

(b) Accept petitions and examine them in consultation with the administering authority;

(c) Provide for periodic visits to the respective trust territories at times agreed upon with the administering authority; and

(d) Take these and other actions in conformity with the terms of the trusteeship agreement.

ARTICLE 88

The Trusteeship Council shall formulate a questionnaire on the political, economic, social and educational advancement of the inhabitants of each trust territory, and the administering authority for each trust territory within the competence of the General Assembly shall make an annual report to the General Assembly upon the basis of such questionnaire.

VOTING

ARTICLE 89

1. Each member of the Trusteeship Council shall have one vote.

2. Decisions of the Trusteeship Council shall be taken by a majority of the members present and voting.

PROCEDURE

ARTICLE 90

1. The Trusteeship Council shall adopt its own rules of procedure, including the method of selecting its president.

2. The Trusteeship Council shall meet as required in accordance with its rules, which shall include provisions for the convening of meetings on the request of a majority of its members.

ARTICLE 91

The Trusteeship Council shall, when appropriate, avail itself of the assistance of the Economic and Social Council and of the specialized agencies in regard to matters with which they are respectively concerned.

313

CHAPTER XIV

THE INTERNATIONAL COURT OF JUSTICE

ARTICLE 92

The International Court of Justice shall be the principal judicial organ of the United Nations. It shall function in accordance with the annexed statute, which is based upon the statute of the Permanent Court of International Justice and forms an integral part of the present Charter.

ARTICLE 93

1. All members of the United Nations are ipso facto parties to the statute of the International Court of Justice.

2. A State which is not a member of the United Nations may become party to the statute of the International Court of Justice on conditions to be determined in each case by the General Assembly upon recommendation of the Security Council.

ARTICLE 94

1. Each member of the United Nations undertakes to comply with the decision of the International Court of Justice in any case to which it is a party.

2. If any party to a case fails to perform the obligations incumbent upon it under a judgment rendered by the court, the other party may have recourse to the Security Council, which may, if it deems necessary, make recommendations or decide upon measures to be taken to give effect to the judgment.

ARTICLE 95

Nothing in the present Charter shall prevent members of the United Nations from entrusting the solution of their differences to other tribunals by virtue of agreements already in existence or which may be concluded in the future.

ARTICLE 96

1. The General Assembly or the Security Council may request the International Court of Justice to give an advisory opinion on any legal question.

2. Other organs of the United Nations and specialized agencies which may at any time be so authorized by the General Assembly, may also request advisory opinions of the court on legal questions arising within the scope of their activities.

CHAPTER XV

THE SECRETARIAT

ARTICLE 97

There shall be a secretariat comprising a secretary general and such staff as the organization may require. The secretary general shall be appointed by the General Assembly on the recommendation of the Security Council. He shall be the chief administrative officer of the organization.

ARTICLE 98

The secretary general shall act in that capacity in all meetings of the General Assembly, of the Security Council, of the Economic and Social Council and of the Trusteeship Council, and shall perform such other functions as are entrusted to him by these organs. The secretary general shall make an annual report to the General Assembly on the work of the organization.

ARTICLE 99

The secretary general may bring to the attention of the Security Council any matter which in his opinion may threaten the maintenance of international peace and security.

ARTICLE 100

1. In the performance of their duties the secretary general and the staff shall not seek or receive instructions from any Government or from any other authority external to the organization. They shall refrain from any action which might reflect on their position as international officials responsible only to the organization.

2. Each member of the United Nations undertakes to respect the exclusively international character of the responsibilities of the secretary general and the staff, and not to seek to influence them in the discharge of their responsibilities.

ARTICLE 101

1. The staff shall be appointed by the secretary general under regulations established by the General Assembly.

2. Appropriate staffs shall be permanently assigned to the Economic and Social Council, the Trusteeship Council, and, as required, to other organs of the United Nations. These staffs shall form a part of the Secretariat.

3. The paramount consideration in the employment of the staff

and in the determination of the conditions of service shall be the necessity of securing the highest standards of efficiency, competence and integrity. Due regard shall be paid to the importance of recruiting the staff on as wide a geographical basis as possible.

CHAPTER XVI

MISCELLANEOUS PROVISIONS

ARTICLE 102

1. Every treaty and every international agreement entered into by any member of the United Nations after the present charter comes into force shall as soon as possible be registered with the Secretariat and published by it.

2. No party to any such treaty or international agreement which has not been registered in accordance with the provisions of Paragraph 1 of this article may invoke that treaty or agreement before any organ of the United Nations.

ARTICLE 103

In the event of a conflict between the obligations of the members of the United Nations under the present charter and any other international obligations to which they are subject, their obligations under the present charter shall prevail.

ARTICLE 104

The organization shall enjoy in the territory of each of its members such legal capacity as may be necessary for the exercise of its functions and the fulfillment of its purposes.

ARTICLE 105

1. The organization shall enjoy in the territory of each of its members such privileges and immunities as are necessary for the fulfillment of its purposes.

2. Representatives of the members of the United Nations and officials of the organization shall similarly enjoy such privileges and immunities as are necessary for the independent exercise of their functions in connection with the organization.

3. The General Assembly may make recommendations with a view to determining the details of the application of Paragraphs 1 and 2 of this article or may propose conventions to the members of the United Nations for this purpose.

CHAPTER XVII
TRANSITIONAL SECURITY ARRANGEMENTS
ARTICLE 106

Pending the coming into force of such special agreements referred to in Article 43, as in the opinion of the Security Council enable it to begin the exercise of its responsibilities under Article 42, the parties to the four-nation declaration, signed at Moscow, Oct. 30, 1943, and France, shall, in accordance with the provisions of Paragraph 5 of that declaration, consult with one another and, as occasion requires, with other members of the organization with a view to such joint action on behalf of the organization as may be necessary for the purpose of maintaining international peace and security.

ARTICLE 107

Nothing in the present charter shall invalidate or preclude action in relation to any state which during the second World War has been an enemy of any signatory to the present charter, taken or authorized as a result of that war by the governments having responsibility for such action.

CHAPTER XVIII
AMENDMENTS
ARTICLE 108

Amendments to the present charter shall come into force for all members of the organization when they have been adopted by a vote of two-thirds of the members of the General Assembly and ratified in accordance with their respective constitutional processes by two-thirds of the members of the United Nations including all the permanent members of the Security Council.

ARTICLE 109

1. A general conference of the members of the United Nations for the purpose of reviewing the present charter may be held at a date and place to be fixed by a two-thirds vote of the General Assembly and by a vote of any seven members of the Security Council. Each member of the United Nations shall have one vote in the conference.

2. Any alteration of the present charter recommended by a two-thirds vote of the conference shall take effect when ratified in

accordance with their respective constitutional processes by two-thirds of the members of the United Nations including all the permanent members of the Security Council.

3. If such a conference has not been held before the tenth annual session of the General Assembly following the coming into force of the present charter, the proposal to call such a conference shall be placed on the agenda of that session of the General Assembly, and the conference shall be held if so decided by a majority vote of the members of the General Assembly and by a vote of any seven members of the Security Council.

CHAPTER XIX

RATIFICATION AND SIGNATURE

ARTICLE 110

1. The present charter shall be ratified by the signatory states in accordance with their respective constitutional processes.

2. The ratifications shall be deposited with the Government of the United States of America, which shall notify all the signatory states of each deposit as well as the secretary general of the organization when he has been elected.

3. The present charter shall come into force upon the deposit of ratifications by the Republic of China, France, the Union of Soviet Socialist Republics, the United Kingdom of Great Britain and Northern Ireland, and the United States of America, and by a majority of the other signatory states.

4. The states signatory to the present charter which ratify it after it has come into force will become original members of the United Nations on the date of the deposit of their respective ratifications.

ARTICLE 111

The present charter, of which the Chinese, English, French, Russian and Spanish texts are equally authentic, shall remain deposited in the archives of the Government of the United States of America. Duly certified copies thereof shall be transmitted by that Government to the Governments of the other signatory states.

In faith whereof the representatives of the United Nations have signed the present charter.

Done in the city of San Francisco the twenty-sixth day of June, one thousand nine hundred and forty-five.

Utah—Frequently called the "Mormon State." State flower, sego lily. Population, 550,310. Area, 84,916 square miles. Capital, Salt Lake City. This area, which once belonged to Spain and later to Mexico, was annexed to the United States in 1848. It was organized as a territory in 1850 and admitted to the Union in 1896. Brigham Young, the leader of the Mormons, was an outstanding character in the affairs of the state and was at one time territorial governor.

Utopia—An ideal political and social state in which provision is usually made for everything except laughter. It was the name given by Sir Thomas More to the imaginary island which he made the seat of his perfect commonwealth. The word is from the Greek and means nowhere. More's *Utopia,* written in Latin, was published in 1516. The epithet "Utopian" is applied to visionary and impracticable schemes.

Vermont—"Green Mountain State." State flower, red clover. Population, 359,231. Area, 9,609 square miles. Capital, Montpelier. Admitted to the Union in 1791. An outstanding personage in the history of Vermont was Ethan Allen, who, as leader of the "Green Mountain Boys," captured Ticonderoga from the English.

Calvin Coolidge, thirtieth President of the United States, was born in Vermont. He took the oath of office in Plymouth, his birthplace.

The state, which is a Republican stronghold, has one representative at large in Congress.

Veto—The power to veto laws passed by Congress which is vested by the Constitution in the Chief Executive alone was rarely used by the early presidents. Up to 1829, when Andrew Jackson became President, it had been exercised only nine times—twice by Washington, six times by Madison, and once by Monroe. During his two terms Jackson vetoed nine bills, and thereafter the power was more frequently employed. It was not until Andrew Johnson's administration that a bill was passed over the presidential veto. Grover Cleveland vetoed more bills than all the presidents before him combined, but they were mostly private pension bills. It is estimated that the veto power has been exercised about 1,750 times.

All bills passed by Congress are sent to the President for his signature. If he wishes to veto a bill he returns it to the house where it originated with his objections. If the bill is then repassed by a two-thirds vote in each house, the veto is overridden and the bill becomes a law. If the President fails to sign or return a bill within ten days (Sundays excepted) it becomes a law just as if he had signed it, unless "Congress by their adjournment prevent its return, in which case it shall not become a law." This last is what is termed the pocket veto (*q.v.*).

The power to veto legislation is generally given to governors of states and mayors of cities, with the proviso that the legislative body may override a veto if a certain number of members, usually two thirds, favor the legislation.

Vice-President—In case of the removal of the President from office, on his death, resignation, or inability to discharge the duties of his office, he is succeeded by the Vice-President, who presides over the Senate but has no vote except in case of a tie. The Vice-President may sit at Cabinet meetings. Like the President, the Vice-President must be a natural-born citizen of the United States, at least thirty-five years old, and a resident of the United States for at least fourteen years. He cannot come from the same state as the President. As in the case of the President, he may be removed from office by impeachment for and conviction of treason, bribery, or other high crimes and misdemeanors.

Formerly each presidential elector voted for two persons, the one receiving the highest number of votes being elected President and the next highest Vice-President (Constitution, Article II, Section 1). But as this method was likely to result in the Vice-President being of a different political party from that of the President, it was changed by the Twelfth Amendment, which provides that distinct ballots be cast for President and Vice-President. In case of the inability of both President and Vice-President the law of 1792 declared that the office of President devolved upon the president pro tempore of the Senate, but this has since been changed. (See *Presidential Succession.*)

Seven vice-presidents have succeeded to the presidency: John

VICE-PRESIDENTS OF THE UNITED STATES

	Name	Born	Took Office	Party	Died
1	John Adams	Quincy, Mass., 1735	1789	Fed.	Quincy, Mass., 1826
2	Thomas Jefferson	Shadwell, Va., 1743	1797	Rep.	Monticello, Va., 1826
3	Aaron Burr	Newark, N. J., 1756	1801	Rep.	Staten Island, N. Y., 1836
4	George Clinton	Ulster Co., N. Y., 1739	1805	Rep.	Washington, D.C., 1812
5	Elbridge Gerry	Marblehead, Mass., 1744	1813	Rep.	Washington, D.C., 1814
6	Daniel D. Tompkins	Scarsdale, N. Y., 1774	1817	Rep.	Staten Island, N. Y., 1825
7	John C. Calhoun	Abbeville, S. C., 1782	1825	Rep.	Washington, D.C., 1850
8	Martin Van Buren	Kinderhook, N. Y., 1782	1833	Dem.	Kinderhook, N. Y., 1862
9	Richard M. Johnson	Louisville, Ky., 1780	1837	Dem.	Frankfort, Ky., 1850
10	John Tyler	Greenway, Va., 1790	1841	Dem.	Richmond, Va., 1862
11	George M. Dallas	Philadelphia, Pa., 1792	1845	Dem.	Philadelphia, Pa., 1864
12	Millard Fillmore	Summerhill, N. Y., 1800	1849	Whig	Buffalo, N. Y., 1874
13	William R. King	Sampson Co., N. C., 1786	1853	Dem.	Dallas Co., Ala., 1853
14	John C. Breckinridge	Lexington, Ky., 1821	1857	Dem.	Lexington, Ky., 1875
15	Hannibal Hamlin	Paris, Me., 1809	1861	Rep.	Bangor, Me., 1891
16	Andrew Johnson	Raleigh, N. C., 1808	1865	Rep.	Carter Co., Tenn., 1875
17	Schuyler Colfax	New York City, N. Y., 1823	1869	Rep.	Mankato, Minn., 1885
18	Henry Wilson	Farmington, N. H., 1812	1873	Rep.	Washington, D.C., 1875
19	William A. Wheeler	Malone, N. Y., 1819	1877	Rep.	Malone, N. Y., 1887
20	Chester A. Arthur	Fairfield, Vt., 1830	1881	Rep.	New York City, N. Y., 1886
21	Thos. A. Hendricks	Muskingum Co., Ohio, 1819	1885	Dem.	Indianapolis, Ind., 1885
22	Levi P. Morton	Shoreham, Vt., 1824	1889	Rep.	Rhinebeck, N. Y., 1920
23	Adlai E. Stevenson	Christian Co., Ky., 1835	1893	Dem.	Chicago, Ill., 1914
24	Garret A. Hobart	Long Branch, N. J., 1844	1897	Rep.	Paterson, N. J., 1899
25	Theodore Roosevelt	New York City, N. Y., 1858	1901	Rep.	Oyster Bay, N. Y., 1919
26	Chas. W. Fairbanks	Unionville Centre, Ohio, 1852	1905	Rep.	Indianapolis, Ind., 1918
27	James S. Sherman	Utica, N. Y., 1855	1909	Rep.	Utica, N. Y., 1912
28	Thos. R. Marshall	No. Manchester, Ind., 1854	1913	Dem.	Washington, D.C., 1925
29	Calvin Coolidge	Plymouth, Vt., 1872	1921	Rep.	Northampton, Mass., 1933
30	Charles G. Dawes	Marietta, Ohio, 1865	1925	Rep.	....
31	Charles Curtis	Topeka, Kan., 1860	1929	Rep.	Washington, D.C., 1936
32	John Nance Garner	Red River Co., Tex., 1869	1933	Dem.	....
33	Henry Agard Wallace	Adair County, Ia., 1888	1941	Dem.	....
34	Harry S. Truman	Lamar, Mo., 1884	1945	Dem.	....

Tyler succeeded William Henry Harrison, who died April 4, 1841; Millard Fillmore succeeded Zachary Taylor, who died July 9, 1850; Andrew Johnson succeeded Abraham Lincoln, who died April 15, 1865; Chester A. Arthur succeeded James A. Garfield, who died September 19, 1881; Theodore Roosevelt succeeded William Mc-Kinley, who died September 14, 1901; Calvin Coolidge succeeded Warren G. Harding, who died August 2, 1923; and Harry S. Truman succeeded Franklin D. Roosevelt, who died April 12, 1945.

In 1791, when some of the Federalists wanted the President to have the title "His Highness, the President of the United States, and Protector of their Liberties," the Democrats humorously suggested that the Vice-President be called "His Superfluous Excellency."

Virginia—Known as the "Old Dominion." State flower, American dogwood. Population, 2,677,773. Area, 40,815 square miles. Capital, Richmond. An original state of the Union.

John Smith, from England, was one of the early settlers, and his life was filled with adventure. In one of his escapades he was rescued by Pocahontas, a thirteen-year-old Indian princess. She later married John Rolfe, an Englishman who settled in Virginia and who discovered a method of curing tobacco.

The state became known as the "Mother of Presidents," having given the nation George Washington, Thomas Jefferson, James Madison, James Monroe, and John Tyler. Patrick Henry, American Revolutionary leader, was born in Virginia.

Clauses in the state constitution require an educational test and payment of poll taxes for a number of years or the possession of property in order to vote. Through this method many whites and Negroes are denied the voting privilege. The city of Staunton adopted the city manager plan in 1908.

The state has nine representatives.

Virginia Influence—By this name is known the influence wielded by the state of Virginia, headed by Jefferson, Madison, Monroe, Taylor, the Randolphs, and others, from the adoption of the Constitution until about 1824. It arose largely from the unanimity of its people on national subjects, owing to a certain clannish feeling

322

among them. The lead taken by the state in opposition to Hamilton's view of the Constitution caused it to be regarded as the head of that opposition, and therefore of the Republican party. This Virginia Influence was a distinct factor in national politics. After John Adams, all the presidents until John Quincy Adams, in 1825, were from Virginia.

Voters, Qualifications of—Each state decides for itself the qualifications of its voters, and the United States follows the state law in Federal elections. The President of the United States is chosen by electors appointed in each state "in such manner as the Legislature thereof may direct." (Constitution, Article II, Section 1.) Senators are elected directly by the people, the voters having "the qualifications requisite for the electors in the most numerous branch of the State Legislatures." (Seventeenth Amendment.) And the same is true in the case of Representatives (Constitution, Article I, Section 2). But the power of the state governments to prescribe qualifications is limited by the Fifteenth and Nineteenth amendments. The Fifteenth Amendment declares: "The right of the citizens of the United States to vote shall not be denied or abridged by the United States or by any State on account of race, color, or previous condition of servitude." The Nineteenth Amendment gives nation-wide suffrage to women by saying that the right shall not be denied or abridged on account of sex.

With each state prescribing its own qualifications for voters, the suffrage in elections varies in the different states, particularly in the matter of residential requirements, as set forth in the following tabular summary:

VOTING QUALIFICATIONS OF THE STATES

General requirements: minimum age, 21 (18 in Georgia); citizen of U.S.; not a convict; literacy; registration. Paupers are excluded in some states.

RESIDENCE REQUIRED

State	In State	In County	In Precinct
Alabama*	2 yrs.	1 yr.	3 mos.
Arizona	1 yr.	30 days	30 days
Arkansas*	1 yr.	6 mos.	30 days

*Indicates that poll tax must be paid.

State	In State	In County	In Precinct
California	1 yr.	90 days	40 days
Colorado	1 yr.	90 days	10 days
Connecticut	1 yr.	6 mos.	......
Delaware	1 yr.	3 mos.	30 days
Florida	1 yr.	6 mos.	30 days
Georgia	1 yr.	6 mos.	......
Idaho	6 mos.	30 days	......
Illinois	1 yr.	90 days	30 days
Indiana	6 mos.	60 days	30 days
Iowa	6 mos.	60 days	10 days
Kansas	6 mos.	30 days	30 days
Kentucky	1 yr.	6 mos.	60 days
Louisiana	2 yrs.	1 yr.	3 mos.
Maine	3 mos.	......	......
Maryland	1 yr.	6 mos.	1 day
Massachusetts	1 yr.	6 mos.	6 mos.
Michigan	6 mos.	20 days	20 days
Minnesota	6 mos.	......	10 days
Mississippi*	2 yrs.	1 yr.	1 yr.
Missouri	1 yr.	60 days	60 days
Montana	1 yr.	6 mos.	......
Nebraska	6 mos.	40 days	10 days
Nevada	6 mos.	30 days	10 days
New Hampshire	6 mos.	......	6 mos.
New Jersey	1 yr.	5 mos.	......
New Mexico	1 yr.	90 days	30 days
New York	1 yr.	4 mos.	30 days
North Carolina	1 yr.	......	4 mos.
North Dakota	1 yr.	90 days	30 days
Ohio	1 yr.	30 days	5 days
Oklahoma	1 yr.	6 mos.	30 days
Oregon	6 mos.	......	......
Pennsylvania	1 yr.	2 mos.	2 mos.
Rhode Island	2 yrs.	6 mos.	......
South Carolina*	2 yrs.	1 yr.	4 mos.
South Dakota	1 yr.	90 days	30 days
Tennessee*	1 yr.	6 mos.	......
Texas*	1 yr.	6 mos.	6 mos.
Utah	1 yr.	4 mos.	60 days
Vermont	1 yr.	3 mos.	3 mos.
Virginia*	1 yr.	6 mos.	30 days
Washington	1 yr.	30 days	10 days
West Virginia	1 yr.	60 days	......
Wisconsin	1 yr.	10 days	10 days
Wyoming	1 yr.	60 days	10 days

*Indicates that poll tax must be paid.

Wall Street, in the heart of the financial district of New York City, is one of the world's most famous streets. Extending from Broadway at Trinity Church to the East River, a distance of approximately half a mile, it was, after the ratification of the Constitution, the earliest seat of the Federal Government. Here were located the most important government offices. The First Congress met in a hall where the Sub-Treasury now stands, and the inauguration of George Washington as our first President took place on the porch of this building. The agricultural members of Congress were dissatisfied with this situation. They were apprehensive of the influence of neighboring financial interests on national legislation and desired a change. Accordingly the national capital was moved from New York to Philadelphia and finally to Washington.

Wall Street has remained the financial center of the country, and the name, which came from the wall or palisade the Dutch built as a protection against the redskins, has become a synonym for the great moneyed interests of the United States. It is often mentioned in political campaigns to give the sinister impression that the financial power represented by the name is being used to influence the outcome of an election. In the Roosevelt-Willkie campaign, Secretary Harold L. Ickes sarcastically referred to Wendell Willkie as "the barefoot Wall Street lawyer."

War Democrats—The Democrats who favored the prosecution of the Civil War and supported the Republican party during the war. At its national convention in 1864, the Democratic party declared the war a failure and demanded a cessation of hostilities. It was overwhelmingly defeated on this issue.

War Department—Henry Knox of Boston was the first Secretary of the War Department, which was created by Congress on August 7, 1789. The Secretary is a civil rather than a military officer. All expenses in connection with the military establishment fall within his sphere—army supply purchases, army maintenance, and transportation. The United States Military Academy at West Point comes under his jurisdiction, as do matters pertaining to land- and coast-defense fortifications and improvements to rivers and harbors and flood control. He approves any plans respecting location of bridges built over any waters of the United States. Under the supervision of the Secretary of War is the governor of the Panama Canal Zone, who has charge of the operation and maintenance of the Canal and the administration, sanitation, and government of the Canal Zone. The General Staff of the War Department, under direction of the Chief of Staff, co-ordinates the development and work of the Army.

Ward Eight—A notorious political ward on the back side of Beacon Hill, Boston, which was benevolently bossed for many years by Martin Lomasney.

A cocktail named after Ward Eight was invented by Billy Kane, a famous old-time Boston bartender at Locke-Ober's in Winter Place. Here is how Billy made his Ward Eight: One jigger of bourbon; one teaspoon of powdered sugar; the juice of half a lemon, a dash of curaçao; grenadine to color; a slice of orange, and a cherry for garnish.

Washington—"Evergreen State." State flower, rhododendron. Population, 1,736,191. Area, 68,192 square miles. Capital, Olympia. Admitted to the Union in 1889. Constitutional amendments put into effect the initiative, referendum, and recall. The state is normally Republican in politics. The Progressive party carried the state in 1912, however, and the Democrats in 1916 and again in 1932, 1940, and 1944. It has six representatives in Congress.

Washington, George, the first President of the United States, was born in Westmoreland County, Virginia, on February 22, 1732. He died at Mount Vernon, Virginia, on December 14, 1799. He was of English descent. His education was obtained in the local schools.

In his early days he was a land surveyor. He inherited considerable property from his father and from his older brother. He distinguished himself during the French and Indian War, when he rose to the rank of colonel and commander of the Virginian forces.

After that war he lived quietly, managing his property and serving in the Virginia House of Burgesses, until sent to the Continental Congress in 1774. In 1759 he married Martha Dandridge Custis, widow of John Parke Custis.

On June 15, 1775, the Continental Congress appointed him Commander in Chief of the American forces engaged in the Revolution; this position he retained to the end of the war. Immediately after the war he resigned his commission and retired to Mount Vernon, whence he emerged as delegate to the convention of 1787, of which he became the presiding officer.

On the adoption of the Constitution framed by that convention he was elected President of the United States, receiving the compliment, unparalleled in our history, of a unanimous vote. He was similarly elected for a second term. During his administration the government's finances were put in order and the Bank of the United States was established; Indian troubles on the frontiers were suppressed after two unsuccessful attempts; Jay's Treaty was concluded with England in the settlement of various matters in dispute, and the Whisky Insurrection in Pennsylvania was crushed.

In 1797 he was once again called from Mount Vernon, whither he had withdrawn at the expiration of his term as President, to act as Commander in Chief of the Army in a war then threatening with France. When the danger of a war had passed by he again retired to his home, where he died in 1799.

With his countrymen, his influence, drawn partly from his military fame and partly from his lofty character, was enormous, and it was always exerted for good. The adoption of the Constitution was in many quarters due to his approval of it. As Commander in Chief of the Revolutionary Army he had refused to accept pay. As President he professed adherence to no party or faction, although his leanings were toward the centralizing tendencies of Hamilton. Personally he was cold, dignified, and aristocratic.

Weather—In horse-and-buggy days, when rural roads were not so good as they are now, the weather on Election Day had a noticeable effect on the returns. Rainy weather was called Democratic weather because it meant there would probably be a falling off in the Republican farm vote, while fair weather was called Republican

327

weather because it meant the rural vote would come out in strength. People still speak of Democratic and Republican weather.

West Virginia—"Mountain State." State flower, rhododendron. Population, 1,901,974. Area, 24,181 square miles. Capital, Charleston. Admitted to the Union in 1863. The state is considered to be normally Republican in national elections but has not always been so in state politics. It is represented in Congress by six representatives.

Westward the Land Is Bright—During World War II Winston Churchill ended a broadcast at a dark hour of his country's history by quoting the last verse of Arthur Hugh Clough's poem *Say Not, the Struggle Naught Availeth,* which expressed the hope of help coming from the United States. American radio stations broadcast the speech, and the quoted verse proved not only prophetic but also that people who claim to care nothing for poetry can be thrilled by it.

> "And not by eastern windows only,
> When daylight comes, comes in the light;
> In front, the sun climbs slow, how slowly,
> But westward, look, the land is bright."

Whig Party—The opposition to Andrew Jackson took the form of the National Republican party on the part of those differing from him on economic principles; to these were added those who had upheld nullification, and factious Democrats in some of the Southern states, notably in Georgia, Alabama, and Tennessee, in the two latter states headed by Hugh L. White.

James Watson Webb, of the New York *Courier and Enquirer,* suggested the name of Whig for this combination, as indicating opposition to "executive usurpation," a meaning it was asserted to have had in England and during the Revolution in America. Under this name were ultimately included the National Republicans and the Southern factions; the Nullifiers were never a portion of them; they formed a separate pro-slavery faction in the Democratic party.

William Henry Harrison was among the first nominees of the

party, and he was endorsed by numerous anti-Masonic and other conventions. Three other candidates were placed in nomination beside the Democratic nominee, Van Buren, who was elected. In 1840 Harrison, a military and anti-Masonic man, was renominated; as Vice-President, Tyler, one of the Southern wing, was named. This combination received an overwhelmingly large electoral vote; the campaign had been a vigorous one, based on Harrison's military services, to the cry of "Tippecanoe and Tyler too." The Whigs had a small majority, also, in both houses.

One month after his inauguration Harrison died. Soon after his accession Tyler broke with his party, the occasion being the veto by him of a national bank bill. The first platform of the party adopted in 1844 meant anything or nothing.

Clay was nominated, and his defeat, to a great extent, was due to the action of the Liberty party. The question of the annexation of Texas foreshadowed the importance that slavery was soon to assume. It was the constant effort of the Northern Whigs to keep this topic out of politics. Opposition to slavery meant rupture with the Southern Whigs, who were first pro-slavery and only then Whigs; advocacy of it meant the displeasure of Northern constituents. The Wilmot Proviso was accordingly supported by Northern Whigs and opposed by the Southerners.

Taylor was the nominee in 1848; no platform was adopted. He was elected largely on his military reputation. The Compromise of 1850 and all other measures affecting slavery found the Southern Whigs acting with the Democrats and against their Northern brothers in the party. These latter made every effort to keep the subject down, and every new piece of legislation on the subject was declared by them to be a "finality." In 1852 the platform contained a plank to that effect, and General Winfield Scott was named for President. Scott was completely defeated.

The Southern Whigs were now practically apart from the party, and many of them soon became so in name also. The Whig party was broken up. A part of it joined the ranks of the American party, but ultimately its Northern elements were swallowed up in the Republican party; the Southern elements joined the Democratic party, while the old Whig desire of keeping slavery out of politics was visible in the Constitutional Union party, composed of Whig remnants in the border states.

Whisky Insurrection—This was a revolt in western Pennsylvania, occasioned by the passage of the excise law of March 3, 1791. Laws of this kind had always been odious, and they were especially so to this community, the greater part of whose grain was converted into whisky.

The tax was suggested by Hamilton for the purpose of exerting the Federal power of direct taxation, and also, as some authorities assert, for the purpose of raising an insurrection of small proportions and of having the Federal power exerted in crushing it. Hamilton saw that the Union could not be a success unless the authority of the Federal Government was recognized, and he thought that a small disturbance speedily suppressed might check a tendency to disunion and separation, which, once fairly entrenched, would prove the end of the government. His forecast was correct. The suppression was practically bloodless; but two persons were killed, and these in brawls with the soldiers. Moreover, the prompt exercise of Federal authority showed the inherent strength and vitality of the Federal Government. Hamilton's purpose was not, of course, avowed—not even known.

The best-known leader in this insurrection was a man named Bradford, but William Findley, a member of Congress, and Albert Gallatin were also concerned in it. The first meeting to oppose the measure was held on July 27. This meeting was peaceful, but disorders followed. Any person taking office under the law was declared a public enemy, and in one case a revenue officer was tarred and feathered.

The opposition continued to increase, and in May 1792 Congress empowered the President to use militia in suppressing disorders within a state. About this time the tax was also reduced. On September 15 a proclamation was issued warning the people to abandon their unlawful combinations.

The disturbance had not yet come to a head. The agitation continued throughout 1793 and 1794. Secret societies were organized to oppose the tax. Under the law only Federal courts had jurisdiction of offenses against it, and this necessitated the transportation of the accused to Philadelphia, a long journey in those days. In June 1794 this just cause of complaint was removed by giving the state courts concurrent jurisdiction in excise offenses.

The issue, on May 31, in Philadelphia, of fifty writs against various western people charged with connection with the disturbances brought the insurrection to a head. The marshal serving the warrants was seized and made to swear that he would serve no more of them. A meeting of seven thousand armed men was held. Those opposed to these proceedings were intimidated, and preparations for armed defense against the United States were made.

The Federal Government acted promptly. A proclamation ordered the insurgents to disperse. A requisition for fifteen thousand militia was made to the governors of New Jersey, Virginia, and Maryland. Meanwhile commissioners were sent ahead to offer amnesty to those who would submit. Their mission was a failure, and on September 25 another proclamation was issued by the President, in which he gave notice of the advance of the troops. President Washington accompanied them part of the way; Hamilton remained with them throughout.

Several meetings were now held declaring submission, but they were not regarded as representative, and the troops continued to advance. On their arrival at the scene of the disorders time was given for submission under the President's proclamation, and all those not submitting were arrested. The violent leaders, including Bradford, had fled; Gallatin was among those who had all along counseled submission. The insurrection was suppressed; all but about twenty-five hundred of the troops returned home; these remained encamped in the region throughout the winter.

Whispering Campaign—Quietly attempting to cut the throat of a political candidate with hints, insinuations, and suggestions reflecting on his character and reputation. This spreading of defamatory gossip behind a candidate's back often extends to the vilification of his family too.

Theodore Roosevelt scotched the persistent rumor that he was a drunkard by hailing a spreader of the tale into court, proving the falsity of the story, and collecting damages.

331

Whitewash—When public officials are charged with wrongdoing and are exonerated without any serious effort being made to ascertain the truth or bring the offenders to justice, they are said to have been whitewashed. It is a prearranged verdict of not guilty regardless of the facts; a bestowal of angels' wings to permit wrongdoers to escape.

Wisconsin—"Badger State." State flower, violet. Population, 3,137,587. Area, 56,154 square miles. Capital, Madison. Admitted to the Union in 1848. Though the Democratic party was in the ascendancy in past times, in recent years it has been under the control of the Republicans and Progressives, the latter guided principally by Senator Robert M. La Follette, Jr., whose father was a political leader of progressives and radicals. The state has generally voted Republican in presidential elections, aside from 1892, 1912, 1932, 1936, and 1940. In 1924 the electoral vote went to the Progressive candidate, Robert M. La Follette, Sr. In 1946 the Progressive party in Wisconsin merged with the Republican party. The state has ten representatives in Congress.

Witch-Hunting—A phrase taken from the Massachusetts witchcraft persecutions in the seventeenth century and now applied to attempts to persecute or discredit persons of unpopular views. (See *Un-American Activities Committee, American Legion.*)

"With Malice towards None"—President Lincoln closed his second inaugural address on March 4, 1865, with these words: "With malice towards none, with charity for all, with firmness in the right, as God gives us to see the right, let us strive on to finish the work we are in; to bind up the nation's wounds; to care for him who shall have borne the battle, and for his widow and his orphan—to do all which may achieve and cherish a just and lasting peace among ourselves and with all nations."

Wizard of Kinderhook—Because he was born at Kinderhook, New York, and was a clever and astute politician, Martin Van Buren was called by many of his contemporaries the Wizard of Kinderhook.

Woman Suffrage—The movement for woman suffrage in the United States began to take shape in 1848, when the first woman's-rights convention was held at Seneca Falls, New York, on July 19. Under New Jersey's constitution of 1776 an act had been passed by that state in 1793 imposing certain restrictions on voters but imposing them equally on both sexes. The act, however, was repealed in 1807. Agitation over the slavery question and the incidental discussion of the rights of man led inevitably to a demand by some women that they be granted the privilege of voting. The Woman's Declaration of Sentiments drawn up at the Seneca Falls convention contained the following terrific indictment of man:

> The history of mankind is the history of repeated injuries and usurpations on the part of man toward woman, having in direct object the establishment of an absolute tyranny over her. To prove this, let facts be submitted to a candid world:
>
> He has never permitted her to exercise her inalienable right to the elective franchise.
>
> He has compelled her to submit to laws, in the formation of which she had no voice.
>
> He has withheld from her rights which are given to the most ignorant and degraded men—both natives and foreigners.
>
> Having deprived her of this first right of a citizen, the elective franchise, thereby leaving her without representation in the halls of legislation, he has oppressed her on all sides.
>
> He has made her, if married, in the eyes of the law, civilly dead.
>
> He has taken from her all right in property, even to the wages she earns.
>
> He has made her, morally, an irresponsible being, as she can commit many crimes with impunity, provided they be done in the presence of her husband. In the covenant of marriage, she is compelled to promise obedience to her husband, he becoming to all intents and purposes, her master—the law giving him power to deprive her of her liberty and to administer chastisement.
>
> He has so framed the laws of divorce, as to what shall be the proper causes, and in case of separation, to whom the guardianship of the children shall be given, as to be wholly regardless of the happiness of the woman—the law, in all cases, going upon a false supposition of the supremacy of man, and giving all power into his hands.

After depriving her of all rights as a married woman, if single, and the owner of property, he has taxed her to support a government which recognizes her only when her property can be made profitable to it.

He has monopolized nearly all the profitable employments, and from those she is permitted to follow, she receives but a scanty remuneration. He closes against her all the avenues to wealth and distinction which he considers most honorable to himself. As a teacher of theology, medicine, or law, she is not known.

He has denied her the facilities for obtaining a thorough education, all colleges being closed against her.

He allows her in Church, as well as State, but a subordinate position, claiming Apostolic authority for her exclusion from the ministry and, with some exceptions, from any public participation in the affairs of the Church.

He has created a false public sentiment by giving to the world a different code of morals for men and women, by which moral delinquencies which exclude women from society, are not only tolerated, but deemed of little account in man.

He has usurped the prerogative of Jehovah himself, claiming it as his right to assign for her a sphere of action, when that belongs to her conscience and to her God.

He has endeavored, in every way that he could, to destroy her confidence in her own powers, to lessen her self-respect, and to make her willing to lead a dependent and abject life.

In October 1850 the first national woman's-rights convention was held at Worcester, Massachusetts. The Equal Rights Association in 1866 laid before Congress a petition on the subject—the first of its kind presented to the House. In 1870 the Massachusetts Republican state convention admitted Lucy Stone and Mary A. Livermore as delegates. At the Republican national conventions of 1872 and 1876 it was resolved that "the honest demands" of this "class of citizens for additional rights . . . should be treated with respectful consideration." Every platform of the Prohibition party from 1872 contained a plank demanding woman suffrage. The Greenback party national platform of 1884 embodied a plank favoring the submission to the people of a woman-suffrage amendment to the Constitution. That same year the Equal Rights party nominated

Mrs. Bella A. Lockwood for the presidency, but she received only about twenty-five hundred votes.

To Wyoming must go the honor of being the first state to extend equal suffrage to women. This was done in 1869, and when the territory was admitted as a state to the Union in 1889 provision was made in the constitution securing women the right to vote. Through the years other states followed suit—Utah, Colorado, Kansas, Oregon, Washington, California, Nevada, Arizona, Montana, Michigan, New York, Oklahoma, and South Dakota—until at length nation-wide suffrage was granted to women by the Nineteenth Amendment to the Constitution, which went into effect on August 24, 1920. It provides:

1. The right of citizens of the United States to vote shall not be denied or abridged by the United States or by any state on account of sex.

2. Congress shall have power, by appropriate legislation, to enforce the provisions of this article.

Two organizations which were active in advocating the cause of suffrage for women were the American Woman's Suffrage Association and the National Woman's Suffrage Association. The former pressed the issue in the individual states, while the latter sought nation-wide suffrage through Federal amendment.

Among the outstanding leaders in the woman-suffrage movement were the following: Lucy B. Stone, Elizabeth Stanton, Lucretia Mott, Susan B. Anthony, Millicent G. Fawcett, Anna H. Shaw, Ellen Key, Carrie Chapman Catt, Sarah P. Decker, Charlotte Gilman, Lady Nancy Astor, and Jeannette Rankin. (See *League of Women Voters.*)

Women in Congress—Miss Jeannette Rankin of Montana was the first woman to be elected to Congress. A Republican, she was elected in 1916, serving one term. She was elected again in 1940. Another Republican, Miss Alice M. Robertson of Muskogee, Oklahoma, was the second woman elected to Congress. She served a single term from 1921 to 1923. Mrs. Rebecca Felton, who was appointed by the governor of Georgia to replace Senator Thomas E. Watson, who died, was the first woman senator. Senator George, who was elected November 7, 1922, to fill the unexpired term of Senator Watson, delayed presenting his credentials until November 22, permitting Mrs. Felton to take part in the Senate sessions on November 21 and 22. The first woman elected to the Senate was Mrs. Hattie Caraway, January 12, 1932. In the Seventy-ninth Congress there were nine women in the House but none in the Senate.

Wyoming—"Equality State." State flower, Indian paintbrush. Population, 250,742. Area, 97,914 square miles. Capital, Cheyenne. Admitted to the Union in 1890. It was ceded to the United States in 1803. Suffrage was extended to women as far back as 1868, the first time women were granted the voting privilege in the United States. The Republicans generally hold sway in state politics. In presidential years, however, the state went Democratic in 1896, 1912, 1916, 1924, 1932, 1936, and 1940. It has one representative in Congress.

X Y Z Mission—During the Revolution the United States secured the valuable aid of France by treaties in 1778. In 1789 monarchy was overthrown in France, and that nation soon found herself at war with England and other European nations. She desired the United States as an ally, and Genêt was sent to accomplish her purpose. His mission failed, Washington persisted firmly in preserving our neutrality, and Jay's Treaty was concluded with England.

The course of our government angered France. In 1797 the Directory, which then governed that country, gave permission to the French Navy to assail our vessels. Following a policy of conciliation, in spite of French insults to our minister and the threat to our commerce, President Adams called a special session of Congress in May 1797, and Charles Cotesworth Pinckney, John Marshall, and Elbridge Gerry were sent to France to arrange matters.

In the spring of the next year the President submitted to Congress dispatches that had been received from these commissioners. They had been kept waiting by Talleyrand, the Minister of Foreign Affairs, and had been approached by three unofficial persons with what was in effect a demand for a bribe and a loan to the Directory before any arrangement could be concluded with the United States. In the dispatches the names of these three persons were indicated merely by the letters X, Y, and Z, and hence the whole affair came to be termed the X Y Z Mission.

To these demands our representatives returned a decided refusal. It is said that Pinckney made use of the phrase, "Millions for defense, but not one cent for tribute." The answer as recorded, however, was, "No, no, no; not a sixpence."

About the time when these dispatches were submitted to Congress, Pinckney and Marshall were ordered to leave France, and Gerry was afterward recalled by our government. A warlike feeling instantly sprang up in the United States. The Federalists, with Adams as leader, desired to defend by force, if necessary, their policy of keeping this country from entangling foreign alliances, and desired to resent French insults. The Democrats (then called Republicans) had always favored an alliance with France and had opposed the creation of a navy for the United States.

Now, however, the popular pressure could not be withstood. Bills were passed for increasing the Navy and separating it from the War Department (April 30, 1798). Provision was made for a national loan and the imposition of a direct tax. The President was authorized to increase the Army in case of a foreign war within three years, and soon Washington was called to be Commander in Chief of the Army and Alexander Hamilton was selected as the active commander. On July 9, 1798, Congress declared the treaties with France no longer binding and authorized our war vessels and privateers to capture armed French vessels. A few naval engagements occurred, but no event of great importance.

The effect on France of our warlike feeling and preparations was excellent. American prisoners were released, and the embargo which had been declared was raised on American ships. Talleyrand now hinted to our minister to Holland, William Vans Murray, that he was willing to receive another American minister. Adams accordingly appointed Murray in February 1799 and soon joined with him Oliver Ellsworth and William R. Davis. The President's action created much stir politically, as he was considered to have become subservient to France and to have changed the former attitude of himself and the Federal party. It was some months after their appointment that our envoys arrived in Paris. Napoleon was then at the head of the government as First Consul and was favorably inclined toward the United States. French commissioners were appointed, and on September 30, 1800, a friendly convention was signed. Both countries ratified it, and it was declared in force December 21, 1801. For a while the safety of our commerce was thus secured.

Youth Movements—Organizations of young voters have played a part in American politics since the eighteenth century. In 1798 there were associations of young Federalists called the Associated Youth. They drew up addresses in support of the Federal party and its principles and worked for it in other ways. It was largely because of their efforts that during the troubles with France the custom of wearing a black cockade in the hat was spread. (See *Black Cockade*.)

Parties and politicians have always encouraged such organizations on the theory that it is good politics to get voters while they are young. College campuses have proved fruitful recruiting grounds. President and Mrs. Franklin D. Roosevelt showed a lively interest in the young voters of the country and did much to interest them in public affairs.